THE GOSPEL ACCORDING TO JOHN
BIBLE STUDY GUIDE

Common People Series

Paula Land

THE PURPOSE OF THIS GUIDE

Mark 12:37...And the common people heard him gladly
The twelfth chapter of Mark begins with Jesus teaching a parable and as usual, the Pharisees, Sadducees and scribes began to flaunt their scholarly knowledge and tried to snare Him in His own words. In the background, is another group of people known as the common people.

.... ***And the common people heard him gladly.***

As in Biblical times, common people are not less intelligent but many do lack confidence and encouragement to read the Word of God. The lack of confidence in our ability to read and learn the scriptures discourages us from actually reading them. What seems as a lack of confidence in ourselves, however, is wrongly placed false humility. It is our lack of FAITH in the Holy Spirit to teach us to skillfully handle the Word of God.

This study guide includes both general Bible knowledge and deeper studies. But it's intent is not just to impart knowledge. Ultimately, it is to help you increase your faith in the Holy Spirit that **He will guide** and teach **you** to skillfully handle the Word of God. You may at first follow this guide to the letter. But it won't be long before you are allowing the Holy Spirit to lead you through your own reading.

John 16:13 Howbeit when he, the Spirit of truth, is come, he will guide you into all truth: for he shall not speak of himself; but whatsoever he shall hear, that shall he speak.

The Bible is the inspired Word of God and consists of 66 books. You can follow this inspiration from one book of the Bible to the next by looking for shadows, patterns, similiarities and cross references. I have included my own studies to help you learn how to recognize some of these.

This guide will also be of great value to those who are searching the scriptures for the deeper things of God. ***1 Corinthians 2:10 But God hath revealed them unto us by his Spirit: for the Spirit searcheth all things, yea, the deep things of God.*** The format enables you to visualize small details that our brains may choose to skip because of information overload. It is invaluable in discerning the proper context of each passage while organizing people, places, dates and sequence of events.

HOW TO USE THIS GUIDE

1. **You must use the King James Bible.** All answers correspond to the King James Bible. There is no substitute.

2. The chapters are divided into sections. Each section has two pages. The lower page is titled NOTES. On this page you will discover words that you overlooked in your reading and write you own study notes. I have intentionally used pictures that are black and white, faceless, and unremarkable to avoid preconceived notions and ideas.

3. The opposite page (GUIDE) has the completed verses. Also written in *script* are my notes. Some of these notes are as simple as definitions of words or phrases that may be unfamiliar and possibly hinder the understanding. Others are deep Bible studies that leaves us in awe of God's Word.

4.   <u>This is very important</u>. Fill-in each blank in numerical order because they are numbered according to the sequence of events. Some pages contain a lot of information and are very busy. Each blank already has the first letter already completed so you don't lose your thoughts trying to figure out what is being asked.

① ② ③

5. <u>Don't try to study outside sources to clarify the meaning</u>. <u>There is no historical or archaeological information from antiquities or Greek/Hebrew lexicons included</u>. These aren't necessary because the King James Bible is plenary meaning complete. If you want to do a deeper study, search the Bible for similiar verses, phrases or ideas. You can find these easily using a concordance (a book that lists words of the Bible in alphabetical order). The Webster's 1828 Dictionary is an excellent source to find definitions to biblical words that may have dropped out of today's vocabulary.

6. Maps are used for general locations only. They are not exactly to scale and serve to keep places and events in context.

THE GOSPEL ACCORDING TO JOHN

Background

The only background we need is provided for us throughout the Bible. We don't need archaelogical evidence, antiquities or whatever. Trust the Bible to be complete in itself. To help gain confidence in the Bible, try to find these facts as your are reading through it.

John wrote The Gospel According to John, The First, Second and Third Epistles of John and The Book of the Revelation. He was one of Jesus' twelve disciples and was with Him at the beginning of His earthly ministry. Be careful not to confuse him with John the Baptist who was beheaded by King Herod near the beginning of Jesus' ministry.

John called himself, "the disciple whom Jesus loved". James and John were brothers, the sons of Zebedee. Jesus called them the "sons of thunder" because they wanted to call fire down from heaven upon some of the enemies of Jesus.

The Gospel According to John bears witness to Jesus as the Son of God and ends almost immediately after the resurrection on the same shore where Jesus first met James and John. Both instances, He said, "Follow me."

The First Epistle of John begins with John and the other disciples bearing witness of what they saw regarding Jesus and the resurrection.This epistle is written to saved people and talks much about fellowship and love. He says he writes these things so that **we may know...** He uses that phrase many times.

The Second and Third Epistles of John are only one chapter each and are addressed to a couple of unknown churches, an individual and how to deal with various types of church members.

The Book of the Revelation was written when John was living in exile on the Isle of Patmos for preaching the Word of God and teaching about Jesus Christ. It is a book of prophecy and the end times.

...and the common people heard him gladly. Mark 12:37

Read John
Chapter 1

CHAPTER 1
V.1
Guide

Each gospel writer describes Jesus differently
Matthew - Jesus as King
Mark - Jesus as a Servant
Luke - Jesus as the Son of Man
John - Jesus as the Son of God

John 1:1 In the beginning Was the Word,

Jesus was with God in heaven but left there to die on the cross.

and the Word Was With God   Jesus was with God

and the Word Was God   created the heaven and the earth. Genesis 1:1

created the heaven and the earth

of the heaven and the earth

Jesus wasn't created because He was already there.

the Word was made flesh (Jesus is) the Word in the flesh)
John 1:14

The 4 Gospels describe Jesus in a different perspective

Jesus as King of Kings
Lineage includes King David

Matthew 1:1 The book of the generation of Jesus Christ, the son of David.

Jesus as a servant
Servants have no lineage

Mark 1:9 And it came to pass in those days, that Jesus came from Nazareth of Galilee.

Jesus as the Son of Man,
Lineage includes the first man, Adam

Luke 3:38 ...which was the son of Seth, which was the son of Adam, which was the son of God.

Jesus as the Son of God
Lineage has no beginning

John 1:2 The same was in the beginning with God.

already was

John 1:1 In the b_____ was the W____,

and the W____ w____ w____ G____

and the W____ w____ G____

Witness of Jesus as God

Jesus was there already in the beginning with God. He is not a being that was created later.

CHAPTER 1
V. 2-5
Guide

A. John 8:43 Why do ye not understand my speech? even because ye cannot hear my word.

B. John 8:47 He that is of God heareth God's words: ye therefore hear them not, because ye are not of God.

A. The Pharisees could not understand Jesus because they could not hear him.
B. They were not of God and could not hear God.
A=B Jesus and God are the same.

was in the beginning with God V.2 (2)

Same is an important word. Jesus and God are the same.

The same V.2 (1)

And the light shineth in darkness; and the darkness comprehended it not. V.5 (5)

comprehend means understand

All things were made by Him V.3 (3)

A. Genesis 1:1 In the beginning God created the heaven and the earth.

B. John 1:3 All things were made by him: (Jesus.)

A. God created
B. All things were made by Jesus.
A=B Jesus and God are the same.

was life; and the life was the light of men. V.4 (4)

Light – A. God is light (1 John 1:15...God is light)
B. Jesus is the light of the world.
John 8:12 ... I am the light of the world:
A=B Jesus and God are the same.

Life – A. Jesus is the quickening spirit.
1Corinthians 15:45 ...the last Adam was made a quickening spirit.
B. God breathed the breath of life into Adam. **Genesis 2:7 And the LORD God...and breathed into his nostrils the breath of life: and man became a living soul.**
A=B Jesus and God are the same.

CHAPTER 1
V. 2-5
Notes

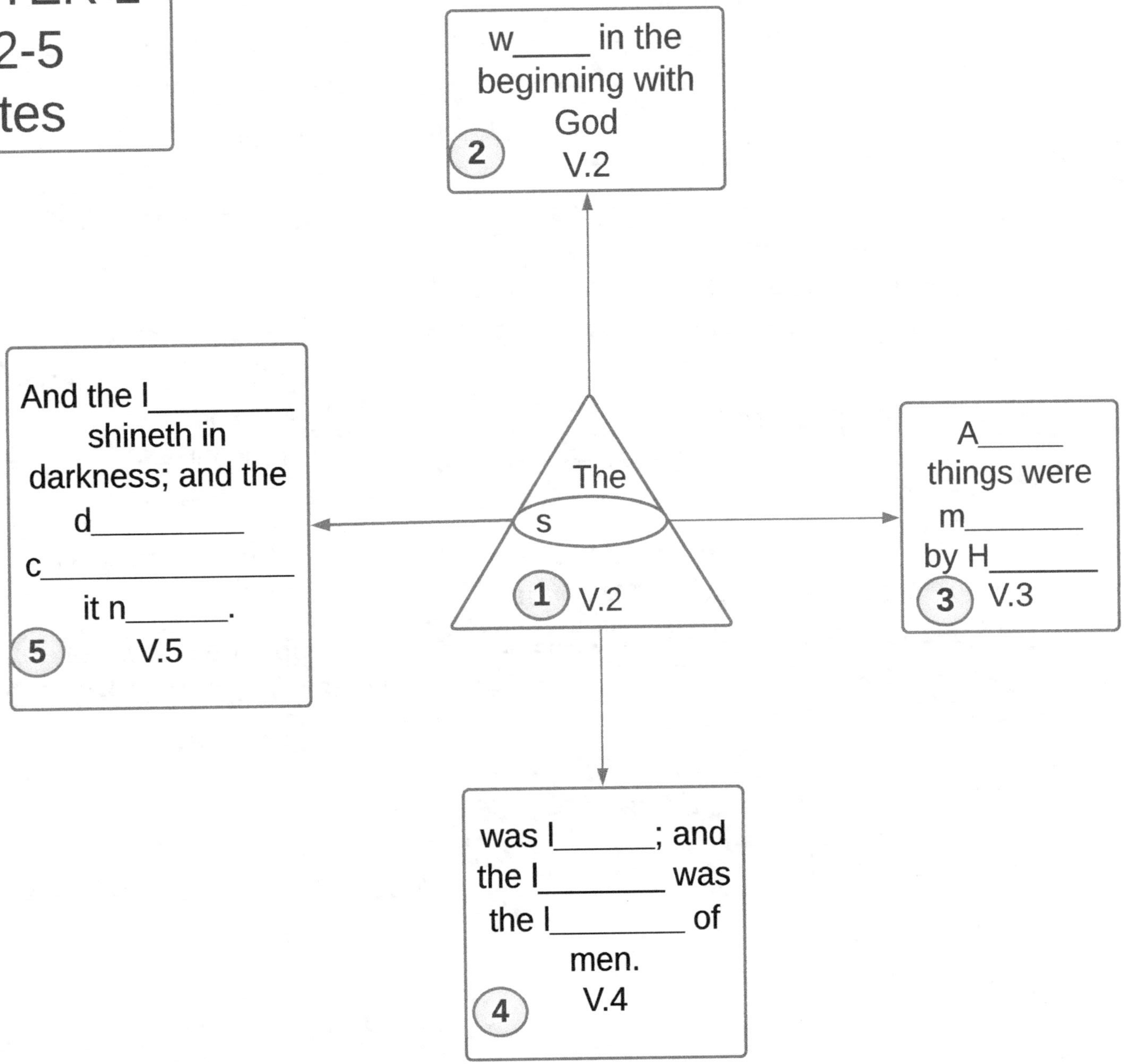

1 V.2

The
s____

2
w____ in the
beginning with
God
V.2

3
A____
things were
m____
by H____
V.3

4
was l____; and
the l____ was
the l____ of
men.
V.4

5
And the l____
shineth in
darkness; and the
d____
c____ it n____.
V.5

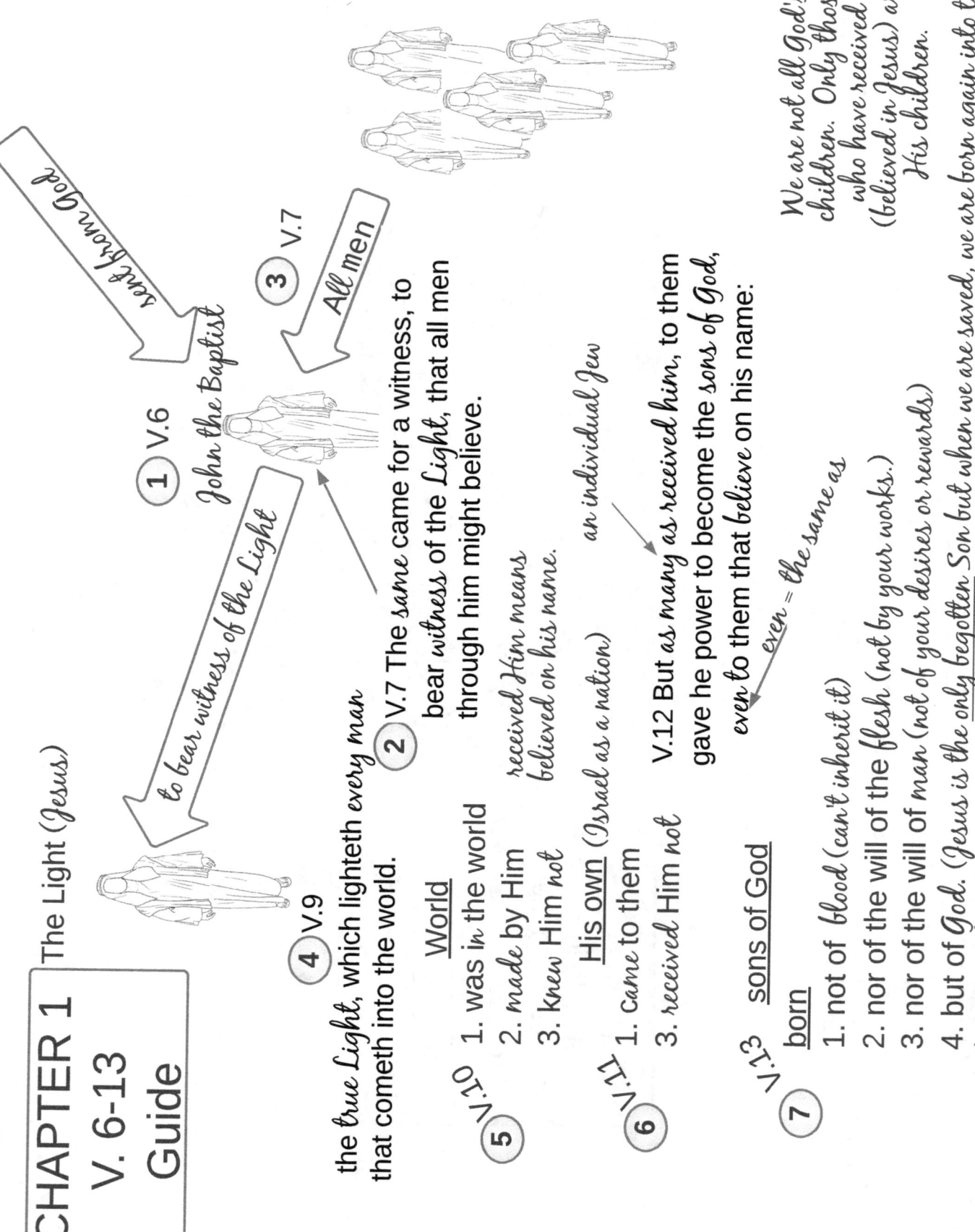

CHAPTER 1
V. 6-13
Guide

sent from God

(1) V.6
John the Baptist

to bear witness of the Light

The Light (Jesus)

(3) V.7
All men

(2) V.7 The same came for a witness, to bear witness of the Light, that all men through him might believe.

*received Him means
believed on his name.*

an individual Jew

(4) V.9

the *true Light*, which lighteth *every man* that cometh into the world.

World

(5) V.10
1. was in the world
2. *made by Him*
3. *knew Him not*

His own *(Israel as a nation)*

(6) V.11
1. came to them
3. *received Him not*

V.12 But as many as received him, to them gave he power to become the sons of God, even to them that believe on his name:

even = the same as

(7) V.13 **sons of God**

born
1. not of *blood (can't inherit it.)*
2. nor of the will of the *flesh (not by your works.)*
3. nor of the will of man *(not of your desires or rewards.)*
4. but of *God. (Jesus is the only begotten Son but when we are saved, we are born again into the kingdom of God.)* **John 3:1 Behold, what manner of love the Father hath bestowed upon us, that we should be called the sons of God: therefore the world knoweth us not, because it knew him not.**

We are not all God's children. Only those who have received (believed in Jesus) are His children.

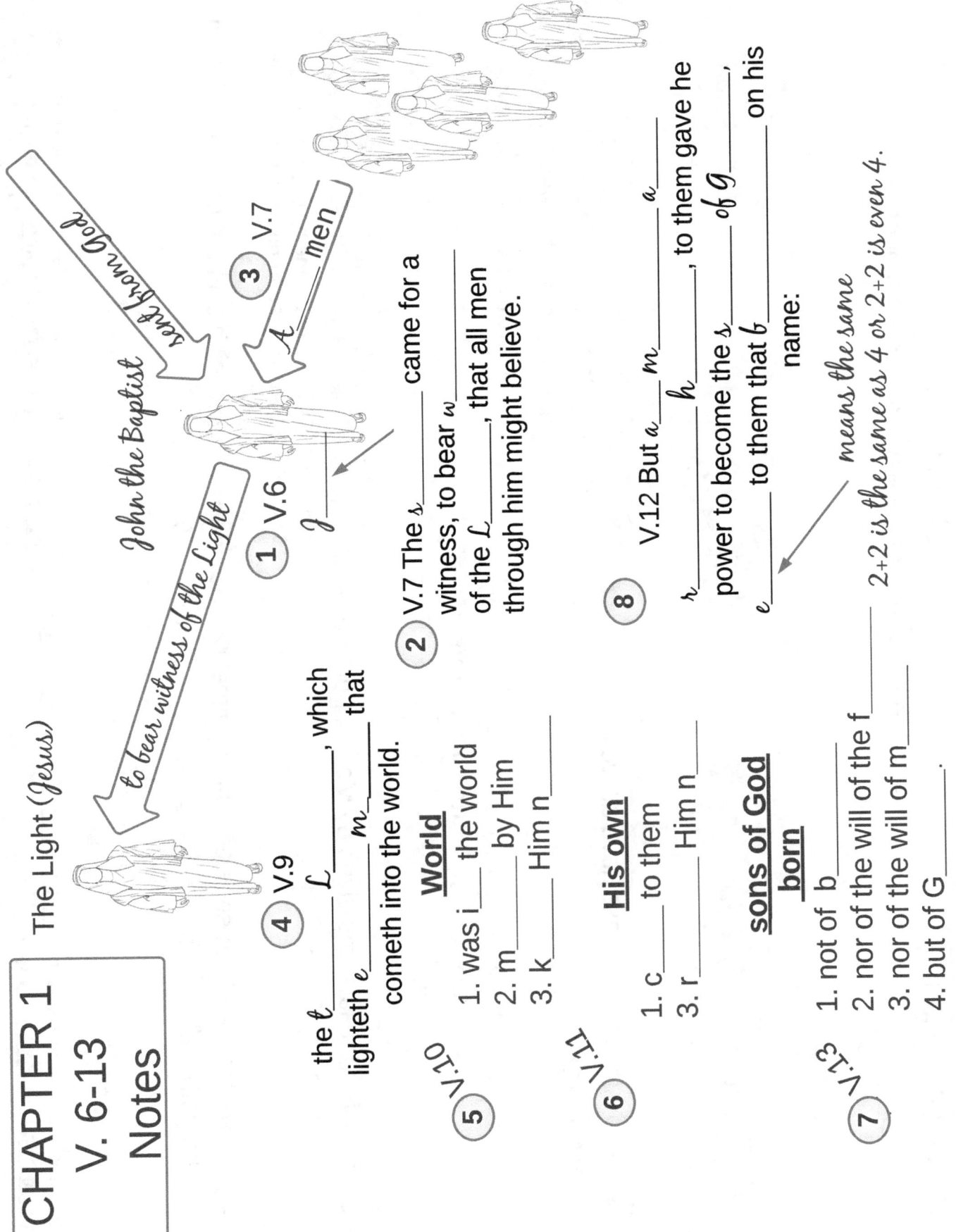

CHAPTER 1
V. 6-13
Notes

The Light (Jesus)

John the Baptist

sent from God

to bear witness of the Light

1 V.6
There was a man s_____ from God, whose name was J_____

2 V.7 The s_____ came for a witness, to bear w_____, that all men of the L_____, through him might believe.

3 V.7
A_____ men might believe.

4 V.9
That was the true L_____, which lighteth e_____ m_____ that cometh into the world.

5 V.10 **World**
1. was i_____ the world
2. m_____ by Him
3. k_____ Him n_____

6 V.11 **His own**
1. c_____ to them
3. r_____ Him n_____

7 V.13 **sons of God born**
1. not of b_____
2. nor of the will of the f_____
3. nor of the will of m_____
4. but of G_____.

8 V.12 But a_____ m_____ a_____, to them gave he p_____ h_____, to them that b_____ of G_____ power to become the s_____ on his name:

e_____

means the same
2+2 is the same as 4 or 2+2 is even 4.

CHAPTER 1
V. 14-18
Guide

The witness that John the Baptist gave to Jesus of Nazareth as the Son of God begins in V. 15.

1 **V.14**

And the *Word* was made *flesh,* and *dwelt* among us,

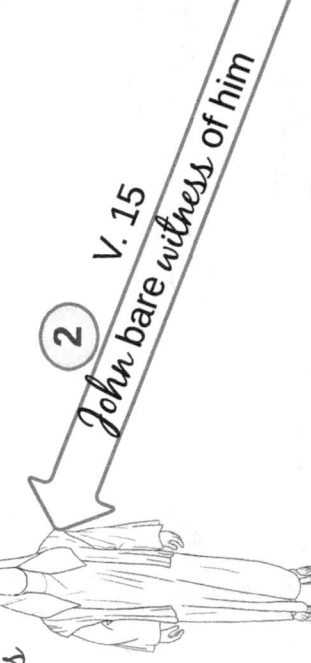

John the Baptist

Jesus

2

John bare witness of him

3 V. 15 ... He that cometh after me is preferred before me: for he was before me.

(was with God in the beginning)

4 V.16 And of his fulness have all we received, and grace for grace.

Because Jesus shows grace to us, we know what grace is and we are, therefore, able to show grace to others.

5 V.17 For the law was given by Moses, but grace and truth came by Jesus Christ.

Jesus was born of a virgin and is the only man with the blood of the heavenly Father.

John 5:6 This is he that came by water and blood, even Jesus Christ; not by water only, but by water and blood.

6 V.18 No man hath seen God at any time, the only *begotten Son,* which is in the bosom of the Father, he hath *declared* him.

Atheist – I don't believe in anyone I can't see.

Answer – You have never seen other historical figures but yet you believe they existed. Jesus was God and spent 33 years upon the earth so He could be looked upon.

to make plain or show

Exodus 33:20 And he said, Thou canst not see my face: for there shall no man see me, and live.

Genesis 32:30 And Jacob called the name of the place Peniel: for I have seen God face to face, and my life is preserved.

—Saw Jesus as God in the Old Testament

CHAPTER 1
V. 14-18
Notes

1 V.14

And the W_____ was made f_____, and d_____ among us,

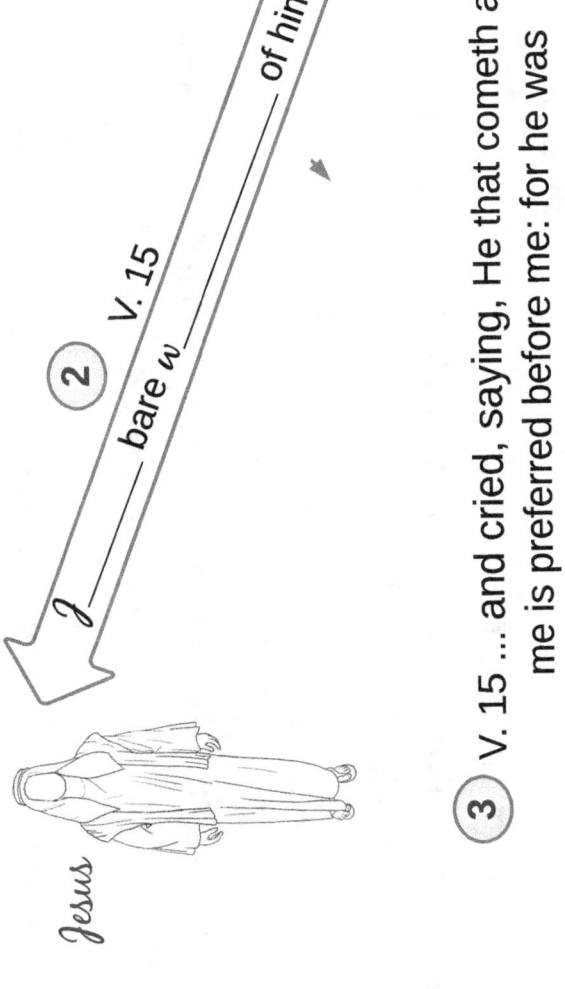

Jesus

John the Baptist

2 V. 15

J_____ bare w_____ of him

3 V. 15 ... and cried, saying, He that cometh after me is preferred before me: for he was b_____ me.

4 V.16 And of his fulness have all we received, and g_____ for g_____.

5 V.17 For the law was given by Moses, but g_____ and t_____ came by Jesus Christ.

6 V.18 No man hath seen God at any time, *the o*_____ b_____ S_____, which is in the b_____ *of the F*_____, he hath d_____ him.

CHAPTER 1
V. 19-24
Guide

The record to the Jews of how John the Baptist knew his witness of Jesus is true (or how it came about) begins in V. 19. He declares it to the Jews in V. 34.

Deuteronomy 18:18 I will raise them up a Prophet from among their brethren, like unto thee, and will put my words in his mouth; and he shall speak unto them all that I shall command him.

Like unto Moses

Jerusalem Jews

Levites— from the tribe of Levi. All priests were Levites. But not all Levites were priests; some had other duties in the temple.

Priests
Levites

John the Baptist

Who art thou?

V. 19
Priests and Levites

V. 24 ..... *of the Pharisees*

① Pharisees— a Jewish religious group that held strictly to traditions and were experts at the law.

⑥

② V.20 ...I am not the Christ.

③ V.21 ...I am not Elias (Elias is Greek for the Hebrew word Elijah)

④ V.21 ...I am not that prophet

Expecting the prophet, like unto Moses, as prophesied in the Old Testament.

Esaias is Greek for the Hebrew word Isaiah.

Voice

⑤ V.23 ...I am the voice of one crying in the wilderness, Make straight the way of the Lord, as said the prophet Esaias.

Isaiah 40:2 Speak ye comfortably to Jerusalem, and cry unto her, that her warfare is accomplished, that her iniquity is pardoned: for she hath received of the LORD's hand double for all her sins.

Isaiah 40:3 The voice of him that crieth in the wilderness, Prepare ye the way of the LORD, make straight in the desert a highway for our God.

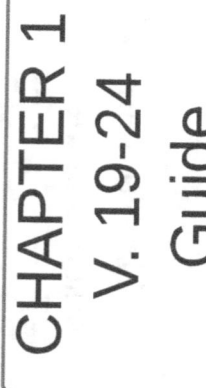

CHAPTER 1
V. 19-24
Notes

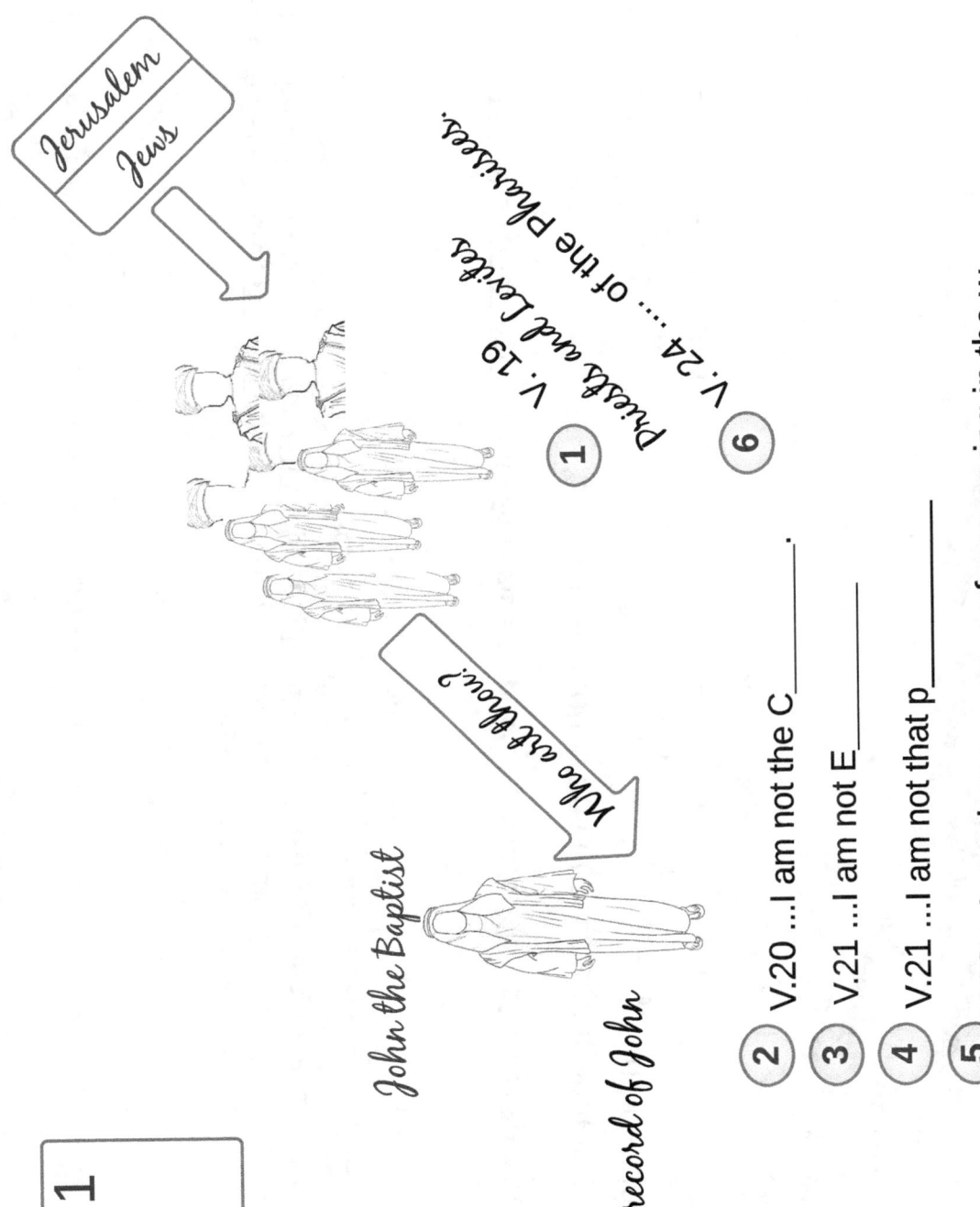

Jerusalem
Jews

John the Baptist

the record of John

Who art thou?

1 V. 19
Priests and Levites

6 V. 24 ..... of the Pharisees.

2 V.20 ...I am not the C_____.

3 V.21 ...I am not E_____

4 V.21 ...I am not that p_____

5 V.23 ....I am the v_____ of one crying in the w_____,
Make straight the way of the Lord, as said the prophet E_____.

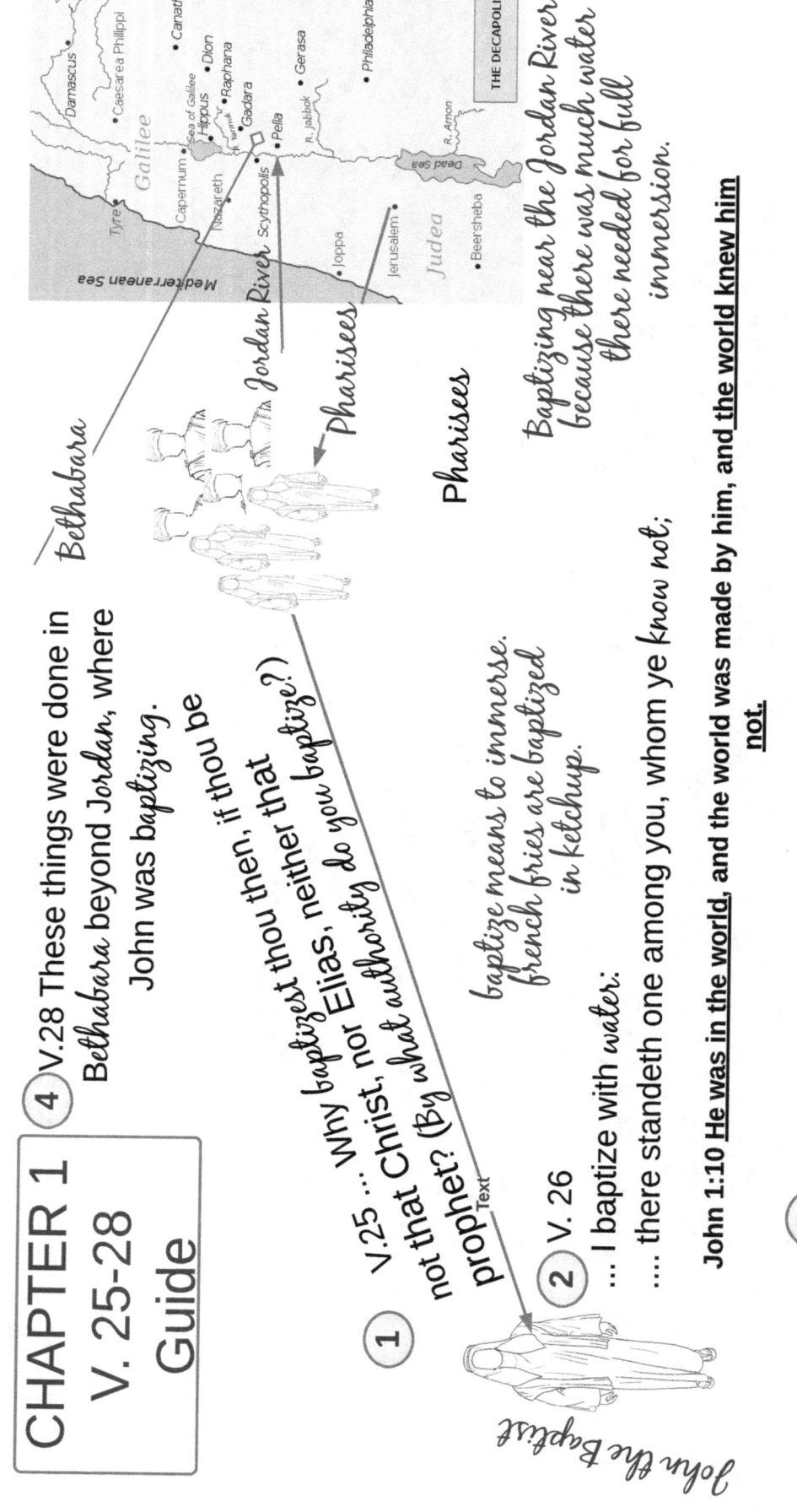

CHAPTER 1
V. 25-28
Guide

4 v.28 These things were done in Bethabara beyond Jordan, where John was baptizing.

Bethabara

THE DECAPOLIS

Jordan River

Pharisees

Pharisees

Pharisees

Baptizing near the Jordan River because there was much water there needed for full immersion.

1 v.25 … Why baptizest thou then, if thou be not that Christ, nor Elias, neither that prophet? (By what authority do you baptize?)

Text

John the Baptist

baptize means to immerse. french fries are baptized in ketchup.

2 V. 26
… I baptize with water:
… there standeth one among you, whom ye know not;

John 1:10 He was in the world, and the world was made by him, and the world knew him not.

3 V.27 He it is, who coming after me is preferred before me, whose shoe's latchet I am not worthy to unloose.

Ruth 4:7-8 Now this was the manner in former time in Israel concerning redeeming and concerning changing, for to confirm all things; a man plucked off his shoe, and gave it to his neighbour: and this was a testimony in Israel. Therefore the kinsman said unto Boaz, Buy it for thee. So he drew off his shoe.

Boaz was the redeemer of Ruth. The tradition of agreeing to a deal was for a man to take off His shoe and give it to his neighbor. The Pharisees were experts in Jewish tradition and knew John was bearing witness, that he himself was not the redeemer. I cannot redeem and I'm not even worthy to loosen the Redeemer's shoe for him.

CHAPTER 1
V. 25-28
Notes

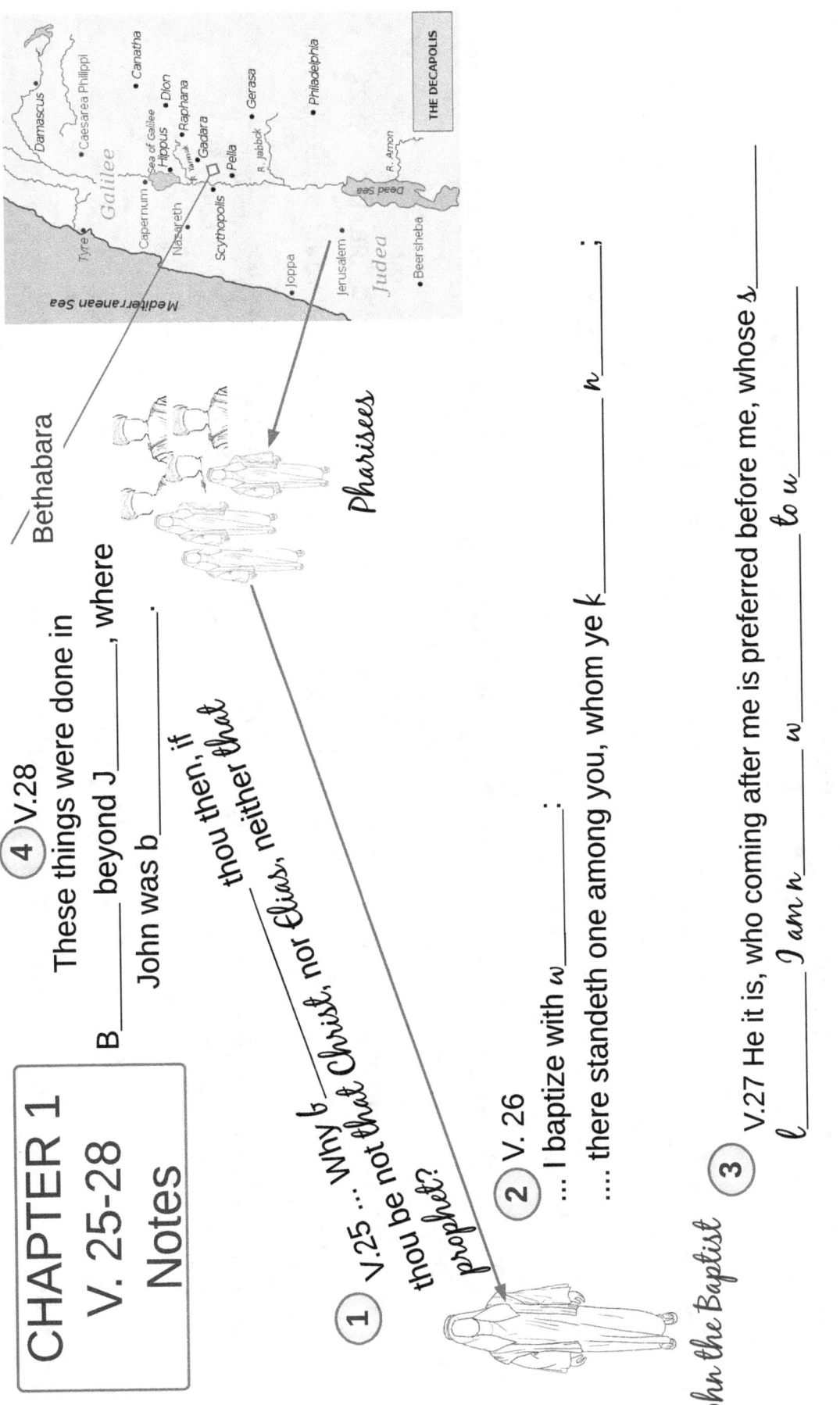

Bethabara

4 V.28

These things were done in

B_____ beyond J_____, where

John was b_____ .

1 V.25 ... Why b_____ thou then, if thou be not that Christ, nor Elias, neither that prophet?

Pharisees

2 V. 26

... I baptize with w_____:

.... there standeth one among you, whom ye k_____ n_____;

John the Baptist **3** V.27 He it is, who coming after me is preferred before me, whose s_____

l_____ w_____ to w_____

I am n_____

CHAPTER 1
V. 29-34
Guide

Jesus

John the
Baptist

1 V. 29 The next day John seeth Jesus coming unto him, and saith Behold the Lamb of God, which taketh away the sin of the world.

In the Old Testament, lambs were sacrificed on the altar for sins. Jesus would be sacrificed on the cross to pay for our sins.

2 V.31 And I knew him not: but that he should be made manifest to Israel, therefore am I come baptizing with water. (baptizing with water makes manifests to others

3 V.32 And John bare record, saying, I saw the Spirit descending from heaven like a dove, and it abode upon him. (A dove is symbolic for the Holy Spirit)

4 V.33 And I knew him not: but he that sent me to baptize with water, the same said unto me, Upon whom thou shalt see the Spirit descending, and remaining on him, the same is he which baptizeth with the Holy Ghost.

As John was baptizing with water. He was looking for the Son of God, which would have the Spirit descending and remaining on Him.

The answer to the Pharisee's question why are you baptizing is because God sent me to bare witness of His Son.

Jesus baptizes with the Holy Ghost. Not all baptisms in the Bible are speaking of water baptism.

5 V.34 And I saw, and bare record that this is the Son of God.

CHAPTER 1
V. 29-34
Notes

Jesus

John the Baptist

(1) V. 29 The next day John seeth J_____ of G_____ coming unto him, and saith Behold the L_____ of the w_____, which taketh away the s_____.

(2) V.31 And I knew him not: but that he should be m_____ m_____ to I_____, therefore am I come b_____ with w_____.

(3) V.32 And John b_____ r_____, saying, I saw the S_____ d_____ from heaven like a d_____, and it a_____ upon h_____.

(4) V.33 And I knew him not: but he that sent me to b_____ with w_____, the same said unto me, Upon whom thou shalt see the S_____ d_____, and r_____ on him, the same is he which b_____ with the H_____ G_____.

(5) V.34 And I saw, and b_____ r_____ that this is the S_____ of G_____.

CHAPTER 1
V. 35-46
Guide

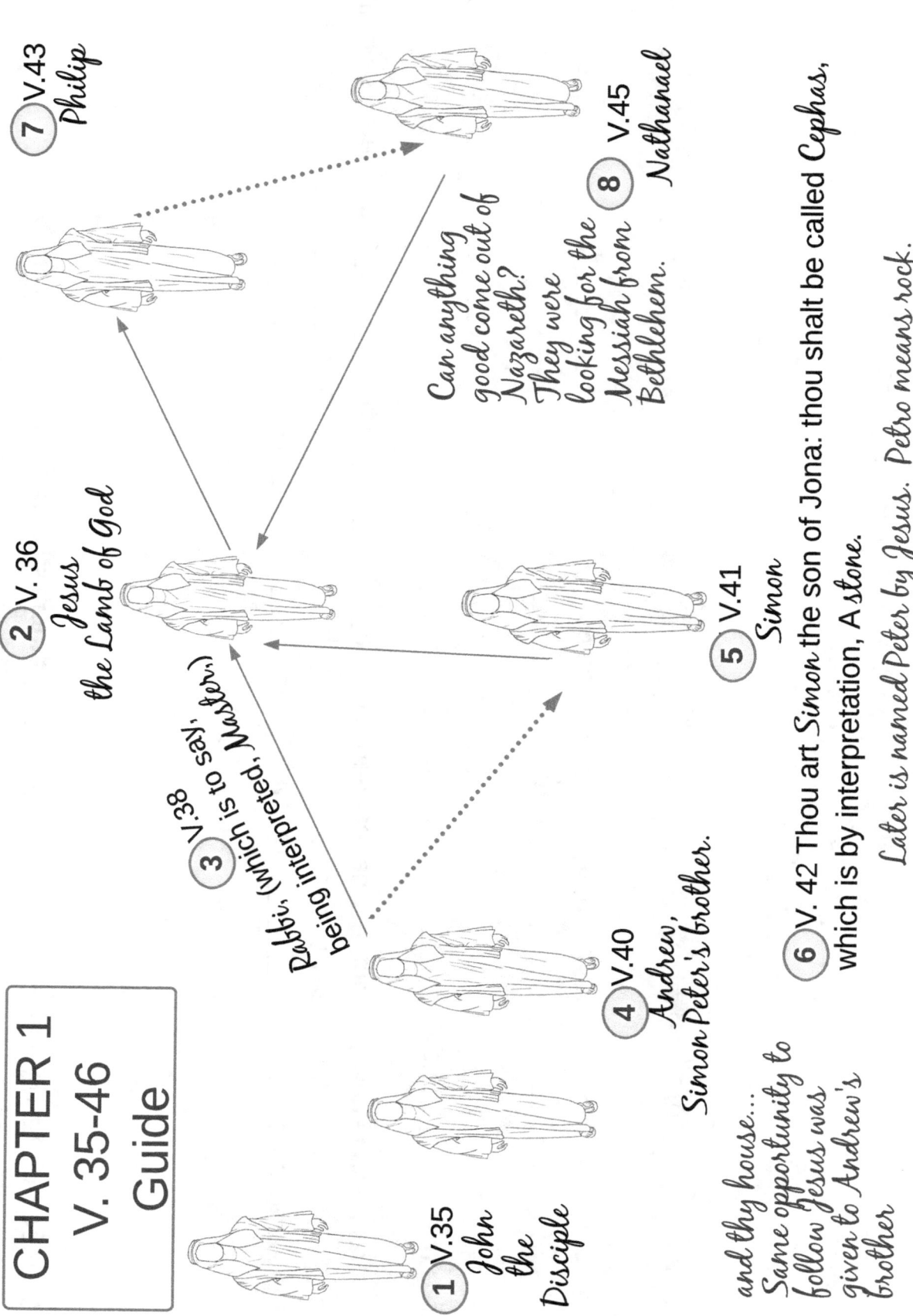

1 V.35
John
the
Disciple

2 V. 36
Jesus
the Lamb of God

3 V.38
Rabbi, (which is to say, Master,)
being interpreted, (Master,)

4 V.40
Andrew,
Simon Peter's brother.

...and thy house...
Same opportunity to
follow Jesus was
given to Andrew's
brother

5 V.41
Simon

6 V. 42 Thou art Simon the son of Jona: thou shalt be called Cephas,
which is by interpretation, A stone.

Later is named Peter by Jesus. Petro means rock.

7 V.43
Philip

8 V.45
Nathanael

Can anything
good come out of
Nazareth?
They were
looking for the
Messiah from
Bethlehem.

CHAPTER 1
V. 35-46
Notes

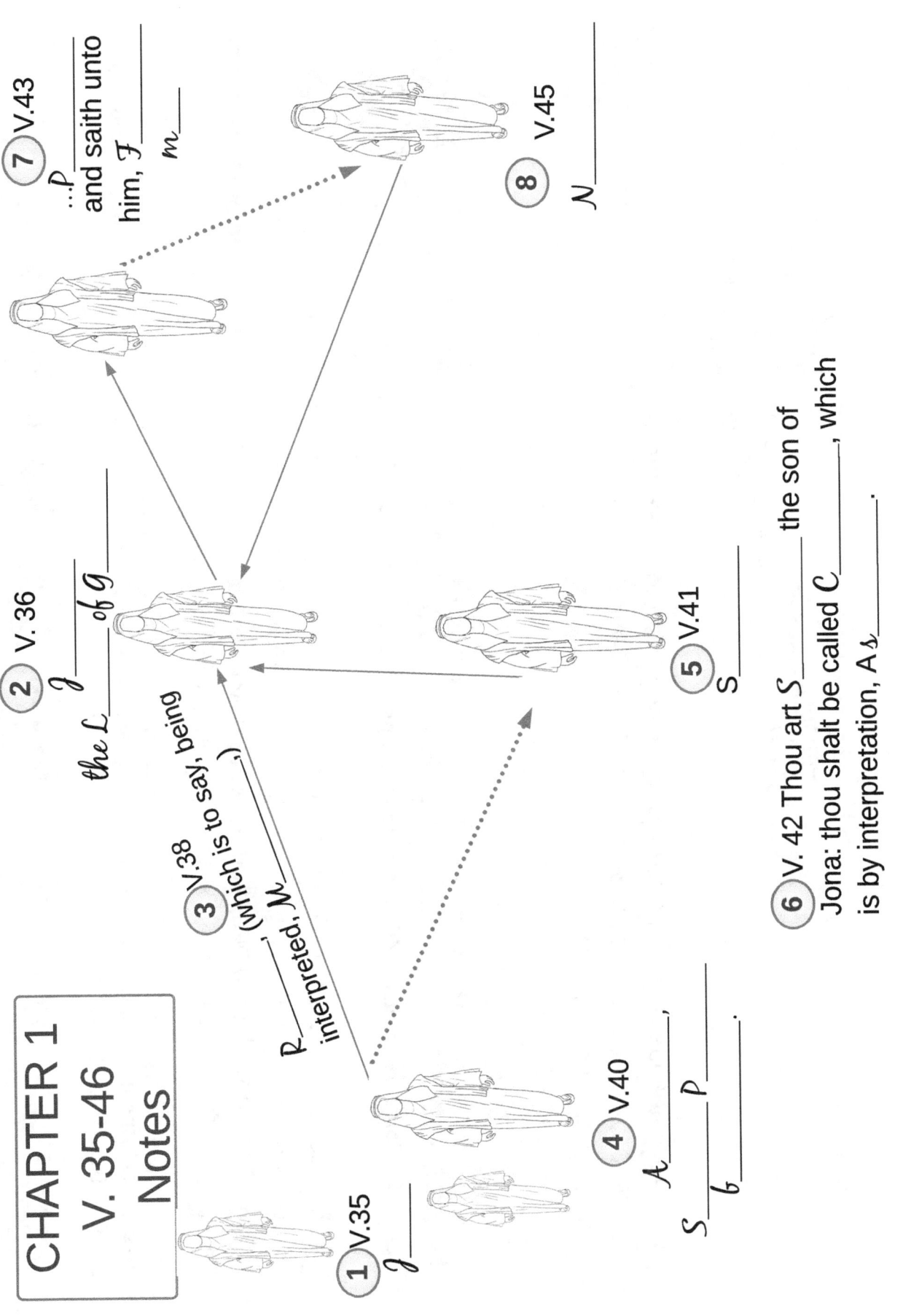

1 V.35

J_____

2 V. 36

J_____ of G_____ the L_____

3 V.38

R_____, interpreted, M_____ (which is to say, being _____,)

4 v.40

A_____, S_____ P_____ b_____.

5 V.41

S_____

6 V. 42 Thou art S_____ the son of Jona: thou shalt be called C_____, which is by interpretation, A s_____.

7 V.43

...P_____ and saith unto him, F_____ m_____

8 V.45

N_____

CHAPTER 1
V. 47-51
Guide

(1) V. 47
Jesus

Behold an Israelite indeed, in whom is no guile!

(3) V. 47
guile means crafty, cunning, deceitful

(2) V. 47
Nathanael

fig tree is symbolic of nation of Israel

— *An Israelite*

(4) V.48 Nathanael saith unto him, Whence knowest thou me? Jesus answered and said unto him, Before that Philip called thee, *when thou wast under the fig tree, I saw thee.*

(5) V.49 Nathanael answered and saith unto him, *Rabbi,* thou art the *Son of God;* thou art the *King of Israel.*

When Jesus was with the woman at the well, she perceived He was a prophet because He told her about her 5 husbands. Then she went and told others.

John 4:29 Come, see a man, which told me all things that ever I did: is not this the Christ?

(6) V.50 Jesus answered and said unto him, *Because I said unto thee, I saw thee under the fig tree, believest thou?* thou shalt see greater things than these.

(7) V.51 And he saith unto him, *Verily, verily, I say unto you,* Hereafter ye shall see heaven open, and *the angels of God ascending and descending upon the Son of man.*

Genesis 28:10 And Jacob went out from Beersheba, and went toward Haran.
Genesis 28:12 And he dreamed, and **behold a ladder** set up on the earth, and the top of it reached to **heaven: and behold the angels of God ascending and descending on it.**

In Jacob's dream, the ladder is a picture of Jesus, the Son of man

CHAPTER 1
V. 47-51
Notes

① V. 47
J_____

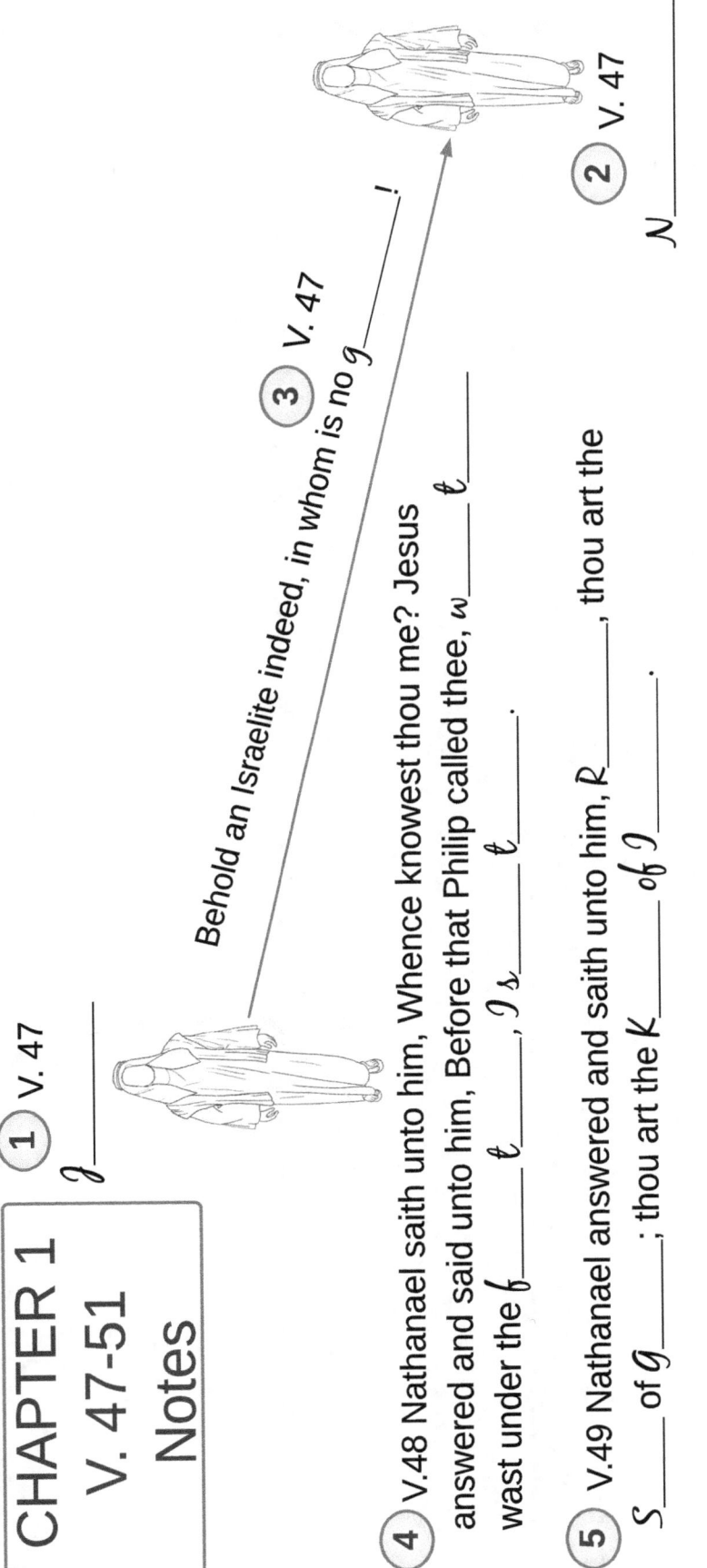

Behold an Israelite indeed, in whom is no g_____!

③ V. 47
_____

② V. 47
N_____

④ V.48 Nathanael saith unto him, Whence knowest thou me? Jesus answered and said unto him, Before that Philip called thee, w_____ t_____ wast under the f_____ t_____, I s_____ t_____.

⑤ V.49 Nathanael answered and saith unto him, R_____, thou art the S_____ of G_____; thou art the K_____ of I_____.

⑥ V.50 Jesus answered and said unto him, B_____ I s_____ unto thee, I saw thee under the fig tree, b_____ t_____? thou shalt see greater things than these.

⑦ V.51 And he saith unto him, V_____, v_____, s_____ unto you, Hereafter ye shall see heaven open, and the a_____ of G_____ a_____ and d_____ upon the S_____ of m_____.

Read John
Chapter 2

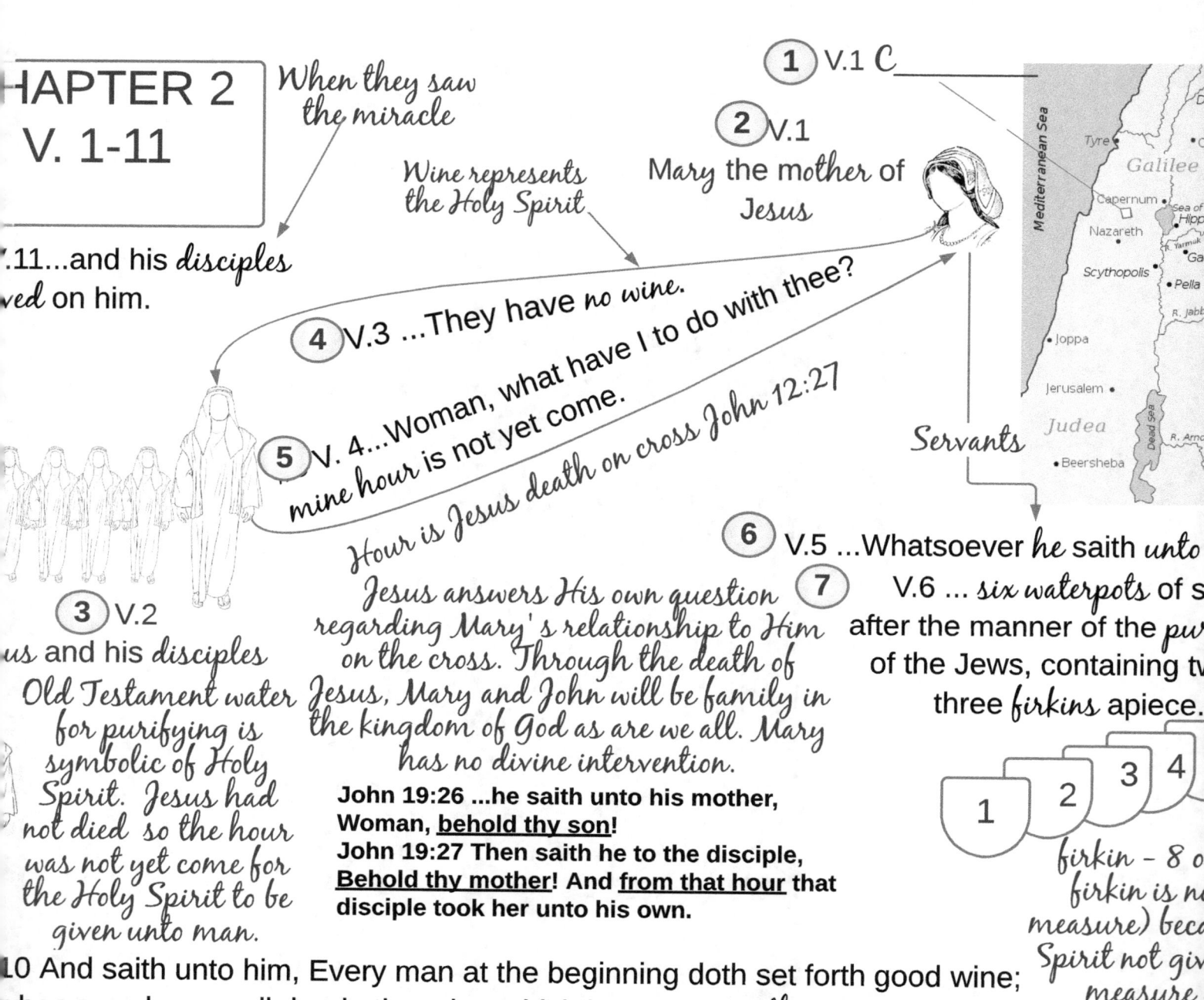

CHAPTER 2
V. 1-11

When they saw the miracle

Wine represents the Holy Spirit

V.11...and his *disciples* ~~ved~~ on him.

(1) V.1 C_____

(2) V.1 Mary the mother of Jesus

(4) V.3 ...They have no wine.

(5) V. 4...Woman, what have I to do with thee? mine hour is not yet come.

Hour is Jesus death on cross John 12:27

Jesus answers His own question regarding Mary's relationship to Him on the cross. Through the death of Jesus, Mary and John will be family in the kingdom of God as are we all. Mary has no divine intervention.

**John 19:26 ...he saith unto his mother, Woman, <u>behold thy son</u>!
John 19:27 Then saith he to the disciple, <u>Behold thy mother</u>! And <u>from that hour</u> that disciple took her unto his own.**

Servants

(6) V.5 ...Whatsoever he saith unto

(7) V.6 ... six waterpots of s~~~~ after the manner of the *pur~~~~* of the Jews, containing t~~~~ three *firkins* apiece.

1 2 3 4

*firkin – 8 o~~
firkin is n~~
measure) beca~~
Spirit not giv~~
measure~~
Filled to the~~
was filled wi~~
Spi~~*

(3) V.2
~~us~~ and his *disciples*

Old Testament water for purifying is symbolic of Holy Spirit. Jesus had not died so the hour was not yet come for the Holy Spirit to be given unto man.

~~1~~0 And saith unto him, Every man at the beginning doth set forth good wine; ~~~~when men have well drunk, then that which is worse: but *thou* hast kept the ~~~~wine until now. *The bridegroom is symbolic of Jesus and the wine is symbolic* ~~~~*Holy Spirit. It was not yet time for the Holy Spirit to be given.*

Mediterranean Sea

Galilee

Tyre
Capernum • Sea of Hipp
Nazareth
Scythopolis • Pella
R. Jabb
• Joppa
Jerusalem •
Judea
• Beersheba
Dead Sea
R. Arno

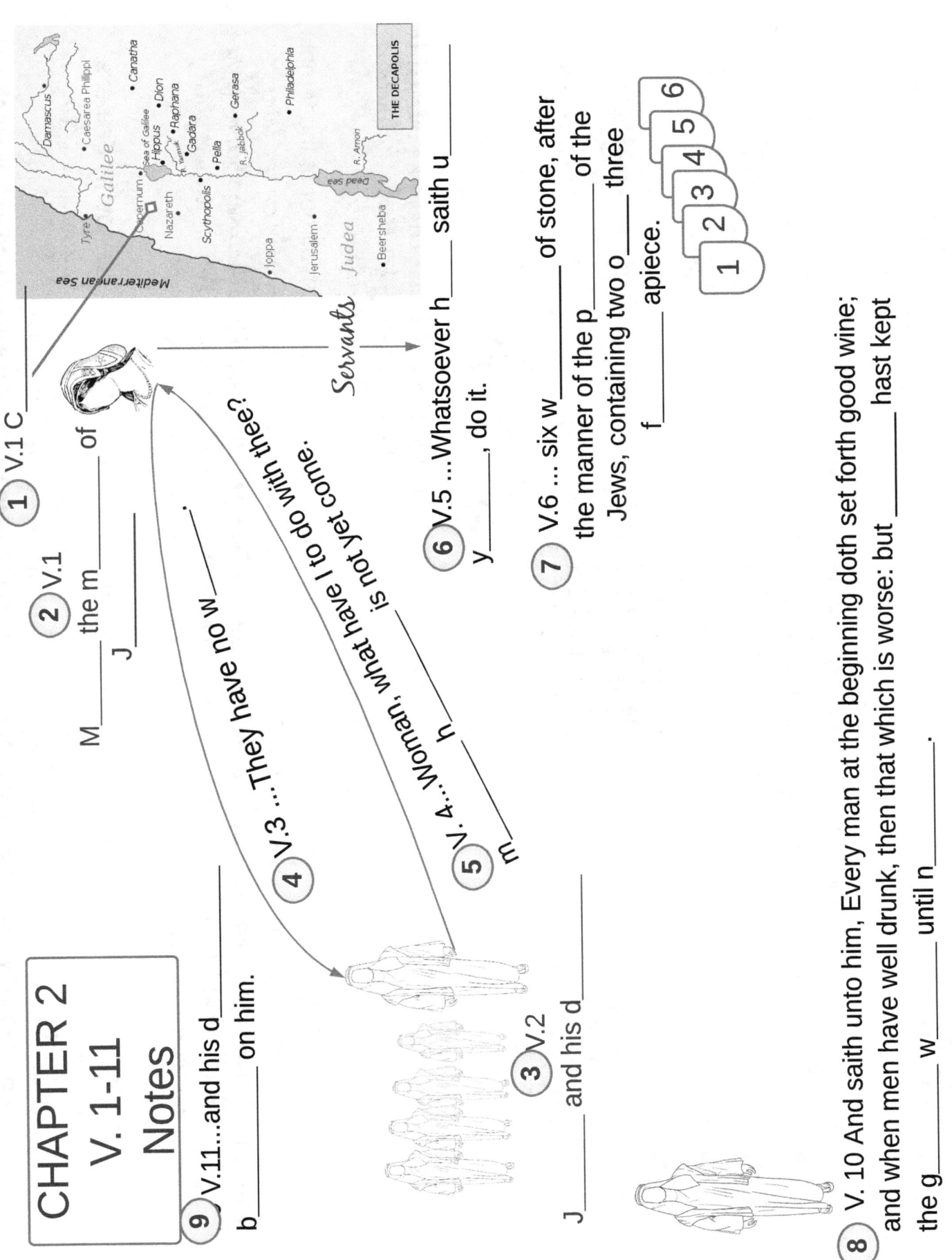

CHAPTER 2
V. 1-11
Notes

1 V.1 C _____

2 V.1 _____ the m _____ J _____ M _____

3 V.2 _____ J _____ and his d _____

4 V.3 …They have no w _____.

5 V. 4 …Woman, what have I to do with thee? m _____ h _____ is not yet come.

Servants →

6 V.5 …Whatsoever h _____ saith u _____ y _____, do it.

7 V.6 … six w _____ of stone, after the manner of the p _____ of the Jews, containing two o _____ three f _____ apiece.

THE DECAPOLIS

8 V. 10 And saith unto him, Every man at the beginning doth set forth good wine; and when men have well drunk, then that which is worse: but _____ hast kept the g _____ w _____ until n _____.

9 V.11…and his d _____ b _____ on him.

CHAPTER 2
V. 12-17
Key

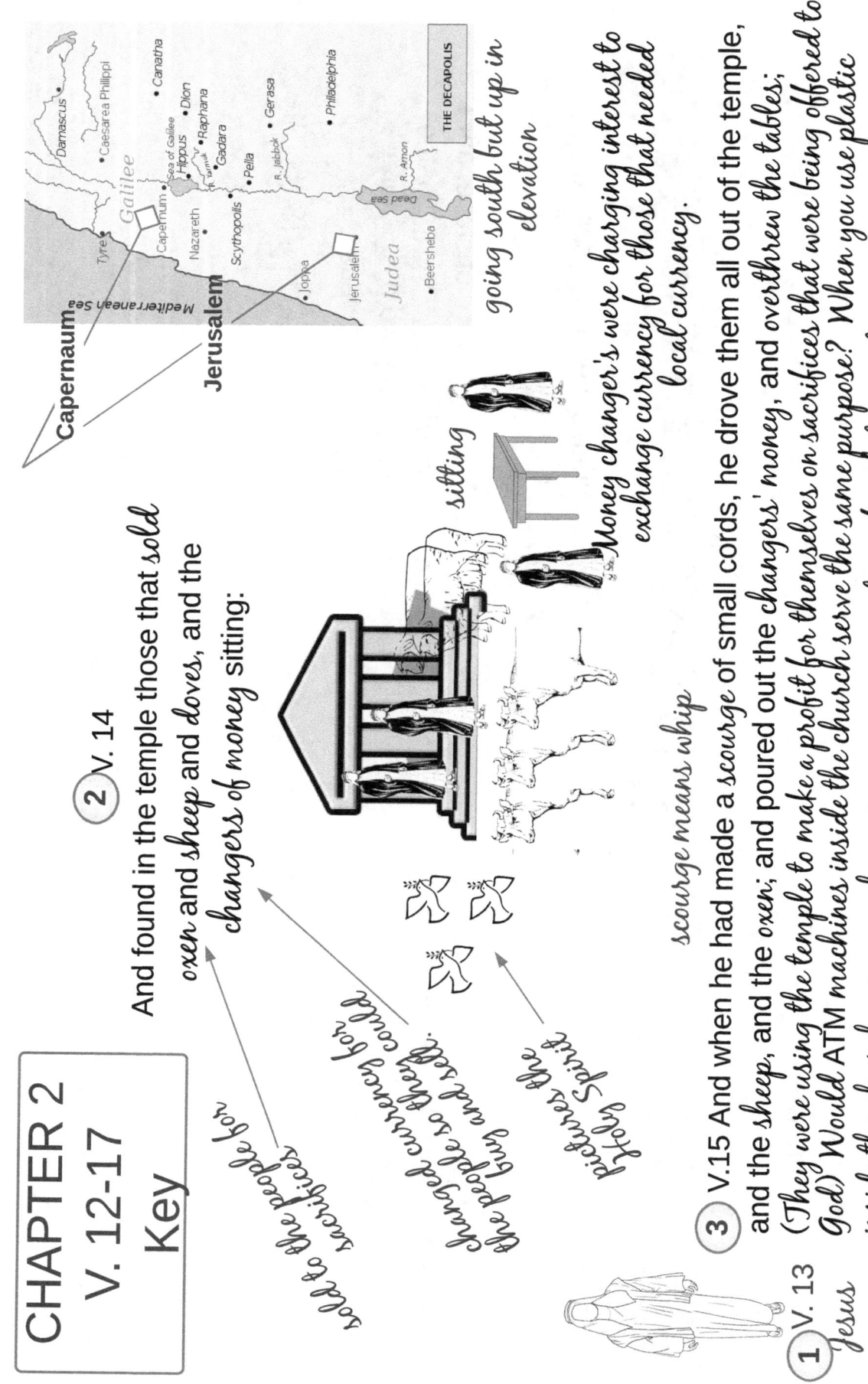

1 V. 13 Jesus

2 V. 14
And found in the temple those that sold oxen and sheep and doves, and the changers of money sitting:

sold for sacrifices

the people so they could buy and sell

Holy Spirit

sitting

money changer's were charging interest to exchange currency for those that needed local currency.

going south but up in elevation

scourge means whip

3 V.15 And when he had made a scourge of small cords, he drove them all out of the temple, and the sheep, and the oxen; and poured out the changers' money, and overthrew the tables; (They were using the temple to make a profit for themselves on sacrifices that were being offered to God) Would ATM machines inside the church serve the same purpose? When you use plastic inside the church a money changer receives a percentage of each transaction.

4 V.16 And said unto them that sold doves, Take these things hence; make not my Father's house an house of merchandise. Doves are mentioned separately because buying and selling a dove at the temple would represent the Holy Spirit could be bought and sold.

Acts 8:20....Thy money perish with thee, because thou hast thought that the gift of God may be purchased with money.

Capernaum

Jerusalem

Mediterranean Sea

Galilee

Judea

THE DECAPOLIS

CHAPTER 2
V. 12-17
Notes

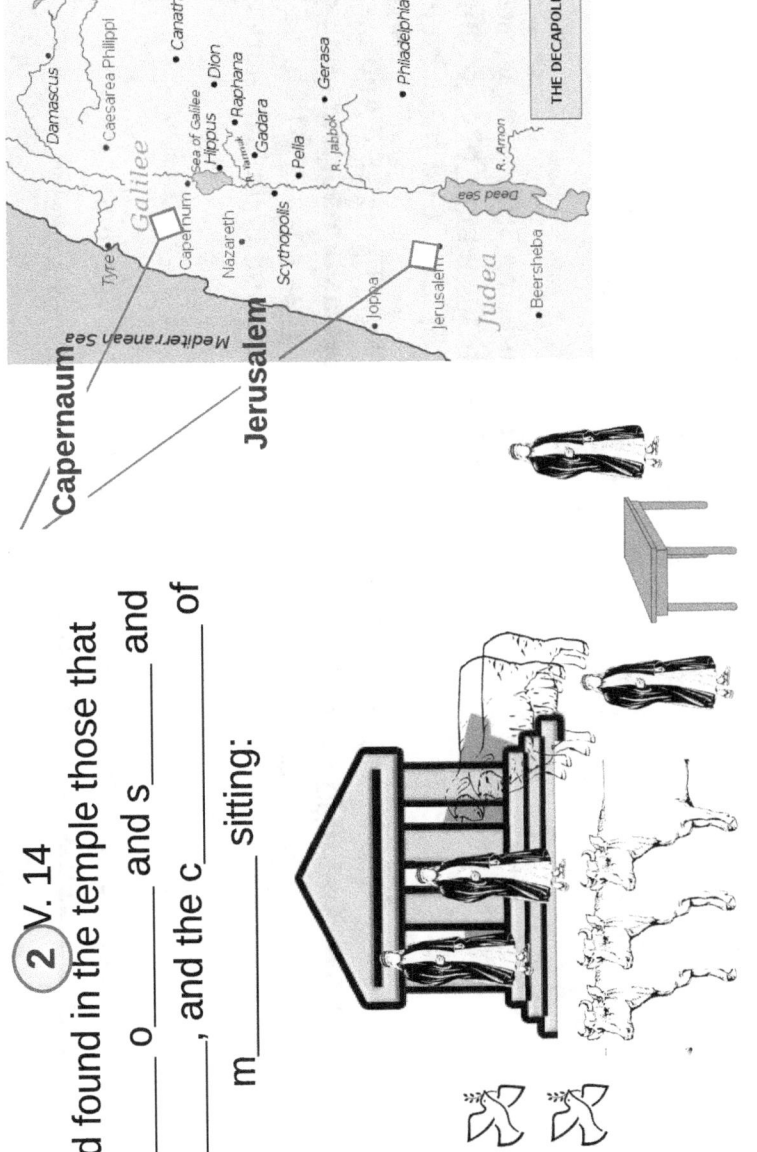

2 V. 14

And found in the temple those that
s_____ o_____ and s_____ and
d_____, and the c_____ of
m_____ sitting:

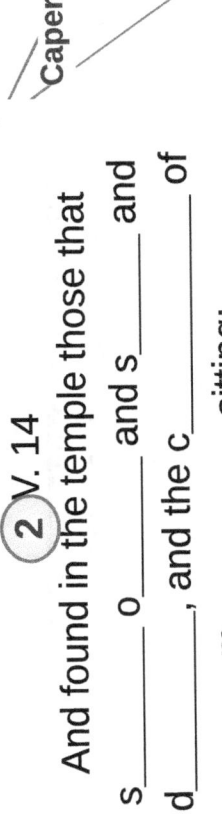

1 V. 13
J

3 V.15 And when he had made a s_____ of small cords, he drove them all out of the
temple, and the s_____, and the o_____; and poured out the c_____
m_____, and o_____ the t_____;

4 V.16 And said unto them that sold d_____, Take these things hence; make not my
Father's house an h_____ of m_____.

CHAPTER 2
V. 18-25
Key

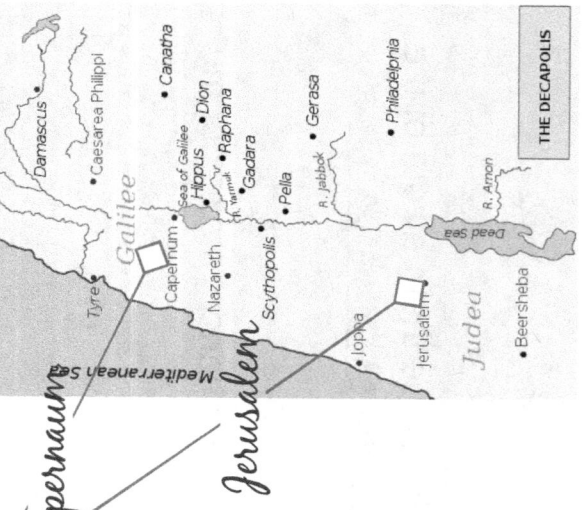

Capernaum

Jerusalem

The Old Testament temple is a picture of the true Temple, the body of Christ.

John the Baptist came as a witness or to testify of Jesus as the Lamb of God. Throughout the Book of John, many will witness or testify that Jesus has been sent from God.

3 V.25 And needed *not* that any should *testify* of man: for he knew what was in man.

prophecy

1 V.18 Then answered the Jews and said unto him, What *sign* shewest thou unto us, seeing that thou doest these things

The sign was that the body of the Holy One would not see corruption (decay).

2 V.19 *Jesus* answered and said unto them, Destroy this *temple*, and in *three days* I will raise it up.

1Corinthians 3:16 Know ye not that <u>ye are the temple of God</u>, and that the Spirit of God dwelleth in you?

1Corinthians 15:4 And that <u>he was buried, and that he rose again the third day according to the scriptures:</u>

Psalm 16:10 For thou wilt not leave my soul in hell; neither wilt thou suffer <u>thine Holy One to see corruption.</u>

CHAPTER 2
V. 18-25
Notes

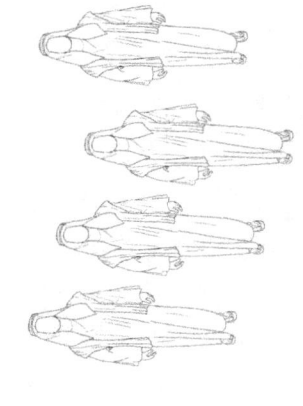

The map showing:
Mediterranean Sea, Galilee, Judea, Dead Sea, Tyre, Damascus, Caesarea Philippi, Canatha, Capernum, Sea of Galilee, Nazareth, Hippus, Dion, Raphana, Gadara, Scythopolis, Pella, Gerasa, Philadelphia, Joppa, Jerusalem, Beersheba, R. Jabbok, R. Arnon, THE DECAPOLIS

Capernaum

Jerusalem

3 V. 25 And needed n_____
that any should
t_____ of
m_____ : for he knew
what was in man.

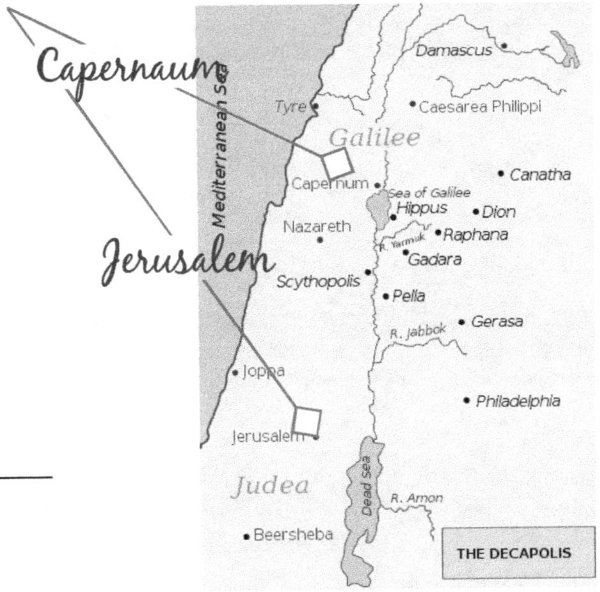

2 V.19 J_____ answered
and said unto them,
Destroy this t_____, and
in t_____ d_____ I will
raise it up.

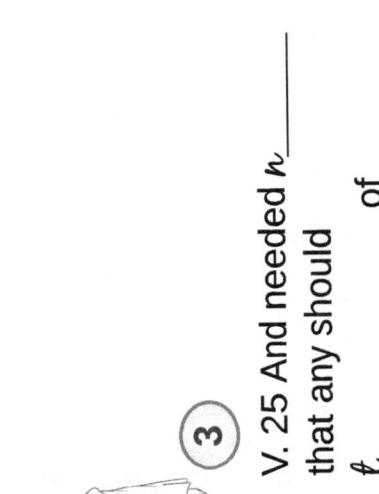

1 V.18 Then answered the
J_____ and said unto him,
What s_____ shewest thou
unto us, seeing that thou doest
these things

Read Chapter 3

2Timothy 3:16 All scripture is given by inspiration of God, and is profitable for doctrine, for reproof, for correction, for instruction in righteousness:

2Timothy 3:17 That the man of God may be perfect, throughly furnished unto all good works.

CHAPTER 3
V. 1-10
Guide

(1) V.1 of the Pharisees, named Nicodemus, a ruler of the Jews:

By night

(2) V.2

(3) unto thee, Except a man be *born again*, he cannot *see* the kingdom of God.

V.3 ... Verily, verily, I say

See means Understand or comprehend.
(Ex. I just can't see it or understand it)

(4) V.4 *How* can a man be *born* when he is old? can he enter the *second time* into his mother's womb, and be born?

Speaking of heavenly things
#1 Physical birth– *Water in the womb gushes out as a baby is born*

#2 *Spiritual birth*

(5) V.5 Jesus answered, Verily, verily, I say unto thee, Except a man be born of *water* and of the *Spirit*, he cannot enter into the kingdom of God.

(6) V.6 That which is born of the *flesh* is *flesh*; and that which is born of the *Spirit* is *spirit*.

Physical birth

Spiritual birth

How can these things be?

chooses

(7) V.8 The *wind* bloweth where it *listeth*, and thou hearest the sound thereof, but canst not tell whence it cometh, and whither it goeth: so is every one that is *born of the Spirit*.
The wind is something that we can't explain or understand. Neither can we explain or understand being born again by the Holy Spirit.

Wind is symbolic for Holy Spirit

Acts 2:2-4 And suddenly there came a sound from heaven as of a rushing mighty wind, and it filled all the house where they were sitting. And there appeared unto them cloven tongues like as of fire, and it sat upon each of them. And they were all filled with the Holy Ghost,

CHAPTER 3
V. 1-10
Notes

1 V.1 of the
P_____,
named
N_____,
a r_____
of the J_____:

By night

2 v.2
J_____

3 V.3 ... V_____, v_____, I say
unto thee, Except a man be
b_____ a_____, he cannot
S_____ the kingdom of God.

4 V.4 H_____ can a man be b_____ when he
is old? can he enter the s_____ t_____
into his mother's womb, and be born?

5 V.5 Jesus answered, V_____, v_____, _____, s_____ unto thee, Except a man be born of
w_____ and of the S_____, he cannot enter into the kingdom of God.

6 V.6 That which is born of the f_____ is flesh; and that which is born of the S_____ is
S_____.

How can these things be?

7 V.8 The w_____ bloweth where it l_____, and thou hearest the sound thereof, but canst not tell
whence it cometh, and whither it goeth: so is every one that is b_____ of the S_____.

CHAPTER 3
V. 11-13
Guide

Who are the plural pronouns in this verse?

Not referring to the disciples. They have never been to heaven.

Singular

V.11 Verily, verily, <u>I say</u> unto thee,

Plural

Plural

<u>We</u> speak that we do know, and testify that <u>we</u> have seen;

Plural

and ye receive not <u>our</u> witness.

The Book of John speaks much of the witness, that Jesus is the Son of God sent from heaven. Whenever the phrase Verily Verily, I say is used, Jesus is testifying of heavenly things only heaven would know.

John 5:7 For there are three that bear record in heaven, the <u>Father</u>, the <u>Word</u>, and the <u>Holy Ghost</u>: and these <u>three</u> <u>are one.</u>

#1 Verily – the Father
#2 Verily – Holy Ghost (Holy Spirit)
#3 I say – the Word (and the Word was made flesh) Jesus

Verily, Verily, I say is found only in John, because the emphasis is on Jesus is come from heaven.

Jesus the Word, is speaking on earth, (I say) but He is speaking for the Father, the Word and the Holy Ghost because they are one. Therefore, He uses the plural. These three are one.

Jesus can testify of heavenly things such as being born again because He has been to heaven and came down from heaven and He is the only one to ever do so.

John 3:12 If I have told you **earthly things, and ye believe not, how shall ye believe, if I tell you of** <u>heavenly things?</u> (such as being sent from heaven, being born again, and prophecy etc.)

John 3:13 And no man hath **ascended up to heaven, but** <u>he that came down from heaven, even the</u> <u>Son of man which is in heaven.</u>

(even means = to or same as)

Jesus

The Father speaks through the Old Testament prophets. In the next few verses of John, Jesus teaches of Moses and the brazen serpent.

Hebrews 1:1 God, who at sundry times and in divers manners <u>spake</u> in time past unto the fathers by the prophets, (example Moses and the Brazen Serpent)

CHAPTER 3
V. 11-13
Notes

Who are the plural pronouns in this verse?

V.11 V_____, v_____, _____ s_____ unto thee,

_____ have seen;

W_____ speak that we do know, and testify that w_____

and ye receive not o_____ witness.

V.12 If I have told you e_____ things, and ye believe not, h_____ shall ye believe, if I tell you of h_____ things?.

V.13 And n_____ man hath a_____ up to h_____, but he that came d_____ from h_____, even the Son of man which is in heaven.

CHAPTER 3
V. 14-17
Guide

Son of Man represents His humanity. He was a sinless man (son of Adam through Mary) and could feel the pain and agony.

Only the Israelites who believed the serpent on the pole could save them, looked to the fiery serpent and lived.

Brass means brazen. (symbolic of sin)

shadow

Body that is casting the shadow.

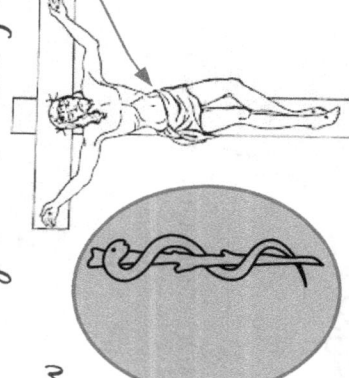

Colossians 2:17 Which are a shadow of things to come; but the **body is of Christ.**

Why does the body of Jesus casts a shadow as a serpent?

2Corinthians 5:21 <u>For he hath made him to be sin for us,</u> who knew no sin; that we might be made the righteousness of God in him

Though, Jesus was sinless, he bore our sins for us upon the cross.

1Peter 2:24 Who <u>his own self bare our sins in his own body on the tree,</u> that we, being dead to sins, should live unto righteousness:

John 3:14 And as Moses lifted up the serpent in the wilderness, even so must the Son of man be lifted up:

Lifted up - lifted up off the earth .

crucified

Numbers 21:8 And the LORD said unto Moses, Make thee a <u>fiery serpent,</u> and set it upon a <u>pole:</u> and it shall come to pass, that every one that is bitten, when he <u>looketh upon it, shall live.</u>

Numbers 21:9 And Moses made a serpent of brass, and put it upon a pole, and it came to pass, that if a serpent had bitten any man, when he beheld the serpent of <u>brass,</u> he lived.

John 3:14 And *as Moses lifted up the serpent in the* wilderness, even so must the *Son of man be lifted up:*

John 3:15 That whosoever believeth in him should not perish, but have eternal life.

John 3:16 For God so loved the world, that he gave his only begotten Son, that *whosoever believeth in him should not perish,* but have everlasting life.

John 3:17 For God sent not his Son into the world to condemn the world; but that the world through him might be saved.

As the Israelites, were already condemned by the fiery serpents, the world was already condemned by the serpent (Satan) when God sent His Son to save it. .

CHAPTER 3
V. 14-17
Notes

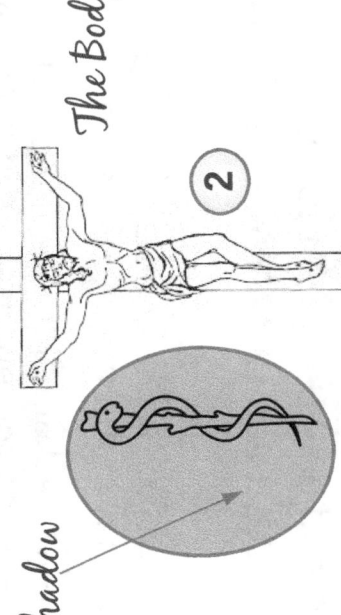

Shadow

②

John 3:14 And as M_____ the serpent in the wilderness, even so must the S_____ of m_____ be _____:

John 3:14 And _____ M_____ l_____ the s_____ in the wilderness, even so must the S_____ of m_____ be l_____ :

John 3:15 That whosoever believeth in him should not perish, but have eternal life.

John 3:16 For God so loved the world, that he gave his only **begotten** Son, that w_____ b_____ should n_____ p_____, but have e_____ l_____ .

John 3:17 For God sent not his Son into the world to condemn the world; but that the world through him might be saved.

Shadow

Numbers 21:8 And the LORD said unto Moses, Make thee a fiery serpent, and set it upon a pole: and it shall come to pass, that every one that is bitten, when he looketh upon it, shall live.

Numbers 21:9 And Moses made a serpent of brass, and put it upon a pole, and it came to pass, that if a serpent had bitten any man, when he beheld the serpent of brass, he lived.

BEGOTTEN?

1John 5:6 This is he that came by water and blood, even Jesus Christ; not by water only, but by water and blood.

(1) water and *blood* → **Jesus Christ** (triangle, "Manifest in the flesh")

Virgin Birth blood of the Heavenly Father

Manifest in the flesh

◇ **1 John 5:6**

(2) water *only* → **All men** (box)

(3) John 1:12 But *as many as received him*, to them gave he power to become *the sons of God*, even to them that believe on his name:

as many as received him

1John 4:1 Beloved, believe not every spirit, but *try the spirits whether they are of God: because many false prophets are gone out into the world.*
1John 4:2 Hereby know ye the Spirit of God: *Every spirit that confesseth that Jesus Christ is come in the flesh is of God:*

Try the spirits of the KJV and the NIV

(4) KJV – John 3:16 *For God so loved the world, that he gave his only begotten Son, that whosoever believeth in him should not perish, but have everlasting life.*

Omits begotten

(5) NIV – John 3:16 *For God so loved the world that he gave his one and only Son, that whoever believes in him shall not perish, but have eternal life.*

The spirit of John 3:16 NIV

(1) If Jesus was God's one and only Son, then we are not sons of Gods and were not <u>begat by the Spirit</u> unto eternal life. **John 1:12, 1 John 3:1, Romans 8:14,19 etc. (James 1:18)**

(2) Omitting only begotten is <u>denying the virgin birth</u> and that Jesus was begotten by the blood of the Heavenly Father. But Jesus came not by water only! Begotten is also omitted in many other verses in the NIV. **1 John 4:9, etc.** This spirit confesseth not that Jesus Christ has come in the flesh. The NIV alludes to Jesus as merely man. Therefore, it is spirit of the antichrist.

BEGOTTEN?

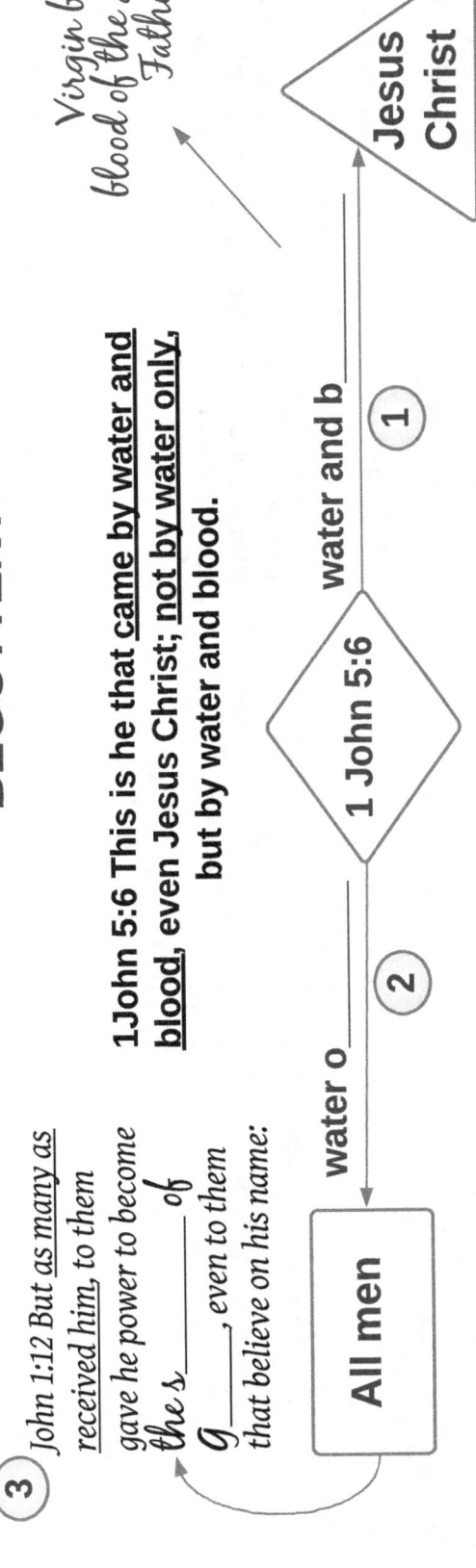

Virgin birth
blood of the Heavenly Father

1John 5:6 This is he that came <u>by water and blood</u>, even Jesus Christ; <u>not by water only, but by water and blood.</u>

Jesus Christ

water and b ___ ①

1 John 5:6

water o ___ ②

All men

③ *John 1:12 But <u>as many as</u> received him, to them gave he power to become <u>the s ___ of G ___</u>, even to them that believe on his name:*

1John 4:1 Beloved, believe not every spirit, <u>but try the spirits whether they are of God: because many false prophets are gone out into the world.</u>
1John 4:2 Hereby <u>know ye the Spirit of God:</u> Every spirit that confesseth that <u>Jesus Christ is come in the flesh is of God:</u>
1John 4:3 And every spirit that confesseth not that Jesus Christ is come in the flesh is not of God: and this is that spirit of antichrist, whereof ye have heard that it should come; and even now already is it in the world.

Try the spirits of the KJV and the NIV

④ *KJV - John 3:16 For God so loved the world, that he gave his only b _____ Son, that whosoever believeth in him should not perish, but have everlasting life.*

⑤ *NIV - John 3:16 For God so loved the world that he gave his o _____ and o _____ Son, that whoever believes in him shall not perish but have eternal life.*

CHAPTER 3
V. 18-33
Guide

fiery serpents had already bitten them, you are a sinner whether or not you believe in Jesus.

1 V.18 He that believeth on him is not condemned: but he that believeth *not is condemned already*, because he hath not believed in the name of the only begotten Son of God.

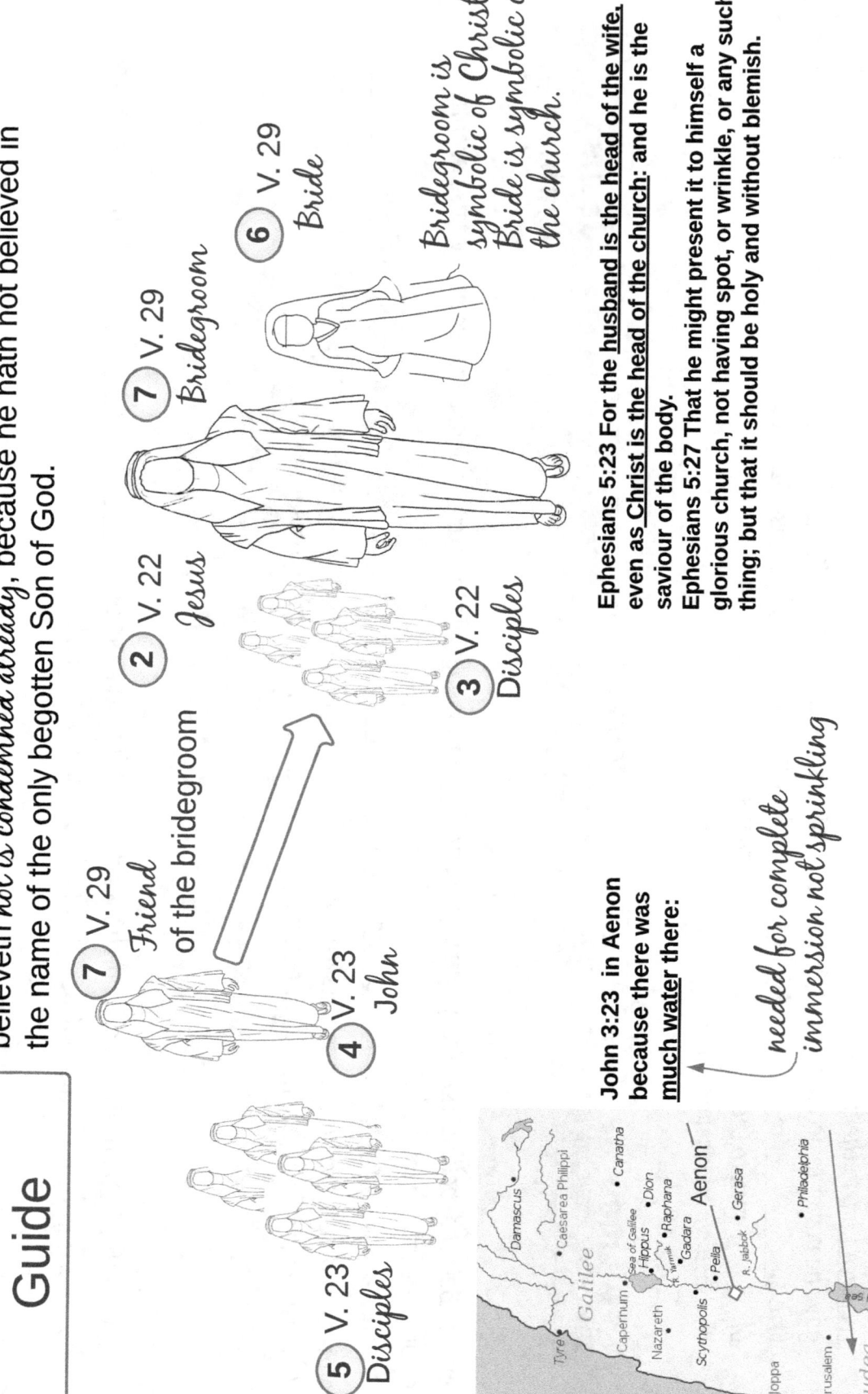

7 V. 29 Friend of the bridegroom

4 V. 23 John

5 V. 23 Disciples

2 V. 22 Jesus

3 V. 22 Disciples

7 V. 29 Bridegroom

6 V. 29 Bride

Bridegroom is symbolic of Christ Bride is symbolic of the church.

John 3:23 in Aenon because there was <u>much water</u> there:

needed for complete immersion not sprinkling

Ephesians 5:23 For the <u>husband is the head of the wife</u>, even as <u>Christ is the head of the church</u>: and he is the saviour of the body.

Ephesians 5:27 That he might present it to himself a glorious church, not having spot, or wrinkle, or any such thing; but that it should be holy and without blemish.

Revelation 19:7 Let us be glad and rejoice, and give honour to him: for <u>the marriage of the Lamb is come, and his wife hath made herself ready.</u>

Christ and the Church

Map: Mediterranean Sea, Tyre, Joppa, Jerusalem, Beersheba, Judea, Galilee, Capernum, Nazareth, Scythopolis, Pella, R. Jabbok, Gerasa, Aenon, Dead Sea, R. Arnon, Philadelphia, Gadara, Hippos, Sea of Galilee, Yarmuk, Raphana, Dion, Caesarea Phillippi, Canatha, Damascus, THE DECAPOLIS

CHAPTER 3
V. 18-36
Notes

1 V.18 He that believeth on him is not condemned: but he that

believeth not ____c____ , because he

hath not believed in the name of the only begotten Son of God.

2 V. 22

J ____a____

8 V. 29

F ____ of the bridegroom

4 V. 23

J ____

5 V. 23

D ____

3 V. 22

D ____

7 V. 29

B ____

6 V. 29

B ____

John 3:23 in Aenon
because there was
<u>much water</u> there:

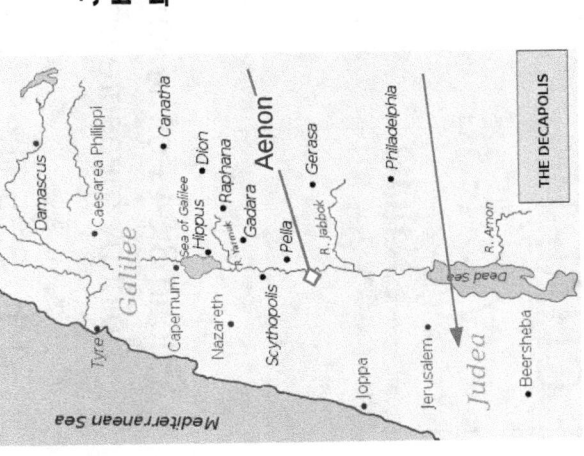

CHAPTER 3
V. 34-36
Guide

Eternal Life

already has sent

John 3:34 For he whom God *hath sent* speaketh the words of God: for God giveth not the Spirit by measure unto him.

already has given

John 3:35 The Father loveth the Son, and *hath given* all things into his hand.

already has everlasting life

John 3:36 He that believeth on the Son *hath* everlasting life: and he that believeth not the Son shall not see life; but the wrath of God abideth on him.

If we can lose your salvation, then we don't already have everlasting life in heaven when we die. But we do have (hath) everlasting life now. We were not saved by works and works cannot keep us saved nor take away our salvation. Our eternal life is not probation depending on our future works.

Eternal Life

John 3:34 For he whom God h_____ s_____ speaketh the words of God: for God giveth not the Spirit by measure unto him.

John 3:35 The Father loveth the Son, and h_____ g_____ all things into his hand.

John 3:36 He that believeth on the Son h_____ e_____ life: and he that believeth not the Son shall not see life; but the wrath of God abideth on him.

Read John
Chapter 4

CHAPTER 4
V.1-26
Guide

Jeremiah 17:13 because they have forsaken the **LORD**, the <u>fountain of living waters.</u>

Jesus baptizes with the Holy Ghost not with water.

(1) V.2 (Though *Jesus* himself *baptized not,* but his disciples,)

Israel Divided into 2 Kingdoms

Southern Kingdom (Judea) Jews
Northern Kingdom (Samaria) Samaritans

Samaria divorced Judea

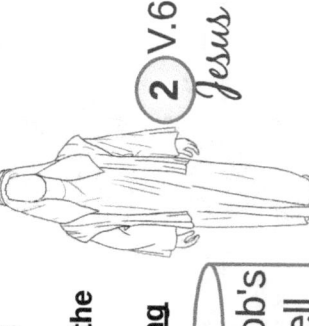

(2) V.6 *Jesus*

Jacob's Well

(4) V.7 Give me to drink.

(6) V.14 But *whosoever* drinketh of the water that I shall give him shall *never thirst;* but the water that I shall give him shall be in him a well of water springing up into *everlasting life.*

(8) V.18 For thou hast had *five husbands;* and he whom thou now hast is not thy husband: in that saidst thou truly.

5 husbands symbolic of married to the law but as a Samaritan had even divorced the Law of Moses.

(10) V. 24 *God* is a *Spirit:* and they that worship him must worship him in spirit and in truth.

They were still worshipping in the temple and the high places but after Jesus' death the believer will become the temple of the Holy Spirit.

(11) V.26 *Jesus* saith unto her, I that speak unto thee am *he.* Told her plainly. Did not do so to Jews.

Believed on Him for the living water (Salvation)

(3) V.7 woman of *Samaria*

(5) V.9 How is it that thou, being a Jew, askest drink of me, which am a woman of *Samaria?* for the Jews have *no dealings* with the Samaritans.

So she won't get thirsty or have to come to draw

(7) V.15 The woman saith unto him, *Sir, give me this water,* that I thirst not, neither come hither to draw

(9) V.19 The woman saith unto him, Sir, I perceive that thou art a *prophet.*

Because He knew all she ever did. She believed like Nathanael when Jesus told him that He saw him under the fig tree.

CHAPTER 4
V.1-26
Notes

(1) v. 2 (Though J _____ himself b _____ n _____, but his disciples,)

(2) V.6
J _____

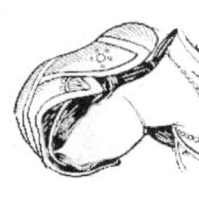

Jacob's Well

(4) V.7 Give me to d _____.

(6) V.14 But w _____ drinketh of the water that I shall give him shall n _____ t _____; but the water that I shall give him shall be in him a well of water springing up into e _____ l _____.

(8) V.18 For thou hast had f _____ h _____; and he whom thou now hast is not thy husband: in that saidst thou truly.

(10) V. 24 G _____ is a S _____; and they that worship him must worship him in spirit and in truth.

(11) V.26 J _____ saith unto her, _____ that speak unto thee am _____.

(3) V.7 woman of S _____

(5) V.9 How is it that thou, being a J _____, askest drink of me, which am a woman of S _____ ? for the Jews have _____ d _____ with the Samaritans.

(7) V.15 The woman saith unto him, Sir, _____ t _____ w _____, that I thirst not, neither come hither to draw g _____

(9) V.19 The woman saith unto him, Sir, I perceive that thou art a p _____ .

CHAPTER 4
V. 27-42
Guide

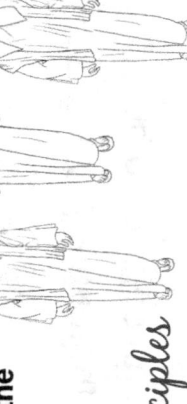

(1) V.28 The woman then left her waterpot, and went her way into the city, and saith to the men,

field in many parables means the world.

Left her waterpot because she won't need it any longer. She has the living water. She'll never thirst or draw again

John 4:8 (For his disciples were gone away unto the city to <u>buy meat</u>.)

Jesus

Disciples

(2) V.31 Master, eat.

(3) V.32 ...I have meat to eat that ye know not of.

(4) V. 34 Jesus saith unto them, My *meat* is to do the *will* of *him* that sent me, and to *finish* his *work*.

(5) V.35 Say not ye, There are yet four months, and then cometh *harvest*? behold, I say unto you, Lift up your eyes, and look on the *fields*; for they are *white already* to harvest. (*There are people ready to be saved today and everyday.*)

(6) V.36 And he that reapeth receiveth wages, and gathereth fruit unto *life eternal*: that *both* he that soweth and he that *reapeth* may *rejoice* together.

Meat doesn't always mean flesh. It can mean fruit and vegs. as in sowing and reaping (harvesting)

(7) V.37 And herein is that saying true, One *soweth*, and another *reapeth*. Jesus sent the disciples to reap where they had not sewn.

(8) V.38 I sent you to *reap* that whereon ye bestowed no labour: other men laboured, and ye are entered into their labours. *Other's had sown seeds about the Messiah. The disciples could have entered into the labors but they didn't testify of Jesus like the woman did. So they did not win souls in the city.*

(9) V.39 And many of the Samaritans of that city *believed* on him for the *saying* of the woman, which *testified*, He told me all that ever I did. *The woman came back with the meat that Jesus was talking about.*

CHAPTER 4
V. 27-42
Notes

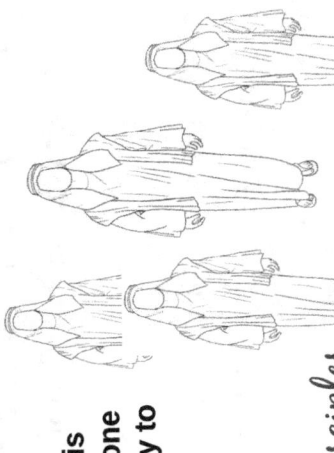

John 4:8 (For his disciples were gone away unto the city to buy meat.)

Disciples

Jesus

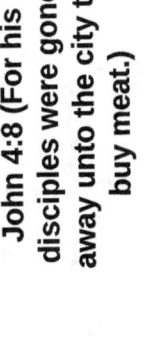

1 V.28 The w_____ then left her w_____, and went her way into the city, and saith to the m_____,

3 V.32 ...I have m_____ to eat that ye know not of.

2 V.31 Master, _____.

4 V. 34 Jesus saith unto them, My m_____ is to do the _____ of h_____ that s_____ _____, and to f_____ his w_____.

5 V.35 Say not ye, There are yet four months, and then cometh h_____? behold, I say unto you, Lift up your eyes, and look on the f_____; for they are w_____ a_____ to h_____.

6 V.36 And he that reapeth receiveth wages, and gathereth fruit unto l_____ e_____: that he that s_____ and he that r_____ may r_____ together.

7 V.37 And herein is that saying true, One s_____, and another r_____.

8 V.38 I s_____ y_____ to r_____ that whereon ye bestowed no labour: other men laboured, and ye are entered into their labours.

9 V.39 And many of the S_____ of that city b_____ on him for the s_____ of the w_____, which t_____, He told me all that ever I did.

CHAPTER 4
V. 43-53
Guide

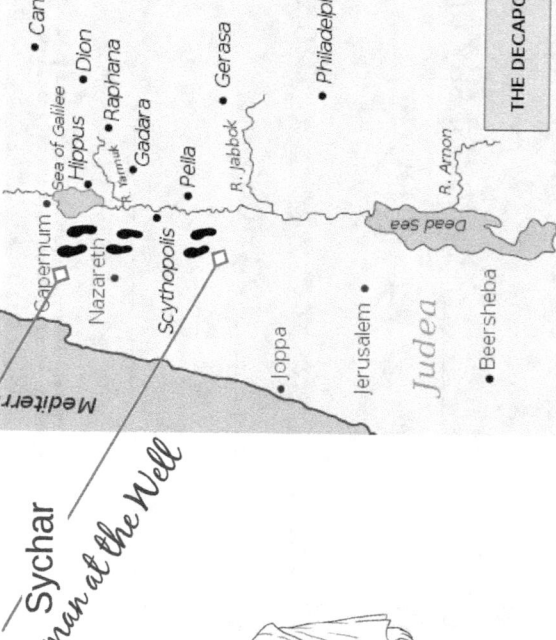

2nd Raised the dead

1st. Water into Wine
— Cana

— Sychar
Woman at the Well

THE DECAPOLIS

① V.44 For Jesus himself testified, that a prophet hath *no honour* in his own country.

Many Samaritans got saved and the Galileans welcomed Him but the Jews of Judea didn't honor Him.

This is why family may not believe you but others can witness to them and they get saved.

certain nobleman – means not any nobleman but a specific one by the providence of God.

② V.46
Jesus

③ V.48 Then said Jesus unto him, Except ye see signs and wonders, ye will not believe.

④ V.46 certain nobleman, whose son was sick at Capernaum.

⑤ V.49 ...Sir, come down *ere* my child die.

means before

⑥ V.50 Jesus *saith* unto him, Go thy way; thy son liveth.

The father believed and then the whole house. Father's have much influence over what their families believe.

⑦ V.53 So the father knew that it was at the same hour, in the which Jesus said unto him, Thy son liveth: and *himself* believed, and his *whole house*.

⑧ V.54 This is again the second miracle that Jesus did, when he was come out of *Judaea* into *Galilee*.
Cana– 1st Miracle turned water into wine (Holy Spirit) 2nd Miracle – Resurrect the dead. (Power over death.)

CHAPTER 4
V. 43-53
Notes

The map shows locations with handwritten labels:

Water into wine — Cana

Sychar
Woman at the Well

Map labels: Mediterranean Sea, Tyre, Damascus, Caesarea Philippi, Galilee, Canatha, Sea of Galilee, Hippus, Dion, Raphana, Gadara, R. Yarmuk, Nazareth, Scythopolis, Pella, Gerasa, R. Jabbok, Capernaum, Philadelphia, R. Arnon, Joppa, Jerusalem, Judea, Dead Sea, Beersheba

THE DECAPOLIS

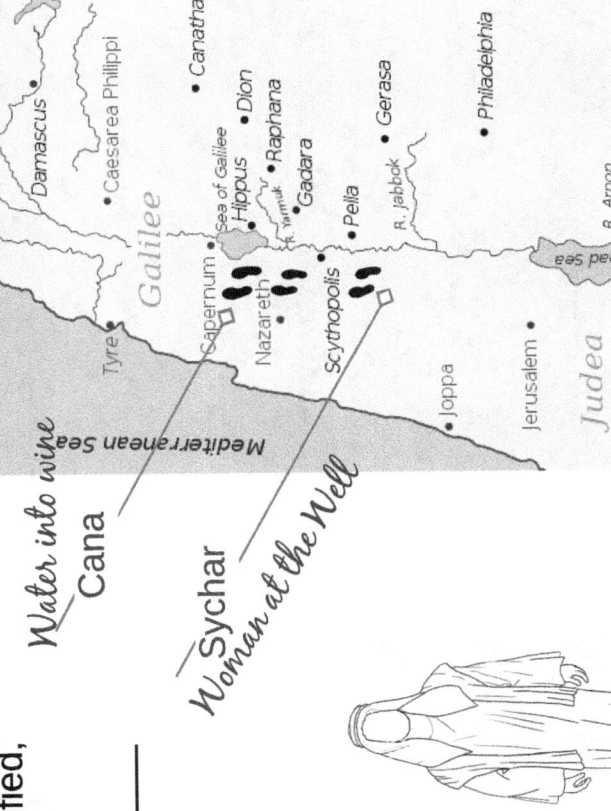

① V.44 For Jesus himself testified, that a prophet hath n_____ h_____ in his o_____ country.

② V.46 l_____

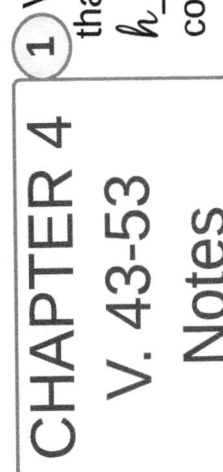

③ V.48 Then said Jesus unto him, Except ye see s_____ *and* w_____, ye will not believe.

④ V.46 c_____ nobleman, whose son was sick at Capernaum.

⑤ V.49 …Sir, come down _____ my child die.

⑥ V.50 Jesus s_____ unto him, Go thy way; thy son liveth.

⑦ V.53 So the father knew that it was at the same hour, in the which Jesus said unto him, Thy son liveth: and h_____ b_____ h_____, and his w_____ _____.

⑧ V.54 This is again the s_____ miracle that Jesus did, when he was come out of l_____ into g_____ .

Read John
Chapter 5

CHAPTER 5
V. 1-8
Guide

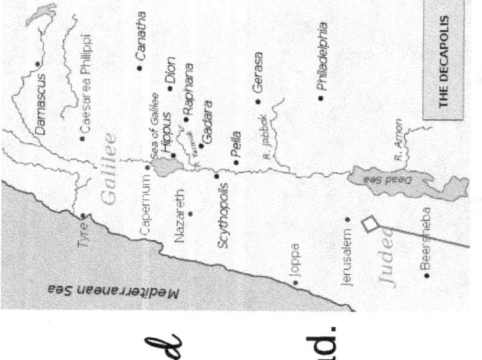

(1) V.2 Now there is at Jerusalem by the sheep market a pool, which is called in the Hebrew tongue Bethesda, having five porches.

Sheep Market

	Porch	
Porch		Porch
Pool (Bethesda)		
Porch		Porch

The impotent folk are pictures of sheep. Sheep are afraid of troubled waters. It took faith for them to get into the waters especially being blind, halt or withered. They were healed by faith the same as we are.

(2) V.3 In these lay a great multitude of impotent folk, of blind, halt, withered, waiting for the moving of the water. (halt mean lame)

Bethesda is a popular name for hospitals

Troubled the water means the angel stirred the water and made it turbulent.

(3) V.4 For an angel went down at a certain season into the pool, and troubled the water: whosoever then first after the troubling of the water stepped in was made *whole of whatsoever disease he had.*

(4) V.5 And a certain man was there, which had an infirmity *thirty and eight years.*

sense of importunity – persistent

Went back to Jerusalem for a feast.

(5) V.8 Jesus saith unto him, *Rise, take up thy bed, and walk.*

Luke 11:8 I say unto you, Though he will not rise and give him, because he is his friend, yet because of his importunity he will rise and give him as many as he needeth.

Psalm 23:1 The LORD is my shepherd; I shall not want.
Psalm 23:2 He maketh me to lie down in green pastures: he leadeth me beside the still waters.

CHAPTER 5
V. 1-8
Notes

Sheep Market

Porch

Pool (Bethsaida)

Porch | Porch

Porch | Porch

1 V.2 Now there is at _J_____ by the _s_____ a _m_____, which is called in the Hebrew tongue _B_____, having _f_____ porches.

2 V.3 In these lay a _g_____ _m_____ of _i_____ _f_____, of blind, halt, withered, _w_____ for the _m_____ of the water.

3 V.4 For an _a_____ went down at a _c_____ season into the pool, and _t_____ the water: _w_____ then first after the troubling of the water stepped in was made _w_____ of _____ disease he had.

4 V.5 And a _c_____ man was there, which had an infirmity _t_____ and _e_____ _y_____.

5 V.8 _J_____ saith unto him, _R_____, _t_____ thy bed, and _w_____.

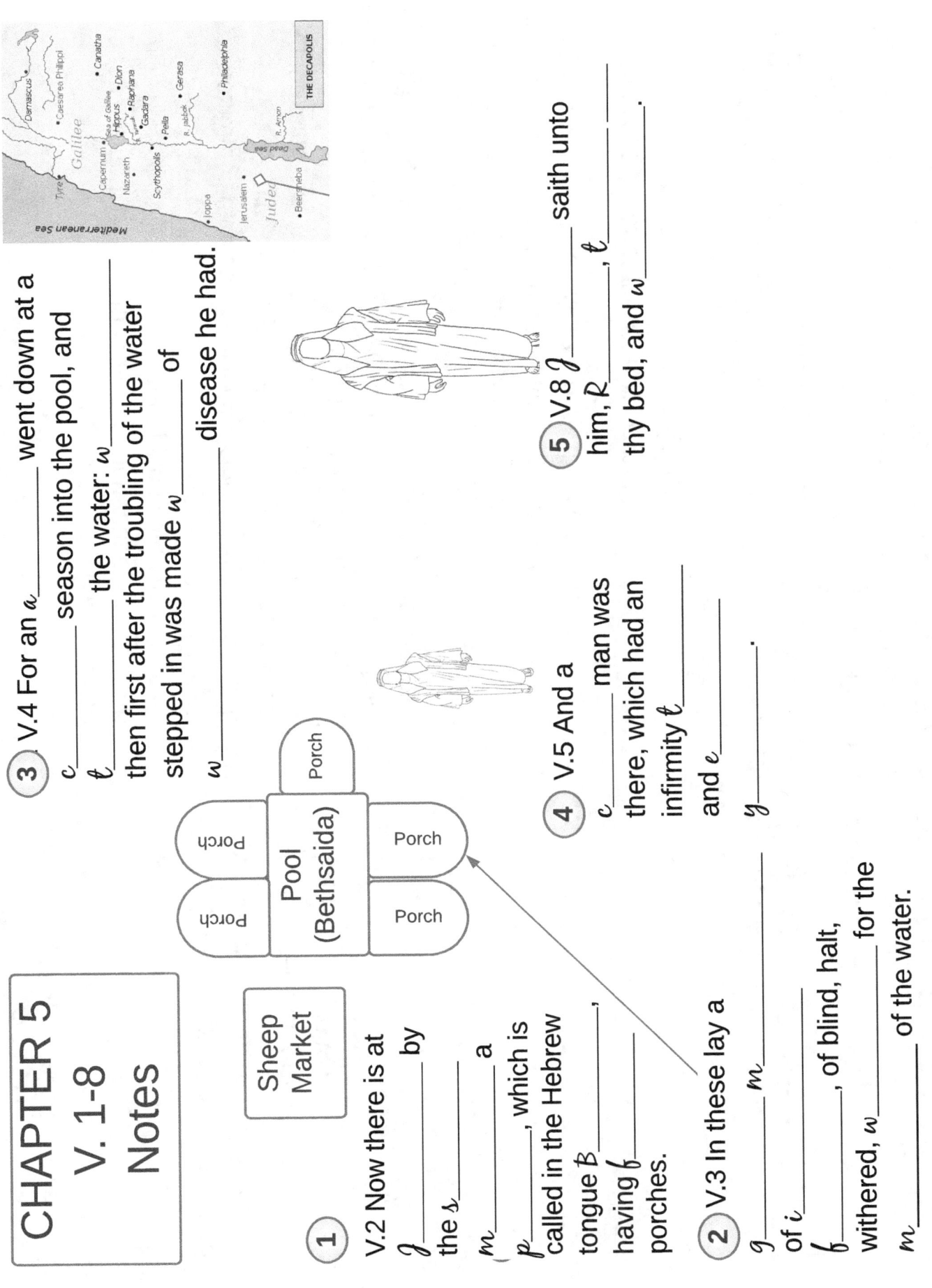

Damascus
Caesarea Philippi
Canatha
Dion
Raphana
Hippos
Sea of Galilee
Capernaum
Gadara
Nazareth
Pella • Gerasa
Scythopolis
Philadelphia
Galilee
R. Jabbok
Tyre
Joppa
Jerusalem
Judea
R. Arnon
Beersheba
Dead Sea
Mediterranean Sea
THE DECAPOLIS

CHAPTER 5
V. 9-23
Guide

1 V.9 And immediately the man was made whole, and took up his bed, and walked: and on the same day was the sabbath.

Authority given by God, My Father

By what authority do you work on the sabbath?

Verily, (God)
Verily, (Holy Spirit)
I Say, (Son)
Answer to that question comes from heaven

6 V.17 But Jesus answered them, My Father worketh hitherto, and I work.

7 V.19 ...Verily, verily, I say unto you, The Son can do nothing of himself, but what he seeth the Father do: for what things soever he doeth, these also doeth the Son likewise.

8 V.20 For the Father loveth the Son, and sheweth him all things that himself doeth: and he will shew him greater works than these, that ye may marvel.
V.21 For as the Father raiseth up the dead, and quickeneth them; even so the Son quickeneth whom he will.
V.22 For the Father judgeth no man, but hath committed all judgment unto the Son:
V.23 That all men should honour the Son, even as they honour the Father. He that honoureth not the Son honoureth not the Father which hath sent him.

2 V.10 Jews

3 V.10 him that was cured,

4 V.12 What man is that which said unto thee, Take up thy bed, and walk?

5 V.16 And therefore did the Jews persecute Jesus, and sought to slay him, because he had done these things on the sabbath day.

Cared more about who told you to work on sabbath than who healed you? Traditional laws over grace.

prophet without honor is His own country. (Jerusalem)

CHAPTER 5
V. 9-23
Notes

1 V.9 And i_____ the _____ man was made whole, and took up his bed, and walked: and on the s_____ day was the s_____.

2 V.10 J_____

3 V.10 h_____ that was c_____

4 V.12 What m_____ is that which said unto thee, T_____ thy bed, and w_____?

5 V.16 And therefore did the J_____ p_____ J_____, and sought to s_____ him, because he had done these things on the s_____ day.

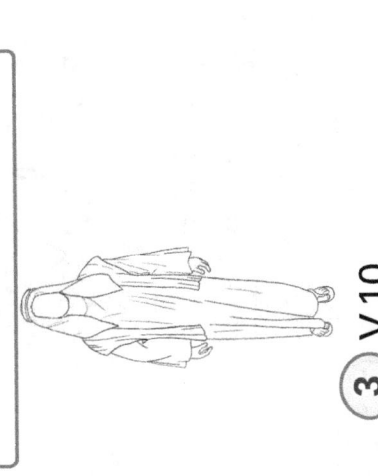

6 V.17 But J_____ answered them, My F_____ w_____ hitherto, and I work.

7 V.19 ...V_____, v_____, say unto you, The S_____ can do nothing of himself, but what he seeth the F_____ do: for what things soever he doeth, these also doeth the Son likewise.

8 V.20 For the F_____ l_____ the S_____, and sheweth him all things that himself doeth: and he will shew him greater works than these, that y_____ m_____ m_____.
V.21 For as the F_____ r_____ up the d_____, and quickeneth them; e_____ so the S_____ whom he will.
V.22 For the F_____ j_____ n_____ m_____, but hath committed a_____ j_____ unto the S_____:
V.23 That all men should h_____ the S_____, e_____ as t_____ h_____ the F_____. He that honoureth not the Son honoureth not the Father which hath sent him.

CHAPTER 5
V. 24-27
Guide

Jesus

Jews

Speaking with authority from heaven.

Prophesy from heaven

1 V.24 Verily, verily, I say unto you, He that *heareth* my word, and *believeth* on him that sent me, hath everlasting life, and shall not come into condemnation; but is passed from death unto life.

2 V.25 *Verily, verily, I say unto you,* The hour is coming, and now is, when the *dead* shall *hear* the voice of the Son of God: and they that hear shall *live.*

3 V.26 For as the *Father* hath life in himself; so hath he given to the Son to have life in himself;

4 V.27 And *hath given him authority* to execute judgment also, *because* he is the *Son of man.* (As a man on earth he has the right to judge men.)

CHAPTER 5
V. 24-27
Notes

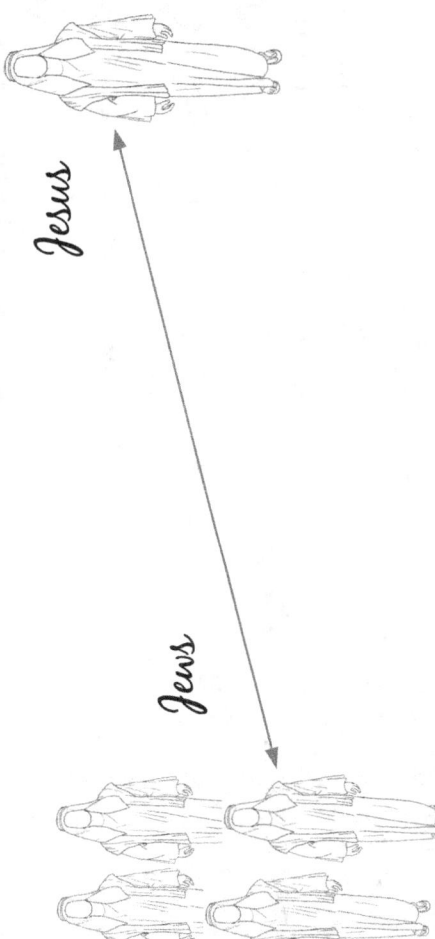

Jesus

Jews

1) V.24 Verily, verily, I say unto you, He that *heareth* my word, and *believeth* on him that sent me, hath everlasting life, and shall not come into condemnation; but is passed from death unto life.

2) V.25 Verily, verily, I say unto you, The hour is coming, and now is, when the *dead* shall *hear* the voice of the Son of God: and they that hear shall *live*.

3) V.26 For as the *Father* hath life in himself; so hath he given to the Son to have life in himself;

4) V.27 And hath given him *authority* to execute judgment also, *because* he is the Son of man. (*As a man on earth he has the right to judge men.*)

CHAPTER 5
V. 28-47
Guide

John the Baptist

(1) V. 28 Marvel not at this: for the hour is coming, in the which all that are in the graves shall *hear* his voice,

V. 29 And shall come forth; they that have *done good*, unto the *resurrection of life*; and they that have *done evil*, unto the resurrection of damnation.

V. 30 I can of mine own self do nothing: as I hear, I judge: and my judgment is just; because I seek not mine own will, but the will of the Father which hath sent me. (*Jesus can do nothing of His own self. Not even judge. As He hears from the Father so will He judge. Jesus seeks the will of the Father even when judging.*)

(3) V.33 Ye sent unto John, and he bare witness unto the truth.

(2) V.31 If I bear witness of myself, my witness is not true.

Healing the man was a mighty work from the Father

In the Old Testament and the works He is doing.

(4) V.36 But I have *greater witness* than that of *John*: for the works which the *Father* hath given me to *finish*

(5) V.37 And the *Father himself*, which hath sent me, hath *borne witness* of me. Ye have neither heard his voice at any time, nor seen his shape.

(6) V.38 And ye have not his word *abiding* in you: for whom he hath sent, him ye believe not.

(7) V.39 *Search* the scriptures; for in them ye think ye have *eternal life*: and they are they which *testify* of me.

witness

Scriptures is the Old Testament Law. They are looking to the law for eternal life and not the new covenant of grace. He tells them to search the scriptures because they prophesy of me, the coming Messiah.

(8) V.45 Do not think that I will accuse you to the Father: there is one that *accuseth* you, even *Moses*, in whom ye trust.

(9) V.46 For had ye believed Moses, ye would have believed me; for *he wrote of me*.

(10) V.47 But if ye believe not his writings, how shall ye believe my words?

Deuteronomy 18:18 I will raise them up a Prophet from among their brethren, like unto thee, and will put my words in his mouth: and he shall speak unto them all that I shall command him.

Deuteronomy 18:19 And it shall come to pass, that whosoever will not hearken unto my words which he shall speak in my name, I will require it of him.

CHAPTER 5

V. 28-47
Notes

(1) V. 28 Marvel not at this: for the hour is coming, in the which all that are in the g_____ shall h_____ his v_____,

V. 29 And shall come forth; they that have d_____ g_____, unto the r_____ of l_____; and they that have d_____ e_____,

unto the r_____ of d_____.

V. 30 I can of mine own self do nothing: as I h_____, I j_____; and my judgment is just; because I seek n_____ m_____ o_____ will, but the will of the Father which hath s_____ m_____.

(2) V.31 If I bear w_____ of m_____, my w_____ is n_____ true.

(3) V.33 Ye sent unto J_____, and he bare w_____ unto the truth.

(4) V.36 But I have g_____ w_____ than that of J_____: for the w_____ which the F_____ hath given me to f_____

(5) V.37 And the F_____ h_____, which hath sent me, hath b_____ w_____ of me. Ye have neither heard his voice at any time, nor seen his shape.

(6) V.38 And ye have not his word a_____ in you: for whom he hath sent, him ye believe not.

(7) V.39 S_____ the s_____ ; for in them ye think ye have e_____ l_____ : and they are they which t_____ of me.

(8) V.45 Do not think that I will accuse you to the Father: there is one that a_____ you, even M_____, in whom ye trust.

(9) V.46 For had ye believed Moses, ye would have believed me; for h_____ w_____ of m_____.

(10) V.47 But if ye believe not his writings, how shall ye believe my words?

Read John
Chapter 6

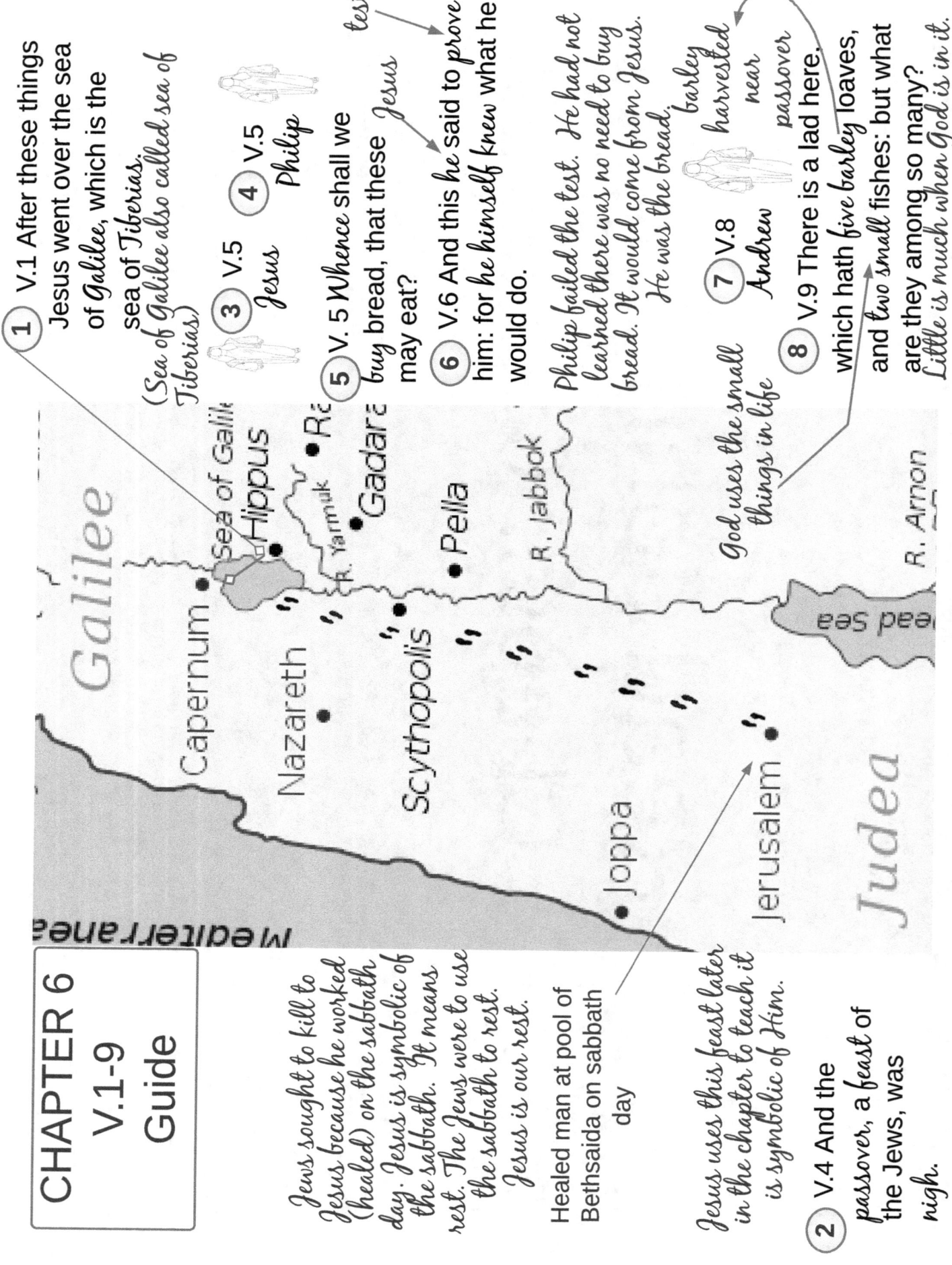

CHAPTER 6
V.1-9
Guide

1 V.1 After these things Jesus went over the sea of *Galilee*, which is the sea of *Tiberias*. (Sea of Galilee also called sea of Tiberias.)

3 V.5 *Jesus*

4 V.5 *Philip*

test

5 V. 5 *Whence* shall we *buy* bread, that these *Jesus* may eat?

6 V.6 And this *he* said to *prove* him: for *he himself knew* what he would do.

Philip failed the test. He had not learned there was no need to buy bread. It would come from Jesus. He was the bread.

barley harvested near passover

God uses the small things in life

7 V.8 *Andrew*

8 V.9 There is a lad here, which hath *five barley* loaves, and *two small* fishes: but what are they among so many? Little is much when God is in it.

Jews sought to kill to Jesus because he worked (healed) on the sabbath day. Jesus is symbolic of the sabbath. It means rest. The Jews were to use the sabbath to rest. Jesus is our rest.

Healed man at pool of Bethsaida on sabbath day

Jesus uses this feast later in the chapter to teach it is symbolic of Him.

2 V.4 And the passover, a feast of the Jews, was nigh.

Map labels
Galilee
Capernum
Nazareth
Sea of Galile
Hippus
R. Yarmuk
Gadara
Pella
Scythopolis
R. Jabbok
Joppa
Jerusalem
Judea
R. Arnon
Dead Sea
Mediterranean

CHAPTER 6
V.1-9
Notes

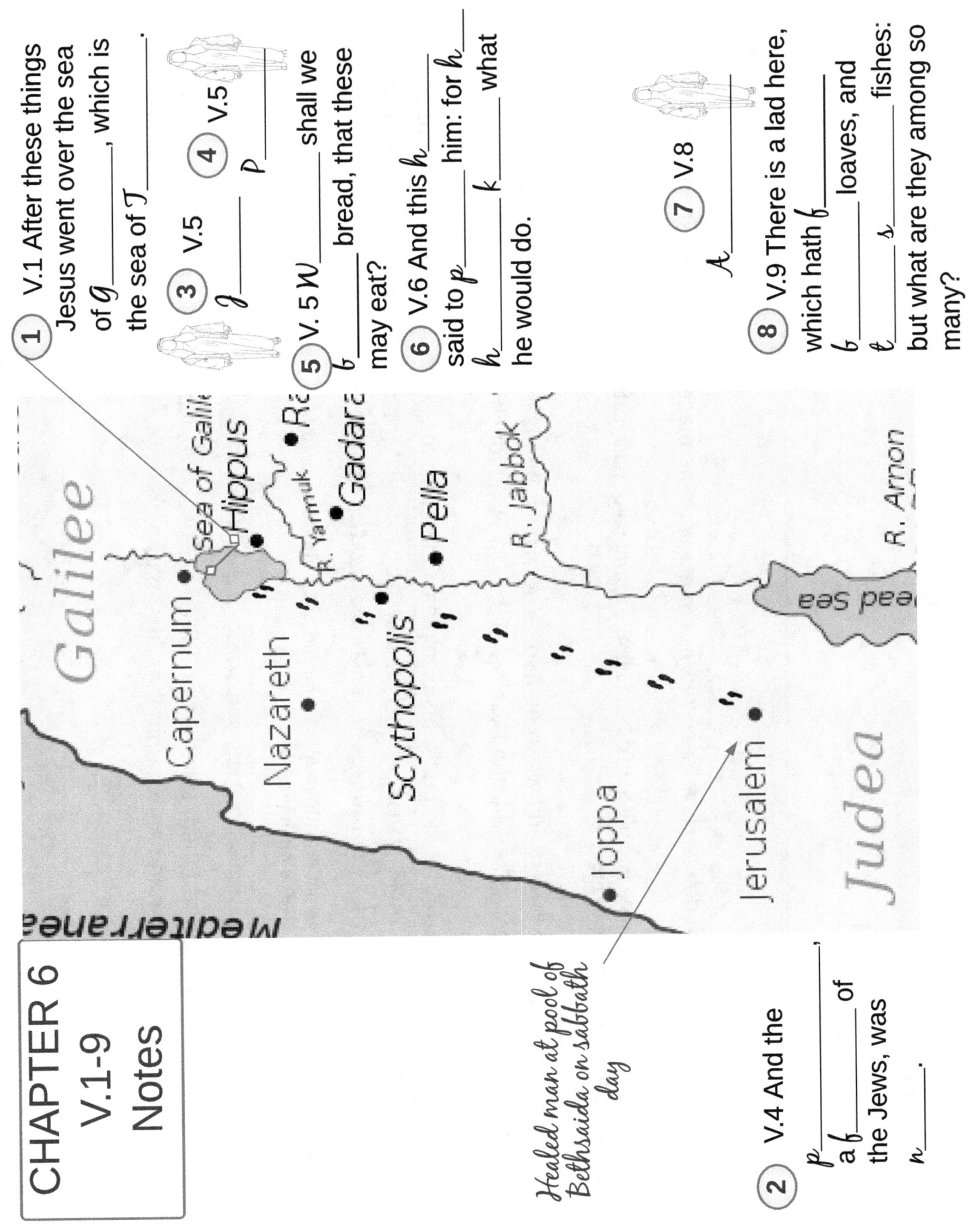

① V.1 After these things Jesus went over the sea of g_____, which is the sea of T_____ .

② V.4 And the p_____ a f_____ of the Jews, was n_____ .

③ V.5 g_____

④ V.5 p_____

⑤ V.5 W_____ shall we b_____ bread, that these may eat?

⑥ V.6 And this h_____ said to p_____ h_____ he would do. him: for h_____ k_____ what

⑦ V.8 A_____

⑧ V.9 There is a lad here, which hath f_____ b_____ loaves, and t_____ s_____ fishes: but what are they among so many?

Healed man at pool of Bethsaida on sabbath day

CHAPTER 6
V.10-13
Guide

1 V.10
Jesus

2 V. 10 Make the men sit down. Now there was *much grass* in the place. So the *men* sat down, in number about *five thousand. Not including women and children*

1Corinthians 11:24 And when he had given thanks, he brake it, and said, Take, eat: this is my body, which is broken for you: this do in remembrance of me.

V. 11 And Jesus took the *loaves;* and when he had given *thanks,* he distributed to the *disciples,* and the disciples to *them* that were *set down;* and likewise of the *fishes* as much as they would.

V. 12 When they were *filled,* he said unto his disciples, Gather up the *fragments* that remain, that <u>*nothing be lost.*</u> (*This bread represented Jesus' body. If it remained it would corrupt or spoil. Nothing was to remain of the passover lamb after eating which also represented His body*)

Exodus 12:11 And thus shall ye eat it; with your loins girded, your shoes on your feet, and your staff in your hand; and ye shall eat it in haste: it is the LORD's passover.

V. 13 Therefore they gathered them together, and filled *twelve* baskets with the *fragments* of the *five barley loaves,* which remained over and above unto them that had eaten. *One basket for each disciple.*

CHAPTER 6
V.10-13
Notes

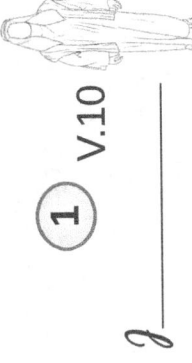

(1) V.10

_g_____

(2) V. 10 Make the men sit down. Now there was _m_____ _g_____ in the place. So the _m_____ sat down, in number about _f_____ _t_____.

V. 11 And Jesus took the _l_____; and when he had _g_____ _t_____, he distributed to the _d_____, and the disciples to _t_____ that were s_____ _d_____; and likewise of the _f_____ as much as they would.

V. 12 When they were _f_____, he said unto his disciples, Gather up the _f_____ _t_____ that remain, that _n_____ be _l_____.

V. 13 Therefore they gathered them together, and filled _t_____ _b_____ with the _f_____ _l_____, which remained over and above unto them that had eaten. of the _f_____ _b_____

John 1:21 And they asked him, What then? Art thou Elias? And he saith, I am not. Art thou that prophet? And he answered, No.

V.14 Then those men, when they had seen the miracle that Jesus did, said, This is of a truth t____ p____ that should come into the world.

Deuteronomy 18:18 I will raise them up a Prophet from among their brethren, like unto thee, and will put my words in his mouth; and he shall speak unto them all that I shall command him. *God is speaking to Moses*

Moses *like unto thee*	Jesus *A Prophet*
Exodus 3:1 Now Moses kept the flock of Jethro his father in law, the priest of Midian: and he led the flock to the backside of the desert, and came to the mountain of God, even to Horeb.	John 10:14 I am the good shepherd, and know my sheep, and am known of mineJohn 10:14 I am the good shepherd, and know my sheep, and am known of mine
Exodus 34:28 And he was there with the LORD forty days and forty nights: he did neither eat bread, nor drink water. And he wrote upon the tables the words of the covenant, the ten commandments.	Matthew 4:2 And when he had fasted forty days and forty nights, he was afterward an hungred.
Exodus 1:22 And Pharaoh charged all his people, saying, Every son that is born ye shall cast into the river, and every daughter ye shall save alive. *(Survived)*	Matthew 2:16 Then Herod, when he saw that he was mocked of the wise men, was exceeding wroth, and sent forth, and slew all the children that were in Bethlehem, and in all the coasts thereof, from two years old and under, *(Survived)*
Exodus 12:5 Your lamb shall be without blemish, a male of the first year: *(Instituted the blood of the Passover Lamb)*	John 1:29 The next day John seeth Jesus coming unto him, and saith, Behold the Lamb of God, which taketh away the sin of the world. *(Was the blood of the Passover Lamb)*
Exodus 19:20 And the LORD came down upon mount Sinai, on the top of the mount: and the LORD called Moses up to the top of the mount; and Moses went up. *(God gave Moses OT Law on a mountain)*	Matthew 5:1 And seeing the multitudes, he went up into a mountain: and when he was set, his disciples came unto him: Matthew 5:2 And he opened his mouth, and taught them, saying, *(Jesus gave NT grace on a mountain)*
Exodus 16:4 Then said the LORD unto Moses, Behold, I will rain bread from heaven for you;	John 6:11 And Jesus took the loaves; and when he had given thanks, he distributed to the disciples, *(Miracle of feeding the 5000)*

many more similiarites

CHAPTER 6

John 1:21 And they asked him, What then? Art thou Elias? And he saith, I am not. Art thou <u>that prophet?</u> And he answered, No.

V.14
Notes

V.14 Then those men, when they had seen the miracle that Jesus did, said, This is of a truth t_____ p_____ that should come into the world.

Deuteronomy 18:18 I will raise them up a Prophet from among their brethren, <u>like unto thee,</u> and will put my words in his mouth; and he shall speak unto them all that I shall command him.

	Jesus
Exodus 3:1 Now Moses *kept the* f_____	John 10:14 I am the *good* s_____,
Exodus 34:28 ....f_____ d_____ and f_____ n_____; he did neither eat *bread, nor drink water.*	Matthew 4:2 And when he had *fasted* f_____ d_____ and f_____ n_____
Exodus 1:22 And Pharaoh charged all his people, saying, *Every son that is born ye shall* c_____ *into the* r_____. (Survived)	Matthew 2:16 Then Herod, ...s_____ *all the* c_____ that were in Bethlehem, and in all the coasts thereof, from two years old and under, (Survived)
Exodus 12:5 Y_____ l_____ shall be without blemish, a male of the first year: *(God used Moses to give the passover lamb to Israel)*	John 1:29 ...*Behold the* L_____ *of* G_____,.... *(Was the Passover Lamb)*
Exodus 16:4 Then said the LORD unto Moses, Behold, I will rain b_____ *from heaven for you;* *(God used Moses to give bread from heaven to Israel)*	John 6:35 And Jesus said unto them, *I am the* b_____ *of life:* *(Jesus was the bread)*

and many more similarities

CHAPTER 6
V.15-25 Guide

① V.16 And when even was now come, his *disciples* went down unto the sea,

② V.17 And entered into a ship, and went over the sea toward *Capernaum*. And it was now *dark*, and Jesus was not come to them.

Holy Spirit

About 3 1/2 miles

③ V.18 And the sea arose by reason of a *great wind* that blew.

V. 19 So when they had rowed about *five and twenty* or *thirty furlongs*, they see *Jesus* walking on the sea, and drawing nigh unto the *ship*: and they were afraid.

V. 20 But he saith unto them, It is I; *be not afraid.* (*Fear Not*)

V. 21 Then they *willingly* received him into the *ship*: and *immediately* the ship was at the land whither they went.

⑤ V.25 Rabbi, when camest thou hither?

④ V.24 When the *people* therefore saw that Jesus was not there, neither his disciples, they also took shipping, and came to *Capernaum*, seeking for Jesus

Seek and ye shall find

CHAPTER 6
V.15-25
Notes

(1) V.16 And when even was now come, his _d_____ went down unto the sea,

(2) V.17 And entered into a ship, and went over the sea toward _C_____. And it was now _____, and _____ Jesus was not come to them.

(5) V.25 Rabbi, when camest thou hither?

(4) V.24 When the _p_____ therefore saw that Jesus was not there, neither his disciples, they also took shipping, and came to _C_____, _____ for _s_____ _J_____

(3) V.18 And the sea arose by reason of a _g_____ _w_____ that blew.

V. 19 So when they had rowed about _f_____ and _t_____ or _f_____, they see _f_____ walking on the _s_____, and drawing nigh unto the _s_____ : and they were afraid.

V. 20 But he saith unto them, It is I; _____ _n_____ _a_____ .

V. 21 Then they _w_____ received him into the _s_____ : and _i_____ the ship was at the land whither they went.

CHAPTER 6
V.26-36
Guide

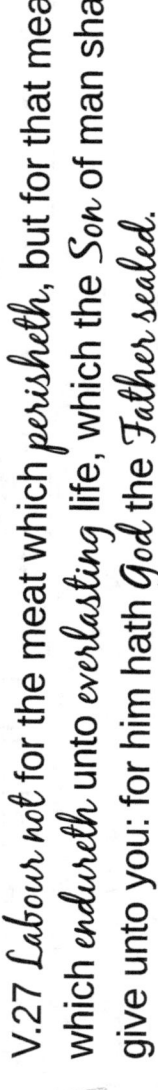

V.27 *Labour not for the meat which perisheth*, but for that meat which *endureth unto everlasting* life, which the *Son of man shall give unto you:* for him hath *God* the *Father sealed.*

Sealed means that it will not rot or spoil.

Exodus 16:19 And Moses said, Let no man leave of it till the morning..... but some of them left of it until the morning, and it bred worms, and stank: and Moses was wroth with them.

Manna from heaven was not everlasting. It would get worms and stink.

V.28 ...What shall we do, that we might *work* the *works* of *God?*
Jesus told them to labour for the meat. They were asking what kind of work do we need to do for this meat.

V.29 This is the *work* of *God,* that *ye believe on him* whom he hath sent.

There is a work we must do to earn the meat that perisheth not. The work is believing on Jesus whom God hath sent. Any other labour, is for the meat which will perish.

V.30 They said therefore unto him, What sign shewest thou then, that we may *see*, and *believe* thee? what dost *thou work*? *Moses fed them manna in the desert, Jesus fed the barley loaves in much grass.*

V. 31 Our fathers did eat *manna* in the *desert*; as it is written, He gave them bread from heaven to eat.

Witness of Trinity

V.32 Then Jesus said unto them, *Verily, verily, I say* unto you, Moses gave you not that bread from heaven; but my Father giveth you the *true bread* from heaven.

V.33 For the bread of God is *he* which *cometh down* from heaven, and *giveth life* unto the world.

V.34 Then said they unto him, Lord, *evermore give us this bread. Manna eventually ceased to be given.*

V.35 And Jesus said unto them, *I am* the *bread of life:* he that *cometh* to me shall never *hunger;* and he that *believeth* on me shall *never thirst.*

CHAPTER 6
V.26-36
Notes

V.27 L_____ n_____ for the meat which p_____,
but for that meat which e_____ unto e_____ life,
which the S_____ of man shall give unto you: for him hath
g_____ the F_____ s_____.

V.28 ...What shall we do, that we might w_____ the w_____ of g_____?

V.29 This is the w_____ of g_____, that ye b_____ on h_____ whom he
hath sent.

V.30 They said therefore unto him, What sign shewest thou then, that we may s_____, and b_____
thee? what dost t_____ w_____?

V. 31 Our fathers did eat m_____ in the d_____; as it is written, He gave them bread from
heaven to eat.

V.32 Then Jesus said unto them, V_____, v_____, s_____ unto you, Moses gave
you not that bread from heaven; but my Father giveth you the t_____ b_____ from heaven.

V.33 For the bread of God is which c_____ d_____ from heaven, and giveth life unto the world.

V.34 Then said they unto him, Lord, e_____ u_____ t_____ g_____ of l_____ b_____ : he that c_____ to me shall
V.35 And Jesus said unto them, _____ a_____ the b_____ of l_____ : he that c_____ to me shall
n_____ h_____; and he that b_____ on me shall n_____ t_____.

CHAPTER 6
Passover Lamb
Guide

Exodus 12:7-10 And they shall take of the blood, and strike it on the two side posts and on the upper door post of the houses, wherein they shall eat it. And they shall eat the flesh in that night, roast with fire, and unleavened bread; and with bitter herbs they shall eat it. Eat not of it raw, nor sodden at all with water, but roast with fire; his head with his legs, and with the purtenance thereof. And ye shall let nothing of it remain until the morning; and that which remaineth of it until the morning ye shall burn with fire.

V.53 Then Jesus said unto them, Verily, verily, I say unto you, Except **ye** eat the flesh of the Son of man, and drink his blood, **ye** have no life in **you**.

V.54 Whoso eateth my flesh, and drinketh my blood, hath eternal life; and I will raise him up at the last day. *The chapter begins with the Passover being nigh (V.5). The Passover Lamb was instituted as part of the law. The passover lamb is a shadow of the true Lamb of God. Jesus is referring to His body that He sacrifices on the cross.*

V.56 He that eateth my flesh, and drinketh my blood, dwelleth in me, and I in him. *(Abide in me 15:4)*

V.57 As the living Father hath sent me, and I live by the Father: so he that eateth me, even he shall live by me. *(I am the way, the truth and the life)*

V.58 This is that bread which came down from heaven: not as your fathers did eat manna, and are dead: he that eateth of this bread shall live for ever. *(Jesus is the true bread from heaven not the manna in the wilderness)*

V.60 Many therefore of his disciples, when they had heard this, said, This is an *hard* saying; *who can hear it.* *(Not everyone with ears can hear. He who hath ears to hear.... Hear with your heart.)*

V.61 When Jesus knew in himself that his disciples murmured at it, he said unto them, Doth this offend you? *(offend means to cause anger or dislike, hinder from obedience.)*

V.63 It is the spirit that quickeneth; the flesh profiteth nothing: the *words* that I speak unto you, they are spirit, and they are life. *(He explains to them literally eating His body will do nothing. They must receive the Holy Spirit by believing Words.) Quickeneth means to make alive.*

CHAPTER 6
Passover Lamb
Notes

V.53 Then Jesus said unto them, V_____, v_____, s_____ unto you, Except ye

e_____ the f_____ of the S_____ of m_____, and d_____ h_____ b_____, ye

h_____ n_____ l_____ i_____ y_____ b_____.

V.54 W_____ e_____ m_____ f_____, and d_____ m_____ b_____, hath

e_____ l_____; and I will raise him up at the last day.

V.55 For my flesh is meat i_____, and my blood is drink i_____.

V.56 He that eateth my flesh, and drinketh my blood, d_____ in me, and _____ in him.

V.57 As the living Father hath sent me, and I live by the Father: so he that eateth me, even he shall live by me.

V.58 This is that bread which came down from heaven: not as your fathers did eat manna, and are dead: he that eateth of this bread shall live for ever.

V.60 Many therefore of his disciples, when they had heard this, said, This is

an h_____ saying; w_____ can hear it?

V.61 When Jesus knew in himself that his disciples murmured at it, he said unto them, Doth this

o_____ you?

V.63 It is the s_____ that q_____ s_____; the flesh profiteth nothing: the w_____ that

I speak unto you, they a_____, and t_____ a_____ l_____.

CHAPTER 6
V. 37-65
Guide

(1) V.37 *All* that the Father giveth me shall <u>**come to me**</u>; and him that **cometh to me** I will in *no wise cast out.*

(2) V.38 For I came down from heaven, *not to do mine own will,* but the *will of him that sent me.*

(3) V. 40 **And this is the** *will* **of him that sent me, that** *every one which* **seeth the** *Son,* **and** *believeth* **on him, may have everlasting life: and** <u>**I will raise him up at the last day**</u>

(4) V.44 *No man* <u>**can come to me**</u>, *except the Father which hath* sent me *draw* him: and <u>**I will raise him up at the last day.**</u>

(5) V.45 It is written in the prophets, And they shall be *all* taught of God. *Every man* therefore that hath heard, and hath learned of the Father, <u>**cometh unto me.**</u>

Isaiah 54:13 **And all thy children shall be taught of the LORD; and great shall be the peace of thy children.**

Old Testament Witness (God) is a witness that Jesus is the Son.

(6) V.47 Verily, verily, I say unto you, He that *believeth* on me hath everlasting life.

(7) V.54 *Whoso* eateth *my flesh,* and drinketh *my blood,* hath eternal life; and <u>**I will raise him up at the last day.**</u>

(8) V.64 But there are some of you that *believe not.* For Jesus knew from the beginning who they were that believed not, and who should betray him.

(9) V.65 And he said, *Therefore said I unto you,* that no man <u>**can come unto me,**</u> *except it were given unto him of my Father.*

Because if you believe, the Father will draw you to Jesus and He will raise you up at the last day.

Believed

Unbelief

Did they believe? Therefore they were not drawn...

X

CHAPTER 6
V. 37-65
Notes

(5) V.45 It is written in the prophets, And they shall be a_____ taught of God. E_____ m_____ therefore that hath heard, and hath learned of the Father, **cometh unto me.**

(7) V.54 W_____ m_____ eateth m_____ b_____, and drinketh m_____ b_____, hath eternal life; and **I will raise him up at the last day.**

Believed

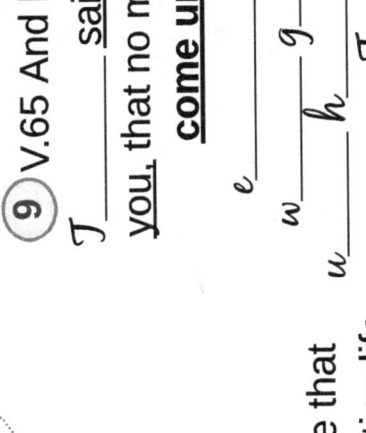

Unbelief

(8) V.64 But there are some of you that b_____ n_____. For Jesus knew from the beginning who they were that believed not, and who should betray him.

(9) V.65 And he said, T_____ said I unto you, that no man **can come unto me,** e_____ w_____ g_____ w_____ h_____ m_____ F_____ .

(6) V.47 Verily, verily, I say unto you, He that b_____ on me hath everlasting life.

(4) V.44 N_____ m_____ **can come to me,** e_____ the F_____ which hath sent me d_____ him: and **I will raise him up at the last day.**

(3) **V. 40 And this is the w_____ o_____ e_____ which seeth the S_____, and b_____ on him, may have life: and I will raise him up at the last day** of him that sent me, that e_____ **on him, may have life: and I will raise him up at the last day**

(1) V.37 A_____ that the Father giveth me shall **come to me;** and him that **cometh to me** I will in n_____ w_____ c_____ o_____ .

(2) V.38 For I came down from heaven, n_____ m_____ o_____ w_____ of h_____ t_____ m_____, but the w_____ o_____ h_____ t_____ s_____ m_____ .

Read John
Chapter 7

CHAPTER 7
V. 1-7
Guide

Temple
Feast of Tabernacles

(1) V.1 After these things Jesus walked in *Galilee*: for he would not walk in *Jewry*, because the Jews sought to *kill* him.

Judea is Jewry

(2) V.2 Now the Jew's *feast* of *tabernacles* was at hand.

The feast of tabernacles celebrates that God dwells with man. When Solomon finished building the temple a dark cloud appeared above signaling God's presence. This was at the time of the feast of tabernacles. Now Jesus is using this feast to tell them He is, going back to the Father but teaches them about the Living Water, Holy Spirit.

His own kin

(3) V.3 His *brethren* therefore said unto him, Depart hence, and go into Judaea, that thy disciples also may see the *works* that thou doest.

Matthew 5:15 Neither do men light a candle, and put it under a bushel, but on a candlestick; and it giveth light unto all that are in the house.
Matthew 5:16 Let your light so shine before men, that they may see your good works, and glorify your Father which is in heaven.

(4) V.4 For there is no man that doeth any thing in *secret*, and he himself seeketh to be known *openly*. If thou do these things, shew thyself to the world.

(5) V.5 For neither did his *brethren* believe in him.

Mark 6:4 But Jesus, said unto them, A prophet is not without honour, but in his own country, and among his own kin, and in his own house.

But they did believe him after His resurrection. Acts 1:17

Map labels:

Mediterranean Sea

Damascus

Caesarea Philippi • Canatha

Galilee

Tyre

Capernum

Sea of Galilee • Dion
Hippus • Raphana
R. Yarmuk • Gadara
• Gerasa

Nazareth

Pella

Scythopolis

R. Jabbok

• Joppa

Jerusalem

Dead Sea

Judea

• Philadelphia

R. Arnon

• Beersheba

THE DECAPOLIS

CHAPTER 7
V. 1-7
Notes

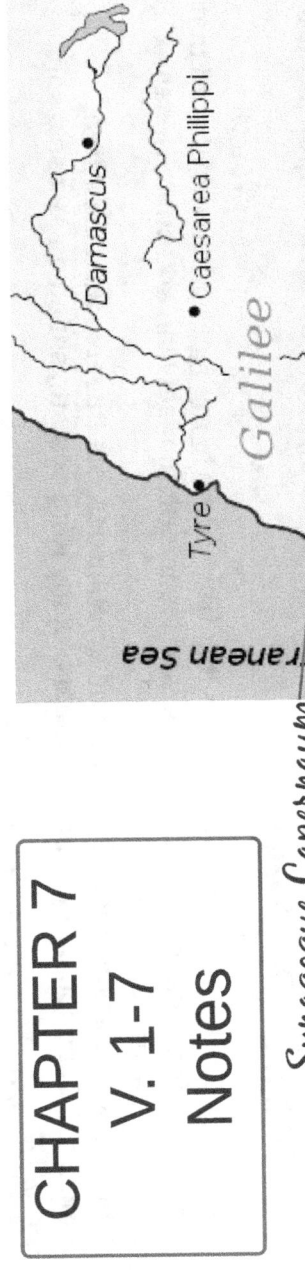

Synagogue Capernaum
6:59

Temple
Feast of Tabernacles

Map labels:

Mediterranean Sea

Tyre

Damascus

Caesarea Philippi

Galilee

Capernum

Nazareth

Sea of Galilee

Hippus

R. Yarmuk

Canatha

Dion

Raphana

Gadara

Pella

Gerasa

R. Jabbok

Philadelphia

Scythopolis

Joppa

Jerusalem

Judea
Judea is Jewry

Beersheba

Dead Sea

R. Arnon

THE DECAPOLIS

---

1 V.1 After these things Jesus walked in g_____: for he would not walk in J_____, because the Jews sought to k_____ him.

2 V.2 Now the Jew's f_____ of t_____ was at hand.

3 V.3 His b_____ therefore said unto him, Depart hence, and go into Judaea, that thy disciples also may s_____ the w_____ that thou doest.

4 V.4 For there is no man that doeth any thing in s_____, and he himself seeketh to be known o_____. If thou do these things, shew thyself to the world.

5 V.5 For neither did his b_____ believe in him.

CHAPTER 7
V. 8-10
Guide

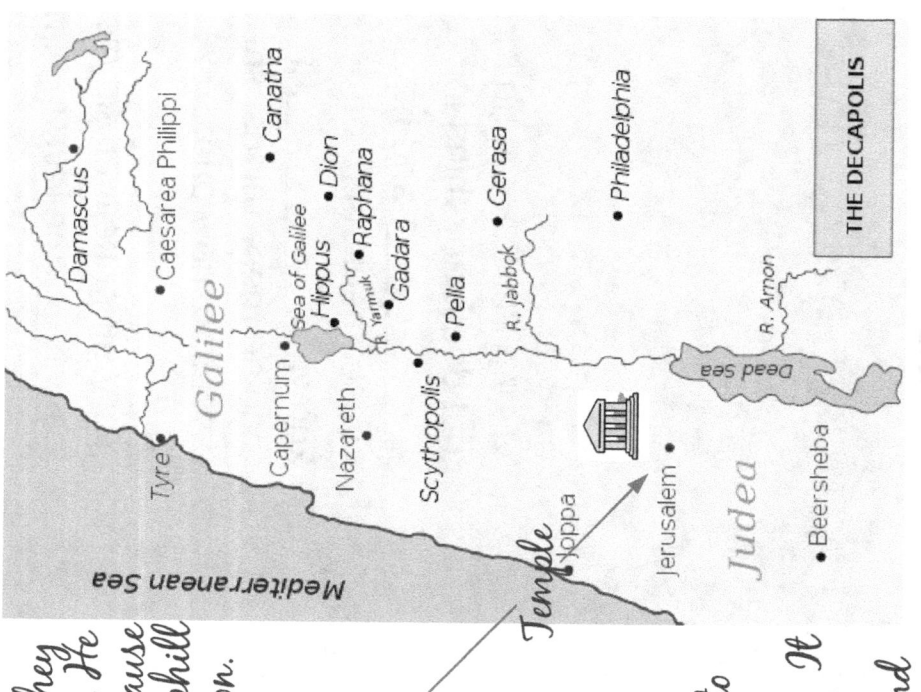

THE DECAPOLIS

His time will come at the Passover Feast.

The feast of tabernacles is celebrated in Jerusalem at the temple.

Up– Even though they were heading south, He said, Go ye up. Because they were walking uphill to a higher elevation.

V.8 Go ye up unto this feast: I go not up yet unto this feast: for my time is not yet full come.

openly

V.9 When he had said these words unto them, he abode still in Galilee.

Explained

V.10 But when his brethren were gone up, then went he also up unto the feast, not openly, but as it were in secret.

Old Testament prophecy was that He would come riding openly into Jerusalem on a donkey which was fulfilled in John 12-13. His brethern wanted him to go openly but it was not at the wrong feast. It would happen at the Passover Feast.

Jesus was referring to I cannot go to Jerusalem openly with you and make myself known. He did not lie when He arrived in secret.

Passover

Zechariah 9:9 Rejoice greatly, O daughter of Zion; shout, <u>O daughter of Jerusalem:</u> behold, thy King cometh unto thee: he is just, and having salvation; lowly, and riding upon an ass, and upon a colt the foal of an ass.
(Old Testament Prophecy)

John 12:12 On the next day much people that were come <u>to the feast,</u> when they heard that Jesus was coming to Jerusalem,
John 12:13 Took branches of palm trees, and went forth to meet him, and cried, Hosanna: Blessed is the King of Israel that cometh in the name of the Lord.
John 12:14 And Jesus, when he had found a young ass, sat thereon; as it is written,
John 12:15 Fear not, daughter of Sion: behold, thy King cometh, sitting on an ass's colt.
(Fulfilled in the New Testament)

Temple

CHAPTER 7
V. 8-10
Notes

V.8 Go ye _____ unto this f_____: I go not up y_____ unto t_____ f_____: for m_____ t_____ is n_____ y_____ f_____ c_____.

V.9 When he had said these words unto them, he abode still in g_____.

V.10 But when his brethren were gone up, then went he also up unto the feast, n_____ o_____, but as it were in s_____.

CHAPTER 7
V. 11-24
Guide

(1) V.13 Howbeit no man spake openly of him for *fear of the Jews.*

This is why He went in secret. No Triumphant Entry as prophesied.

Exodus 20:8 Remember the sabbath day, to keep it holy.

V.19 Did not Moses give you the *law*, and yet none of you keepeth the law? Why go ye about to kill me?

Perform circumcisions which is working on the sabbath day

Temple

V.20 The people answered and said, Thou hast a devil: who goeth about to kill thee? *They sought to kill Him when he had healed on the sabbath day.* **John 5:18 Therefore the Jews sought the more to kill him, because he not only had broken the sabbath, but said also that God was his Father, making himself equal with God.**

V.21 Jesus answered and said unto them, I have done one *work*, and ye all marvel. (*Healed on the sabbath day*).

V.22 Moses therefore gave unto you *circumcision*; (not because it is of Moses, but of the *fathers*;) and ye on the *sabbath* day *circumcise* a man.

V.23 If a man on the sabbath day receive circumcision, that the law of Moses should not be broken; are ye angry at me, because I have made a man *every whit whole* on the sabbath day? **John 5:6 When Jesus saw him lie, …. he saith unto him, Wilt thou be made whole?**

V.24 *Judge* not according to the *appearance, but judge righteous judgment.*

Acts 7:51 Ye stiffnecked and uncircumcised in heart and ears, ye do always resist the Holy Ghost: as your fathers did, so do ye.

The Covenant of Circumcision was given to Abraham. The Law of Moses allowed the Jews to perform circumcision on the sabbath day even though it is work. But they refused to accept Jesus healing on the sabbath day because it was work. The Jews could not discern circumcision is a picture of spiritual circumcision, being made every whit whole.

THE DECAPOLIS

Mediterranean Sea

Tyre

Galilee

Damascus
Caesarea Philippi
Canatha
Dion
Raphana
Sea of Galilee
Hippus
Gadara
Yarmuk
Pella
R. Jabbok
Gerasa
Philadelphia
R. Arnon

Capernum
Nazareth
Scythopolis
Dead Sea

Joppa
Jerusalem
Judea
Beersheba

Mediterranean Sea
Galilee
Damascus
Caesarea Philippi
Canatha
Dion
Raphana
Hippos
Sea of Galilee
Gadara
Pella
Gerasa
Philadelphia
R. Jabbok
R. Arnon
Dead Sea
Tyre
Capernum
Nazareth
Scythopolis
Joppa
Jerusalem
Judea
Beersheba
THE DECAPOLIS
Temple

CHAPTER 7
V. 11-24
Notes

1 V.13 Howbeit no man spake o_____ of him for
f_____ of the J_____ .

2 V.19 Did not Moses give you the l_____, and yet none of you
k_____ the law? Why go ye about to kill me?
V.20 The people answered and said, Thou hast a devil: who goeth about to kill thee?
V.21 Jesus answered and said unto them, I have done one w_____, and ye all marvel. .
V.22 Moses therefore gave unto you c_____; (not
because it is of Moses, but of the f_____;) and ye on the s_____ day c_____ a man.
V.23 If a man on the sabbath day receive circumcision, that the law of Moses should not be broken; are ye angry at me, because I have made a man e_____ w_____ on the sabbath day?
V.24 J_____ not according to the a_____,
b_____ judge r_____ j_____ .

Circumcision Guide

testament means covenant (a contract or agreement.)

OLD TESTAMENT (Physical)

Genesis 17 – God's Everlasting Covenant with Abraham
1. *Abraham would be the father of many nations*
2. *God would be a God unto him and his seed*
3. *God would give unto Abraham and his seed a land where they were strangers (called Canaan) for an everlasting possession*

bought (redeemed)
NT bought with the blood of Jesus and not money.

Genesis 17:12 And he that is eight days old shall be circumcised among you, every man child in your generations, he that is born in the house, or bought with money of any stranger, which is not of thy seed.

Genesis 17:13 He that is *born in thy house,* and he that is *bought with thy money, must needs be circumcised:* and my covenant shall be in your flesh for an *everlasting covenant.*

Genesis 17:14 And the *uncircumcised* man child whose flesh of his foreskin is not circumcised, that soul shall be *cut off from his people;* he hath broken my covenant.

Deuteronomy 30:6 And the LORD thy God will *circumcise* thine *heart,* and the *heart* of thy *seed,* to love the LORD thy God with all thine heart, and with all thy soul, that thou mayest live.

Jeremiah 4:4 *Circumcise* yourselves to the LORD, and take away the *foreskins* of your *heart,* ye men of Judah and inhabitants of Jerusalem: lest my fury come forth like fire, and burn that none can quench it, because of the *evil* of your doings.

NEW TESTAMENT (Spiritual)

Gentiles

Galatians 3:29 And if ye be *Christ's,* then are ye *Abraham's seed,* and heirs according to the promise.

Romans 2:29 But he is a *Jew,* which is one *inwardly;* and *circumcision* is that of the *heart, in the spirit,* and not in the *letter;* whose praise is not of men, but of God.

The Law

Colossians 2:9 For in him dwelleth all the fulness of the Godhead bodily.
Colossians 2:10 And ye are complete in him, which is the head of all principality and power:
Colossians 2:11 In whom also ye are circumcised with the circumcision made without hands, in putting off the body of the sins of the flesh by the circumcision of Christ:

When Jesus healed a sinner, He often said your sins are forgiven (putting off the body of the sins of the flesh) which is the circumcision made without hands.

Circumcision Notes

OLD TESTAMENT
(Physical)

Genesis 17:12 And he that is e_____ days old shall be circumcised among you, every man child in your generations, he that is born in the house, or bought with money of any stranger, which is not of thy seed.

Genesis 17:13 He that is b_____ i___ t___ h_____, and he that is b_____ w___ t___ m_____, ; and my covenant m____ n___ b___ c____ shall be in your flesh for an e_____ c_____.

Genesis 17:14 And the u_____ man child whose flesh of his foreskin is not circumcised, that soul shall be c_____ o_____ f_____ h___ p_____; he hath broken my covenant.

Deuteronomy 30:6 And the LORD thy God will c_____ thine h_____, and the h_____ of thy s_____, to love the LORD thy God with all thine heart, and with all thy soul, that thou mayest live.

<u>Jeremiah 4:4</u> C_____ yourselves to the LORD, and take away the f_____ of your h_____, ye men of Judah and inhabitants of Jerusalem: lest my fury come forth like fire, and burn that none can quench it, because of the e_____ of your doings.

NEW TESTAMENT
(Spiritual)

Galatians 3:29 And if ye be C_____ s__, and then are ye A_____ s__, and heirs according to the promise.

Romans 2:29 But he is a _____, which is one i_____; and c_____ is that of the h_____, in the s_____, and not in the letter; whose praise is not of men, but of God.

CHAPTER 7
V. 25-32
Guide

Jesus spoke in the open. He was not acting in secret. It was His entry into Jerusalem that was secret. So that prophecy would be filled later.

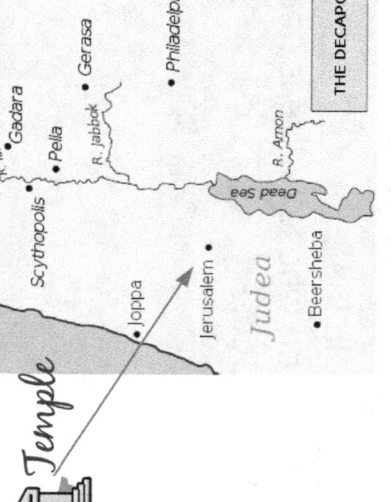

THE DECAPOLIS

Temple

(1) V. 26 But, lo, he speaketh boldly, and they say nothing unto him

They know but they don't know where Jesus is from.

(2) V. 28 Then cried Jesus in the temple as he taught, saying, Ye both know me, and ye know whence I am: and I am not come of myself, but he that sent me is true, whom ye know not. V.29 But I know him: for I am from him, and he hath sent me.

The Word was God, The Word was manifest in the flesh.

Old Testament – Christ will do many miracles

Isaiah 35:5 Then the eyes of the blind shall be opened, and the ears of the deaf shall be unstopped.
Isaiah 35:6 Then shall the lame man leap as an hart, and the tongue of the dumb sing: for in the wilderness shall waters break out, and streams in the desert.

(3) John 7:31 And many of the people believed on him, and said, When Christ cometh, will he do more miracles than these which this man hath done?

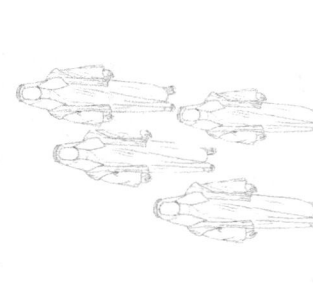

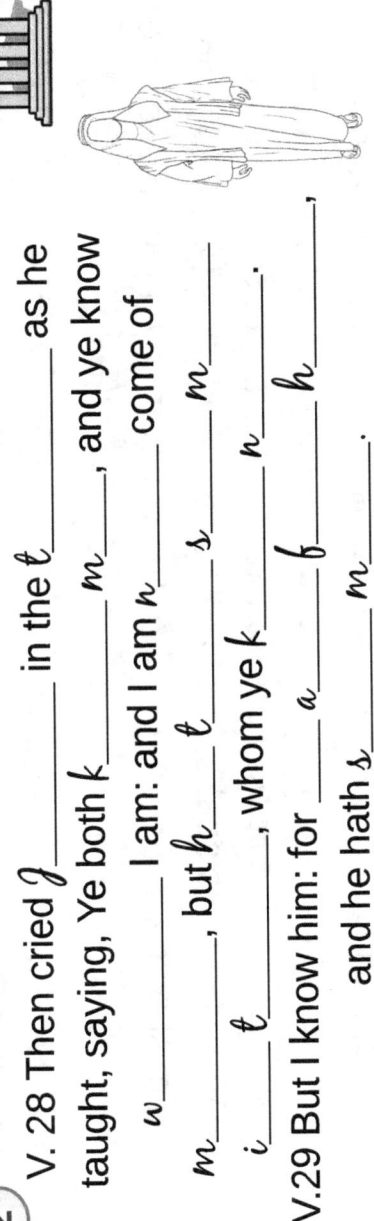

CHAPTER 7
V. 25-32
Notes

1

V. 26 But, lo, he speaketh
b_____, and they say
nothing unto him

Temple

THE DECAPOLIS

2

V. 28 Then cried J_____ in the t_____ as he
taught, saying, Ye both k_____, and ye know
I am: and I am n_____ come of
w_____, but h_____ t_____ s_____ m_____
i_____ t_____, whom ye k_____ n_____,
V.29 But I know him: for a_____ b_____ h_____,
and he hath s_____ m_____.

3

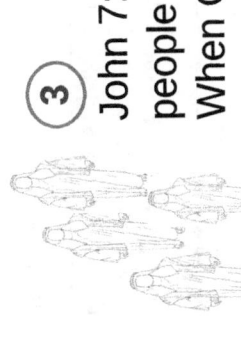

John 7:31 And m_____ of the
people believed on him, and said,
When Christ cometh, will he do
m_____ m_____ than
these which this man hath done?

During feast of tabernacles, Jesus teaches not find him? will he go unto the dispersed among the Gentiles, and teach the them that He will no longer be with them.

V.33 Then said Jesus unto them, Yet a little while am I with you, and then I go unto him that sent me.

V.34 Ye shall seek me, and shall not find me: and where I am, thither ye cannot come.

V.35 Then said the Jews among themselves, Whither will he go, that we shall not find him? will he go unto the dispersed among the Gentiles, and teach the Gentiles?

V.36 What manner of saying is this that he said, Ye shall seek me, and shall not find me: and where I am, thither ye cannot come?

John 7:2 Now the Jew's feast of tabernacles was at hand.

① V. 37 In the last day, that great day of the feast, Jesus stood and cried, saying, If any man thirst, let him come unto me, and drink.

V. 38 He that believeth on me, as the scripture hath said, out of his belly shall flow rivers of living water.

V. 39 (But this spake he of the Spirit, which they that believe on him should receive: for the Holy Ghost was not yet given; because that Jesus was not yet glorified.)

Last day of feast instructions on how He can be with them through the Holy Ghost.

John 4:10 Jesus answered and said unto her, If thou knewest the gift of God, and who it is that saith to thee, Give me to drink; thou wouldest have asked of him, and he would have given thee living water. (Woman at the Well John 4)

Jeremiah 17:13 ....because they have forsaken the LORD, the fountain of living waters. The Father, Son and Holy Spirit are One, the Living Water

Old Testament (Shadow)

New Testament (Body that casts the shadow)

1Corinthians 10:4 And did all drink the same spiritual drink: for they drank of that spiritual Rock that followed them: and that Rock was Christ.

Exodus 17:6 Behold, I will stand before thee there upon the rock in Horeb; and thou shalt smite the rock, and there shall come water out of it, that the people may drink. And Moses did so in the sight of the elders of Israel.

Feast of Tabernacles- God will tabernacle (Live) with man.

CHAPTER 7

V. 33-39

Notes

V.33 Then said Jesus unto them, Yet a little while a_____ with y_____, and then I go unto him that sent me.

V.34 Ye shall seek me, and shall not find me: and w_____ a_____,

t_____ y_____ c_____ c_____.

V.35 Then said the Jews among themselves, Whither will he go, *that we shall*

n_____ f_____ h_____? will he go unto the dispersed among the Gentiles, and teach the Gentiles?

V.36 What manner of saying is this that he said, Ye shall seek me, and shall not

find me: and w_____ a_____, t_____ ye c_____ c_____?

① V. 37 In the l_____ d_____, that great day of the f_____, Jesus

stood and cried, saying, If any man t_____, let him come unto me,

and d_____.

V. 38 He that b_____ on me, as the s_____ hath said,

out of h_____ b_____ s_____ f_____ r_____ o_____

l_____ w_____.

V. 39 (But this spake he of the S_____, which t_____ t_____

b_____ on him should r_____: for the H_____

g_____ was not yet given; because that J_____ w_____

n_____ y_____ g_____.)

CHAPTER 7
V. 40-43
Guide

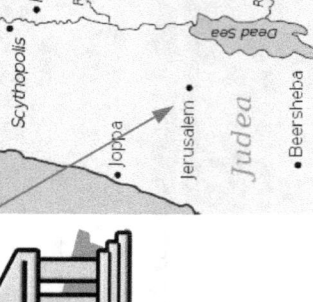

THE DECAPOLIS

Temple

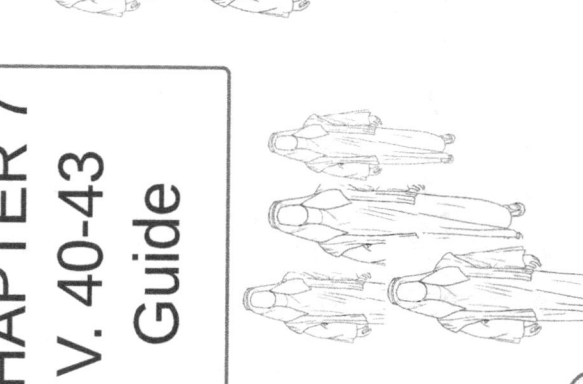

1

V. 40 *Many* of the people therefore, when they heard this saying, said, Of a *truth* this is *the Prophet*.

Deuteronomy 18:15 *Believed He was the prophet like unto Moses. Would be raised up from among the brethren.*

2

Saw the miracles and believed.

V.41 *Others* said, This is the *Christ*.

3

V. 41 ....But some said, Shall Christ come out of *Galilee?*

John 7:42 Hath not the *scriptures* said, That *Christ* cometh of the *seed* of *David*, and out of the town of *Bethlehem*, where David was?

4

This group thought they knew Jesus but they did not. They knew the scriptures but they did not know Jesus. Common today. It is possible to know the Bible but not really know who Jesus is. Jesus was born in Bethlehem but they did not even ask Him, How can you be the Christ?

V.43 So there was a *division* among the people *because of him.*

Jesus causes division. Division is not always bad. Separates the sheep from the goats.

5

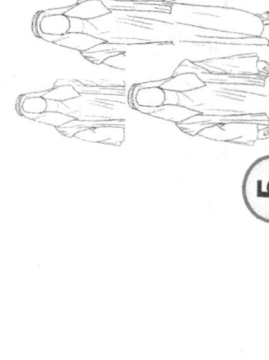

V.44 And some of them would have taken him;
Unbelieving Jews

CHAPTER 7
V. 40-43
Notes

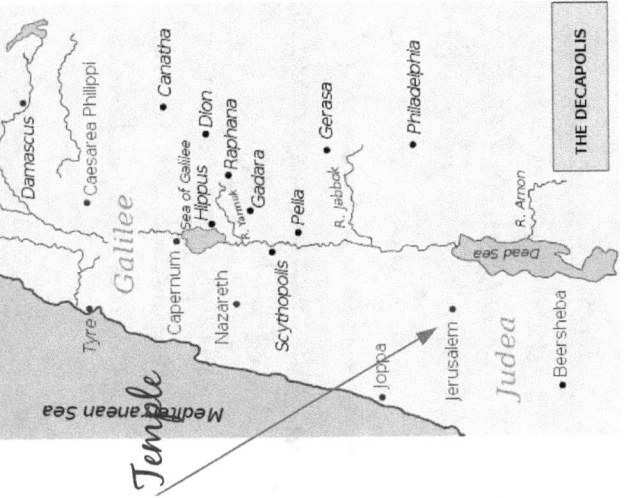

Temple

THE DECAPOLIS

1

V. 40 M_____ of the people therefore, when they heard this saying, said, Of a t_____ this is t_____ P_____.

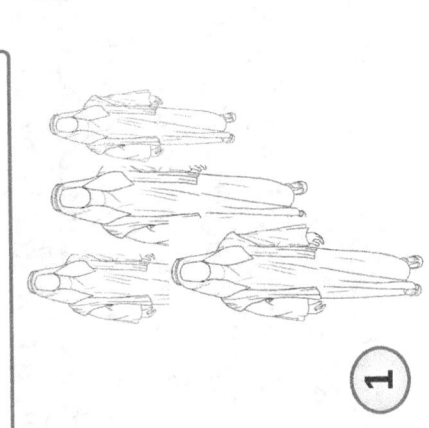

2

V.41 O_____ said, This is the C_____.

3

V. 41 ....But some said, Shall Christ come out of G_____?

John 7:42 Hath not the s_____ said, That C_____ cometh of the s_____ of D_____, and out of the town of B_____, where David was?

4

V.43 So there was a d_____ among the people b_____

5

V. 44 And s_____ of them would have taken him;

CHAPTER 7
V. 44-53
Guide

Officers

chief
priests
and
Pharisees

V.45 Then came the officers to the chief priests and Pharisees; and they said unto them, Why have ye not brought him?

V.46 The officers answered, Never man spake like this man.
V.47 Then answered them the Pharisees, Are ye also deceived?

V.48 Have any of the rulers or of the Pharisees believed on him?
V.49 But this people who knoweth not the law are cursed.

V.50 Nicodemus saith unto them, (he that came to Jesus by night, being one of them,)
V.51 Doth our law judge any man, before it hear him, and know what he doeth?
V.52 They answered and said unto him, Art thou also of Galilee? Search, and look: for out of Galilee ariseth no prophet.
Jesus did not arise out of Nazareth of Galilee. He arose out of Bethlehem-Judah. He was in Nazareth because Joseph took Him there after coming back out of Egypt. They had fled from King Herod when he slaughtered all the babies.

V. 53 And every man went unto his own house. ——→ the feast is over

The feast of tabernacles is also called the feast of booths. Booths means tents. During the feast, the Jews would live in tents and then go to their own homes on the last day of the feast.

There is nothing new under the sun! The rulers believed the common people could not discern truth. They wanted to censure Jesus! Nicodemus was a ruler and he knew the law. What he did not know was that Jesus did not arise out of Galilee.

THE DECAPOLIS

Mediterranean Sea

Tyre
Damascus
Caesarea Philippi
Canatha
Dion
Sea of Galilee
Hippus
Raphana
Capernaum
R. Yarmuk
Gadara
Galilee
Nazareth
Pella
Scythopolis
R. Jabbok
Gerasa
Philadelphia
Joppa
Dead Sea
R. Arnon
Jerusalem
Judea
Beersheba

CHAPTER 7
V. 44-53
Notes

Officers

chief
priests
and
Pharisees

THE DECAPOLIS

V.45 Then came the o_____ to the c_____ p_____ and
P_____; and they said unto them, Why have ye not brought him?

V.46 The officers answered, Never man spake like this man.

V.47 Then answered them the P_____, Are ye also d_____?

V.48 Have any of the r_____ or of the P_____ b_____
on him?

V.49 But this people who knoweth not the law are cursed.

V.50 N_____ saith unto them, (he that came to Jesus by
night, being one of them,)

V.51 Doth our law judge any man, before it hear him, and know what he doeth?

V.52 They answered and said unto him, Art thou also of Galilee? Search, and
look: for out of G_____ a_____ no p_____.

V. 53 And every man went unto h_____ o_____ h_____.

Read John
Chapter 8

CHAPTER 8
V. 1-11
Guide

Doing the works of Satan, their father by accusing their brethern.

Revelation 12:10... for the accuser of our brethren is cast down, ...

The accusers knew Jesus would not participate in stoning the woman. So they not only were accusing the woman but they also were there to accuse Him of not following the law of Moses of stoning. Jesus stooped down in their presence. He did not do as expected and climb on His throne. God uses His finger to write commandments and perform miracles. He wrote the 10 commandments with His finger on clay tablets. Whatever He wrote, it convicted the accusers of their own conscience. Jesus could have cast the first stone so He alone was left. He could have stoned her and she would have died in her sin. But He came to save her not condemn her.

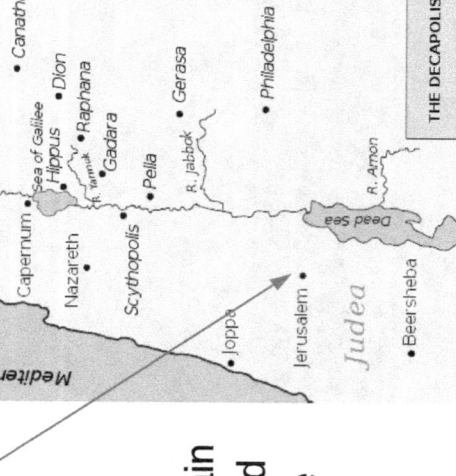

1 V.1 Jesus went unto the mount of Olives.

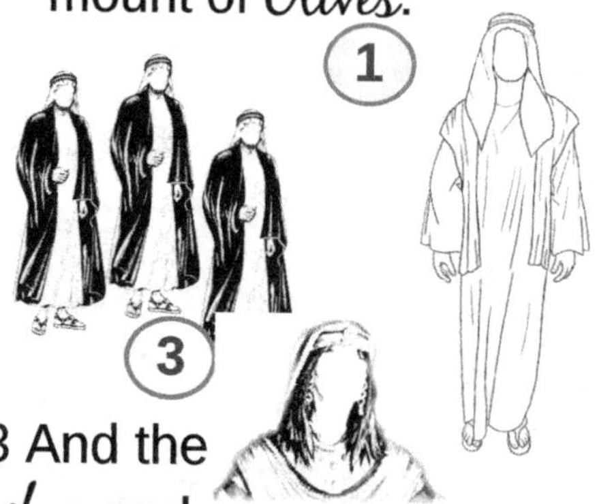

3 V.3 And the scribes and Pharisees

woman taken in adultery

2 V.2... he came again into the temple, and all the people came unto him;

After the feast the people went to their homes, Jesus went to the Mount of Olives

THE DECAPOLIS

Map labels: Mediterranean Sea, Tyre, Damascus, Caesarea Philippi, Canatha, Galilee, Sea of Galilee, Capernum, Nazareth, Hippus, Dion, Raphana, R. Yarmuk, Gadara, Pella, R. Jabbok, Gerasa, Scythopolis, Philadelphia, Dead Sea, R. Arnon, Joppa, Jerusalem, Judea, Beersheba

4 V. 5 Now Moses in the law commanded us, that such should be stoned: but what sayest thou?
V.6 This they said, tempting him, that they might have to accuse him. But Jesus stooped down, and with his finger wrote on the ground, as though he heard them not.
V.7 So when they continued asking him, he lifted up himself, and said unto them, He that is without sin among you, let him first cast a stone at her.
V.8 And again he stooped down, and wrote on the ground.
V.9 And they which heard it, being convicted by their own conscience, went out one by one, beginning at the eldest, even unto the last: and Jesus was left alone, and the woman standing in the midst. had lived the longest and had the most sin. Therefore most convicted.

CHAPTER 8
V. 1-11
Notes

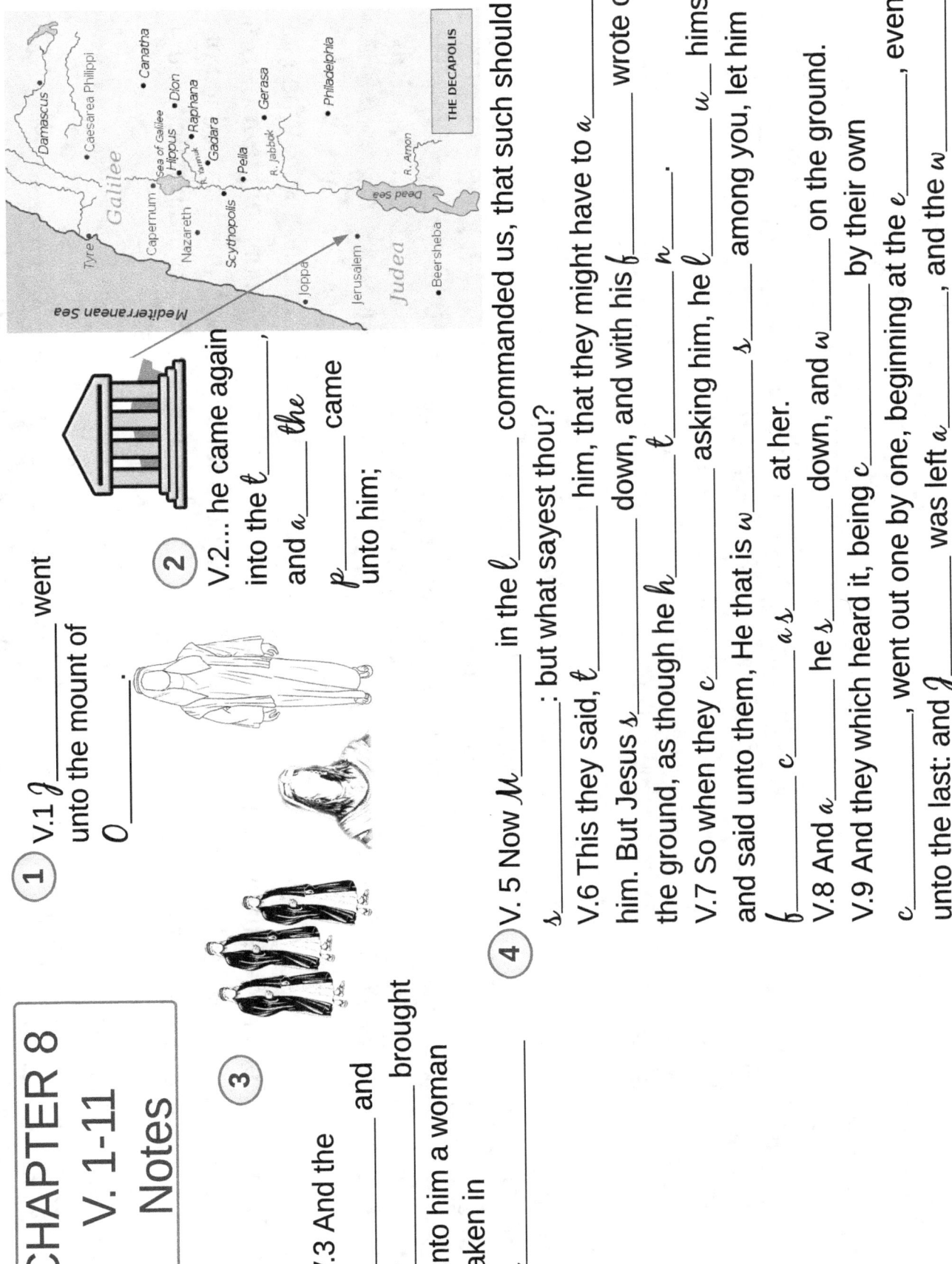

Map labels: Mediterranean Sea · Tyre · Galilee · Damascus · Caesarea Philippi · Canatha · Sea of Galilee · Dion · Hippos · Raphana · Capernum · Nazareth · Gadara · Scythopolis · Pella · Gerasa · R. Jabbok · Philadelphia · Joppa · Jerusalem · Judea · Beersheba · Dead Sea · THE DECAPOLIS

1 v.1 J____ went unto the mount of O____.

2 V.2... he came again into the t____ the ____, and a____ the came p____ unto him;

3 V.3 And the s____ and P____ brought unto him a woman taken in a____

4 V. 5 Now M____ in the l____ commanded us, that such should be s____; but what sayest thou?

V.6 This they said, t____ him, that they might have to a____ him. But Jesus s____ down, and with his f____ wrote on the ground, as though he h____ t____ n____.

V.7 So when they c____ asking him, he l____ u____ himself, and said unto them, He that is w____ s____ among you, let him f____ c____ a s____ at her.

V.8 And a____ he s____ down, and w____ on the ground.

V.9 And they which heard it, being c____ by their own c____, went out one by one, beginning at the e____, even unto the last: and J____ was left a____, and the w____ standing in the midst.

CHAPTER 8
V. 12-31
Guide

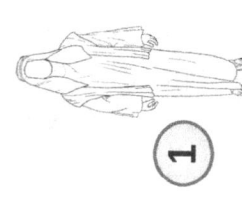

(2) V.13 The *Pharisees* therefore said unto him, Thou *bearest record of thyself;* thy record is not true.

There is no one that can bear record of Jesus other than John the Baptist whom God sent.

(4) V.21 Then said Jesus again unto them, I go my way, and ye shall seek me, and shall die in your sins: whither I go, ye cannot come.

Answer → *They could not come unto Him. They would die in their sin because they did not believe in Him and would not be saved.*

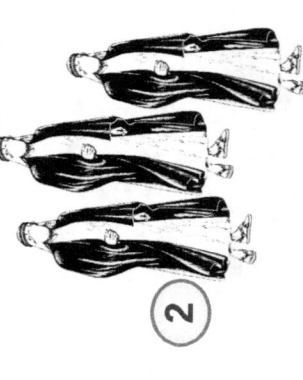

(1) V.12 Then spake Jesus again unto them, saying, *I am the light of the world;* he that followeth me shall not walk in darkness, but shall have the light of life.

(3) V.17 It is also written in your law, that the testimony of *two men* is true.

V.18 *I am one that bear witness of myself, and the Father that sent me beareth witness of me.*

Jesus counts the Father and Himself as two. Other men could not bear record of themself because they are only one. But Jesus is two.

(5) V.28 Then said Jesus unto them, When ye have *lifted up* the Son of man, *then shall ye know* that I am he, and that I do nothing of myself; but as my Father hath taught me, I speak these things.

Prophecy →

Lifted up means crucified. After He was crucified, He would be resurrected from the dead. That was proof the Father was with Him. We have no excuse for not believing today because we know He was crucified and risen from the dead.

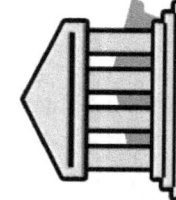
THE DECAPOLIS

CHAPTER 8
V. 12-31
Notes

THE DECAPOLIS

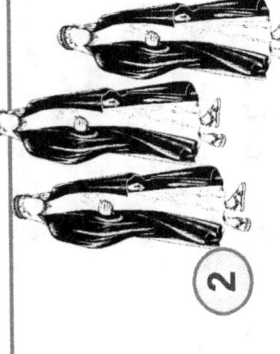

1 V.12 Then spake Jesus again unto them, saying, _I_ _a_____ _t___ _l___ _o_ _t___ _w_____: he that followeth me shall not walk in darkness, but shall have the light of life.

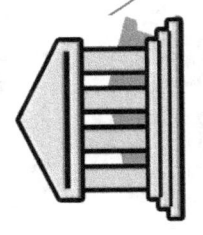

2 V.13 The P_____ _r___ therefore said unto him, Thou _b_____ _r_____ of _t_____; thy record is not true.

3 V.17 It is also written in your law, that the testimony of _t___ _m___ is true.

V.18 _I_ _a__ _o__ _that_ bear witness of myself, _a__ _the F_____ _that_ _s____ _me b____ _w_____ of me.

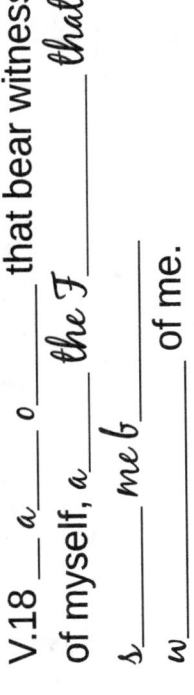

4 V.21 Then said Jesus again unto them, I go _m_ _w___, and ye shall seek me, and _s____ _d__ _in y____ _s____: whither I go, ye _c_____ _c____.

5 V.28 Then said Jesus unto them, When ye have _l_____ _u_ the Son of man, _t___ _s____ _y_ _k___ that I am he, and that I do nothing of myself; but as my Father hath taught me, I speak these things.

CHAPTER 8
V. 32-53
Guide

God made Abraham the Father of the Jewish Nation. Genesis 12

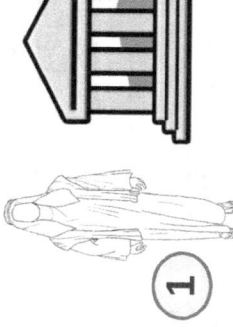

Whosoever does the deeds of Jesus will live free. Whosoever does the deeds of sin will live in bondage and be the servant of that sin.

(1)

V.32 And ye shall know the *truth*, and the truth shall make you *free*.

V.33 They answered him, We be Abraham's seed, and were never in bondage to any man: how sayest thou, Ye shall be made free?

(2)

(3)

V.34 Jesus answered them, Verily, verily, I say unto you, Whosoever committeth sin is the servant of sin.

An unsaved person is in bondage to sin.

(4) V.39 They answered and said unto him, *Abraham is our father.* Jesus saith unto them, If ye were *Abraham's children, ye would do the works of Abraham.*
V.40 But now ye seek to kill me, a man that hath told you the truth, which I have heard of God: *this did not Abraham.* (*Jesus appeared before Abraham in the Old Testament*)

(5) V.52 Then said the Jews unto him, Now we know that thou hast a devil. *Abraham is dead,* and the prophets; and thou sayest, If a man keep my saying, he shall *never taste of death.*
V.53 Art thou *greater* than our father Abraham, which is dead? and the prophets are dead: *whom makest thou thyself? Even Abraham and the prophets, which they considered the greatest among them, died. Jesus was claiming He was better than even they were because He would never taste death.*

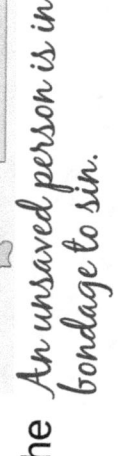

THE DECAPOLIS

CHAPTER 8
V. 32-53
Notes

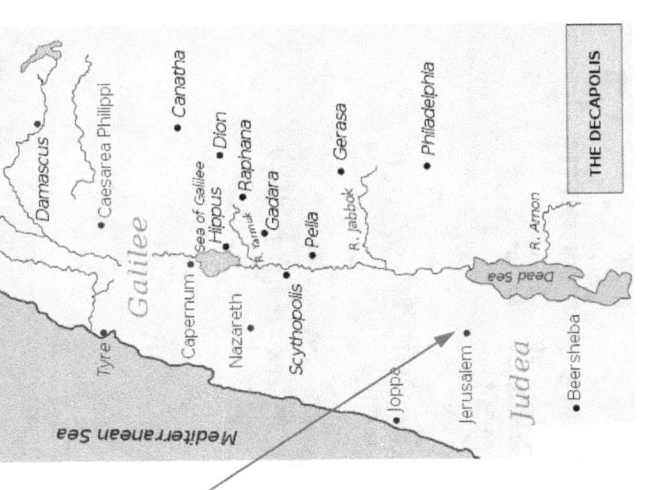

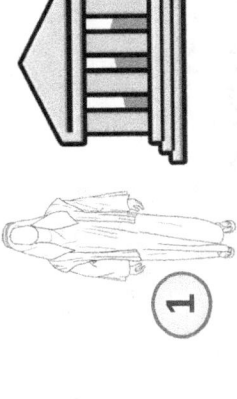

1 V.32 And ye shall know the *truth*, and the truth shall make you *free*.

2 V.33 They answered him, We be A_____ s_____, and were _____ to any man: how sayest thou, Ye shall be made free?

3 V.34 Jesus answered them, Verily, verily, I say unto you, W_____ c_____ sin is the s_____ of sin.

4 V.39 They answered and said unto him, A_____ is our father. Jesus saith unto them, If ye were A_____ c_____, ye would do the w_____ o_____ A_____.

V.40 But now ye s_____ t_____ k_____ m_____, a man that hath told you the truth, which I have heard of God: t_____ d_____ n_____ A_____.

5 V.52 Then said the Jews unto him, Now we know that thou hast a devil. A_____ d_____, and the p_____ of d_____; and thou sayest, If a man k_____ my s_____, he shall n_____ t_____ t_____ g_____ t_____ t_____.

V.53 A_____ t_____ g_____ t_____ than our father Abraham, which is dead? and the prophets are dead: w_____ m_____ t_____ t_____?

CHAPTER 8
V. 54-57
Guide

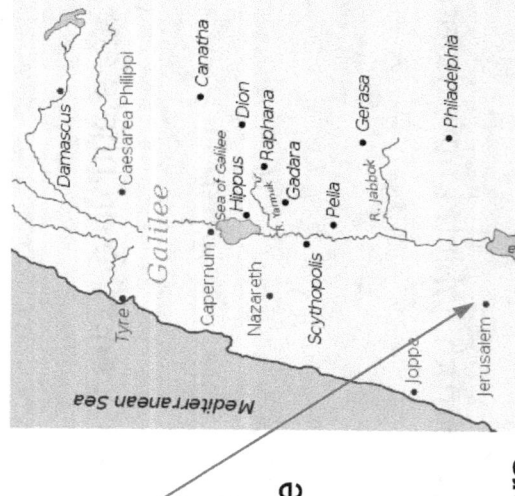

THE DECAPOLIS

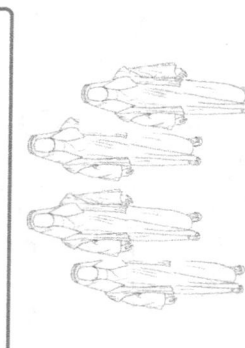

① V.56 Your father Abraham rejoiced to see my day: and he saw it, and was glad.

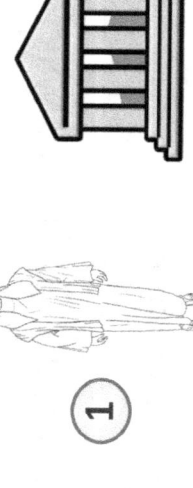

② V.57 Then said the Jews unto him, Thou art not yet fifty years old, and hast thou seen Abraham?

God appeared to Abraham in the Old Testament. When God is in the Old Testament. When God is in the flesh, He is manifested as Jesus so it is Jesus that appeared to Abraham. **John 4:12 No man hath seen God at any time.**

Genesis 18:2 And he lift up his eyes and looked, and, lo, three men stood by him: and when he saw them, he ran to meet them from the tent door, and bowed himself toward the ground. (He had 2 other men with Him and Abraham bowed before Him and called Him, LORD)

Genesis 18:10 And he said, I will certainly return unto thee according to the time of life; and, lo, Sarah thy wife shall have a son. (Only God could do this miracle)

Genesis 18:13 And the LORD said unto Abraham (The Bible itself testifies that it was the LORD speaking to Abraham)

Genesis 18:22 And the men turned their faces from thence, and went toward Sodom: but Abraham stood yet before the LORD (2 of the men were angels and went on to Sodom, but the 3rd was Jesus and again He is called the LORD)

CHAPTER 8
V. 54-57
Notes

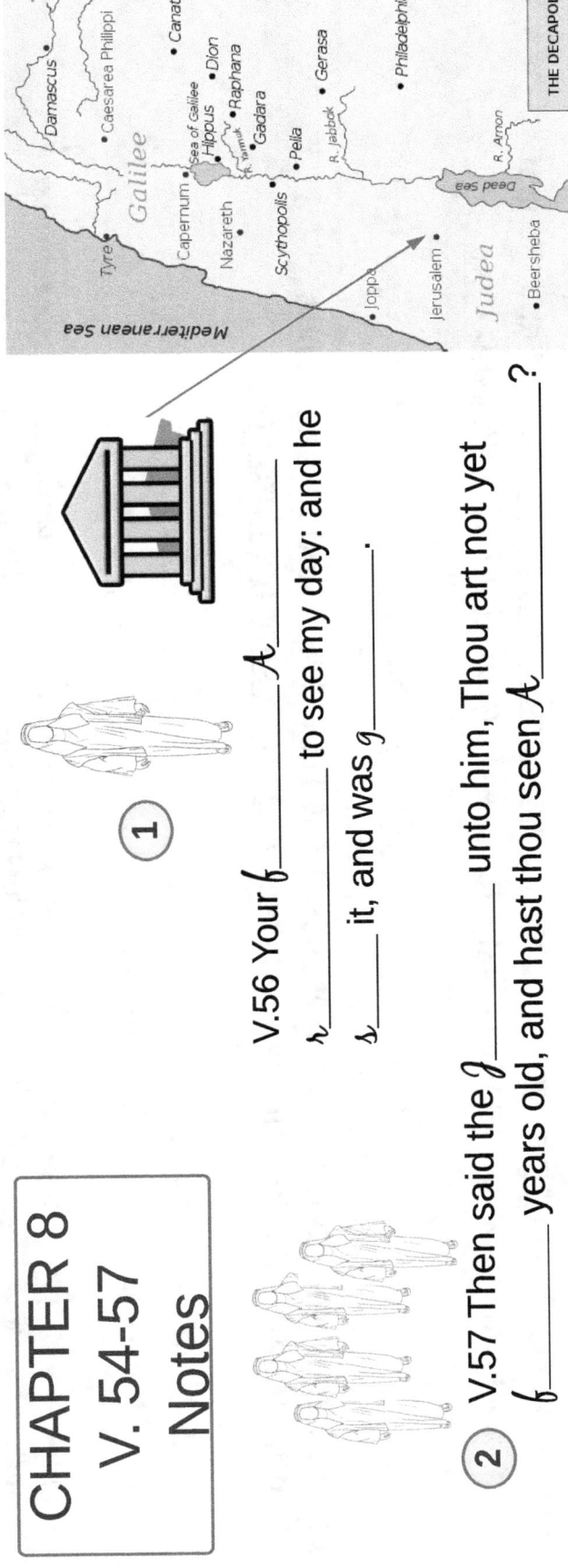

1 V.56 Your f_____ A_____ to see my day: and he

r_____ it, and was g_____ .

2 V.57 Then said the J_____ unto him, Thou art not yet

f_____ years old, and hast thou seen A_____ ?

THE DECAPOLIS

CHAPTER 8
V. 58-59
Guide

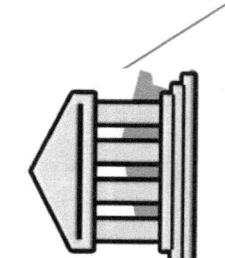

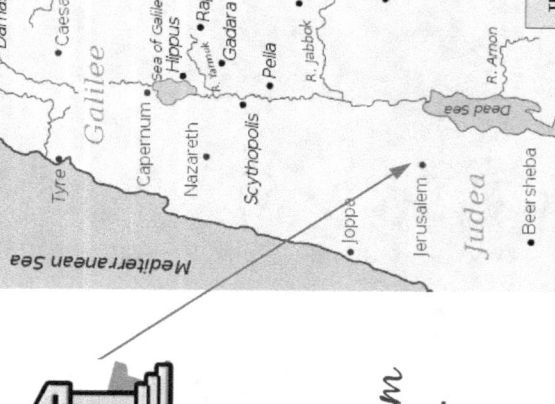

THE DECAPOLIS

Witnessing again for the Father, Son and Holy Ghost.

1. V. 58 Jesus said unto them, Verily, verily, I say unto you, Before Abraham was, I am.

Jesus was in the beginning, Abraham was not born until 2000 years later.

John 1:1 In the beginning was the Word, and the Word was with God, and the Word was God.
John 1:2 The same was in the beginning with God.
John 1:14 And the Word was made flesh, and dwelt among us,

Revelation 22:13 I am Alpha and Omega, the beginning and the end, the first and the last.
(Alpha and Omega are the first and last letters of the Greek alphabet). He says I am.

2. *Jesus did not say before Abraham was, I was but He said, I Am. That is the name that God called Himself when talking to Moses at the burning bush.*

Exodus 3:14 And God said unto Moses, I AM THAT I AM: and he said, Thus shalt thou say unto the children of Israel, I AM hath sent me unto you.

2. V.59 Then took they up stones to cast at him: but Jesus hid himself, and went out of the temple, going through the midst of them, and so passed by.

They wanted to stone Him because He was making Himself equal to God. Jesus called Himself by God's name and says that He was the LORD that appeared to Abraham and others.

CHAPTER 8
V. 58-59
Notes

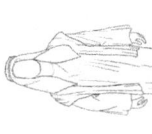

V. 58 Jesus said unto them, V_____,

v_____, s_____, A_____, w_____,

B_____, a_____.

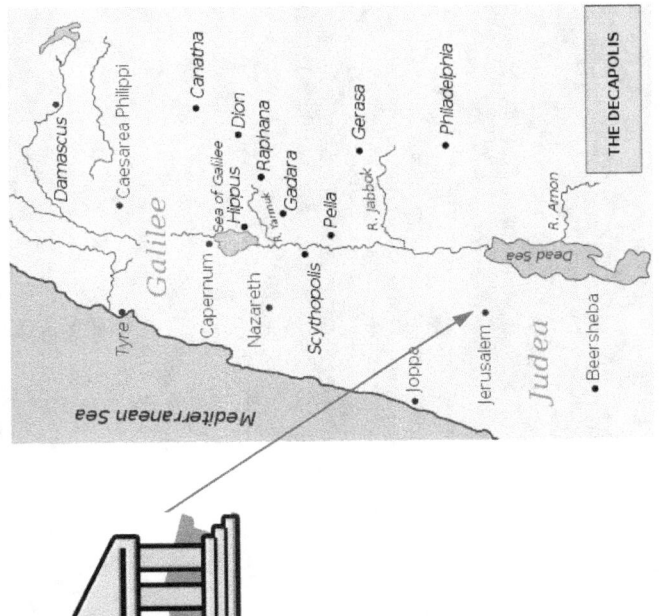

V.59 Then took they up s_____ to cast at him: but J_____ hi_____ h_____, and went out of the temple, going through the midst of them, and s_____ p_____ b_____.

Read John

Chapter 9

CHAPTER 9
V. 1-6
Guide

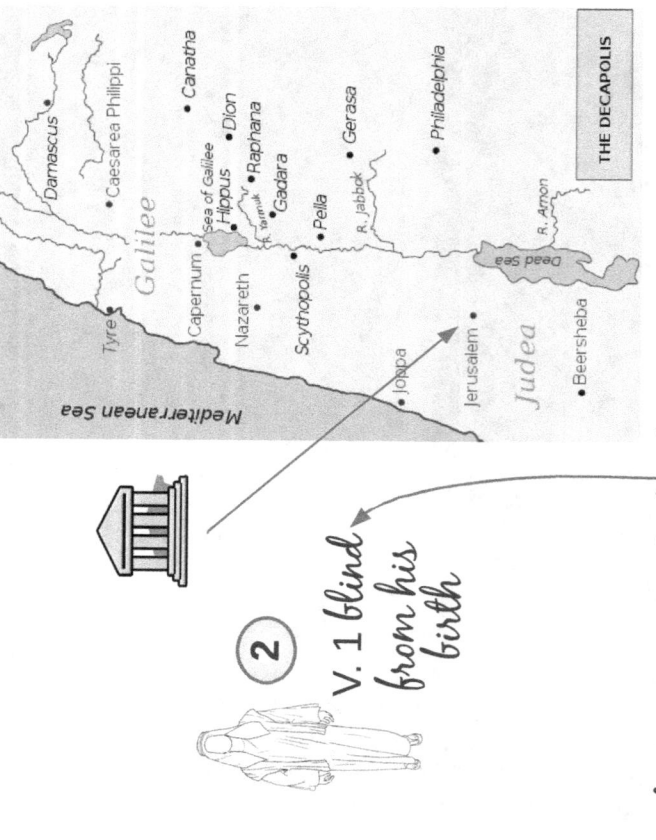

THE DECAPOLIS

V. 1 *blind from his birth*

V. 1 *Jesus* *The man needed light, he was in darkness*

②

①

⑤ V.5 As long as I am in the world, I am the *light* of the world.

③ V.2 And his disciples asked him, saying, *Master*, who did *sin*, this *man*, or his *parents*, that he was *born blind?*

④ V.3 Jesus answered, *Neither* hath this man *sinned*, nor his parents: *but* that the *works* of *God* should be made *manifest* in him.

⑥ V.6 When he had thus spoken, he spat on the ground, and *made clay* of the spittle, and he *anointed the eyes* of the blind man with the *clay,*

Jeremiah 18:4 And the vessel that he made of clay was marred in the hand of the potter: so he made it again another vessel, as seemed good to the potter to make it.

Jeremiah 18:5 Then the word of the LORD came to me, saying,

Jeremiah 18:6 O house of Israel, cannot I do with you as this potter? saith the LORD. Behold, as the clay is in the potter's hand, so are ye in mine hand, O house of Israel.

CHAPTER 9
V. 1-6
Notes

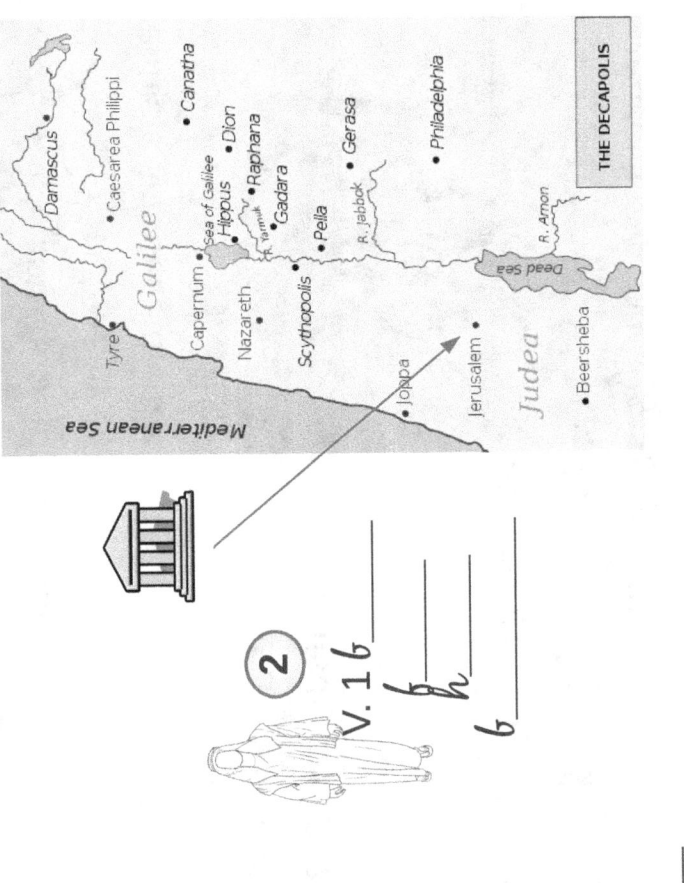

THE DECAPOLIS

③

V.2 And his disciples asked him, saying, M_____, who did s____, this m____, or his p____ b_____ b_____, that he was born b_____ ?

② V. 1 b_____
b_____
h_____
b_____

① V. 1 J_____

④ V.3 Jesus answered, N_____ hath this man s_____, nor his parents: b_____ that the w_____ of g_____ should be made m_____ in him.

⑤ V.5 As long as I am in the world, I am the l_____ of the world.

⑥ V.6 When he had thus spoken, he spat on the ground, and m_____ c_____ of the spittle, and he a_____ t_____ e_____ of the blind man with the c_____,

Jeremiah 18:4 And the vessel that he made of clay was marred in the hand of the potter: so he made it again another vessel, as seemed good to the potter to make it.

Jeremiah 18:5 Then the word of the LORD came to me, saying,

Jeremiah 18:6 O house of Israel, cannot I do with you as this potter? saith the LORD. Behold, as the clay is in the potter's hand, so are ye in mine hand, O house of Israel.

CHAPTER 9
V. 7-16
Guide

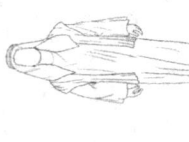

A. Commanded

1 V.7 And said unto him, *Go, wash* in the pool of *Siloam,* (which is by interpretation, Sent.)

near the Temple

B. faith to obey

V.7 He *went* his way therefore, and *washed,* and came seeing.

C. healed

2

3 V.13 They brought to the Pharisees him that aforetime was blind.

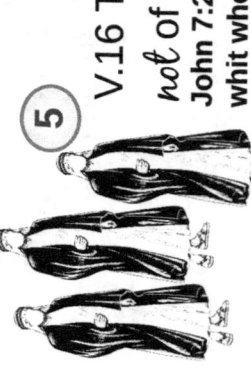

5 V.16 Therefore said *some* of the *Pharisees,* This man is *not* of God, because he keepeth not the *sabbath* day.

John 7:23 are ye angry at me, because I have made a man every whit whole on the sabbath day?

John 7:24 Judge not according to the appearance, but judge righteous judgment.

7 V. 16 And there was a *division* among them.

4 V. 14 And it was the *sabbath day* when Jesus made the clay, and *opened* his eyes.

Jesus healed on the sabbath again

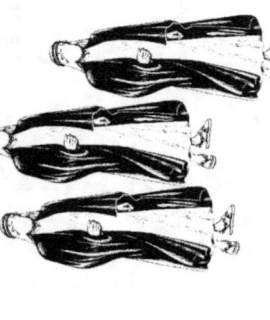

6 V. 16 *Others* said, How can a man that is a sinner do such *miracles?*

Righteous judgement (saw His works.)

THE DECAPOLIS

Mediterranean Sea

Galilee

Judea

Damascus
Caesarea Philippi
Canatha
Dion
Raphana
Hippos
Sea of Galilee
Capernum
Gadara
R. Yarmuk
Pella
Gerasa
Nazareth
Scythopolis
R. Jabbok
Philadelphia
Joppa
Jerusalem
R. Arnon
Dead Sea
Beersheba
Tyre

CHAPTER 9
V. 7-16
Notes

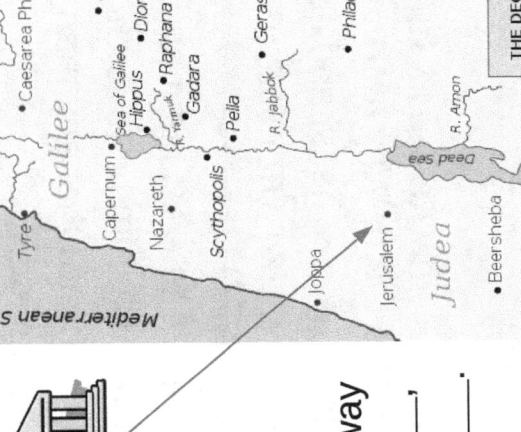

Mediterranean Sea

Tyre

Damascus
• Caesarea Philippi
• Canatha
• Dion
Galilee
Sea of Galilee
Hippus • Raphana
Capernaum • Tarmuk • Gadara
Nazareth •
Scythopolis • Pella • Gerasa
R. Jabbok
• Philadelphia
Judea
• Joppa
• Jerusalem
• Beersheba
Dead sea
R. Arnon

THE DECAPOLIS

1 V.7 And said unto him, *G*_____, *w*_____ (which is by interpretation, Sent.) in the pool of *S*_____

2 V. 7 He *w*_____ his way therefore, and *w*_____, and *c*_____ *s*_____.

3 V.13 They brought to the *P*_____ him that aforetime was *b*_____.

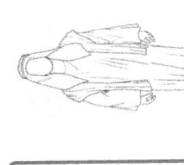

4 V. 14 And it was the *s*_____ *d*_____, when Jesus made the *c*_____, and *o*_____ his *e*_____.

5 V.16 Therefore said *s*_____ of the *P*_____, This man is *n*_____ of God, because he keepeth not the *s*_____ day.

6 V. 16 *O*_____ said, How can a man that is a sinner do such *m*_____?

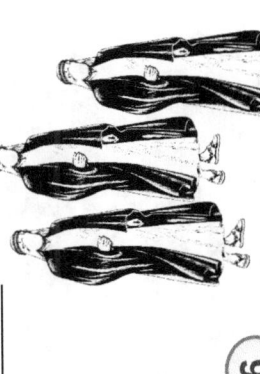

7 V. 16 And there was a *d*_____ among them.

CHAPTER 9
V. 17-33
Guide

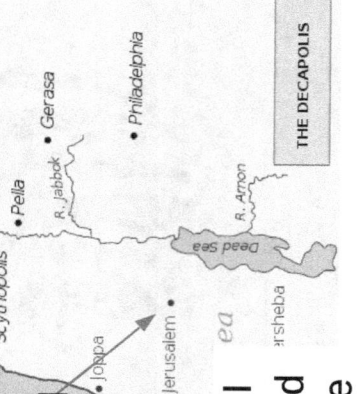

THE DECAPOLIS

1

of age—there is an age of accountability. A child is not accountable but becomes so at a certain age. (When he can understand?)

V.20 His parents answered them and said, We know that this is our son, and that he was born blind:

V.21 But by what means he now seeth, we know not; or who hath opened his eyes, we know not: he is of age; ask him: he shall speak for himself.

Because they feared the Jews V.22

2

V.26 Then said they to him again, What did he to thee? how opened he thine eyes?

They knew that God spake to Moses because of scriptures and miracles. But refused to recognize Jesus though he did the same.

3

V.27 He answered them, I have told you already, and ye did not hear: wherefore would ye hear it again? will ye also be his disciples?

4

V. 29 We know that God spake unto Moses: as for this fellow, we know not from whence he is. (strange, wonder)

whence means (from where)

5

V. 30 The man answered and said unto them, Why herein is a marvellous thing, that ye know not from whence he is, and yet he hath opened mine eyes. (The man was mocking the unbelieving Jews who could not see Jesus was from God)

herein means (in this)

V. 31 Now we know that God heareth not sinners: but if any man be a worshipper of God, and doeth his will, him he heareth.

V. 32 Since the world began was it not heard that any man opened the eyes of one that was born blind.

John 9:33 If this man were not of God, he could do nothing.

The man that was born blind and healed (a common man) could not believe they could not know Jesus was from God. If He was not from God, He could do nothing. He did the works of God. No man had healed the blind before.

CHAPTER 9
V. 17-33
Notes

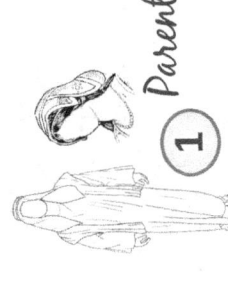

1 Parents

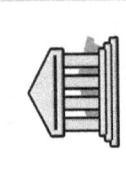

V.20 His p_____ answered them and said, We k_____
is our son, and that he was b_____ b_____:

V.21 But by w_____ m_____ he now seeth, we know not; or who
hath opened his eyes, we know not: h_____ i_____ of a_____; ask him: he
shall s_____ for h_____.

2

V.26 Then said they to him
again, What did he to thee?
h_____ o_____ he thine
eyes?

3

V.27 He answered them, I
have t_____ you
a_____, and ye did
not hear: wherefore would
ye hear it again? will ye
also be his disciples?

that this _____

4

V. 29 We k_____ that
God spake unto
M_____: as for this
fellow, we k_____ n_____
from w_____ he is.

5

V. 30 The m_____ answered and said unto them, Why h_____ is a
m_____ thing, that y_____ k_____ n_____ from _____
w_____ he is, and y_____ he hath o_____ m_____ e_____: but if any
V. 31 Now we know that g_____ h_____ n_____ s_____
man be a w_____ of God, and l_____ his will, him he
h_____.
V. 32 Since the w_____ b_____ was it not heard that any man
opened the eyes of one that was born blind.
John 9:33 If this man were n_____ of g_____, he could do n_____.

CHAPTER 9
V. 34-41
Guide

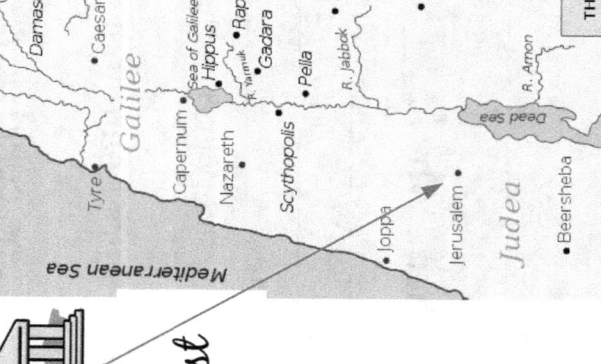

THE DECAPOLIS

(1) V. 34 They answered and said unto him, Thou wast altogether born in sins, and dost thou *teach us?* And they cast him out.

Jesus had explained to his disciples, the man's blindness was not because he or his parents had sinned. The Pharisees were wrong again.

(2) V. 35 Jesus heard that they had cast him out; and when he had *found* him, he said unto him, Dost thou *believe* on the *Son of God*

When the man was cast out. Jesus went looking for him. He doesn't leave you alone.

(3) V. 36 He answered and said, Who is he, Lord, that I might *believe* on him?

(4) V. 37 And Jesus said unto him, Thou hast both *seen him*, and it is he that *talketh* with thee.

(5) V.38 And he said, Lord, *I believe*. And he *worshipped* him.

Because he saw the works of the Father and knew from whence he was. He believed

(6) V. 39 And Jesus said, For *judgment* I am come into this *world*, that they which see not might see; and that they which see might be made blind.

Jesus was come into the world to separate those who would believe on Him.

(7) John 9:41 Jesus said unto them, If ye were *blind*, ye should have no *sin*: but now ye say, We *see*; therefore your *sin remaineth*.

The blind man said, I once was blind but now I see. He confessed to being blind. The Pharisee's are not willing to confess they are spiritually blind and need the light of the world.

CHAPTER 9
V. 34-41
Notes

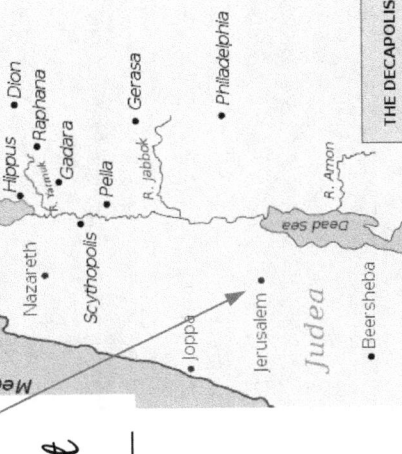

THE DECAPOLIS

1

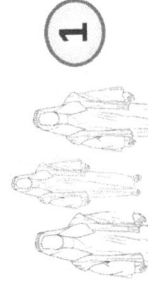

V. 34 They answered and said unto him, Thou wast altogether born in sins, and _dost_ thou t_____ w_____? And they c_____ him o_____.

2

V. 35 Jesus heard that they had cast him out; and when he had f_____ him, he said unto him, Dost thou b_____ on the S_____ of G_____?

3

V. 36 He answered and said, Who is he, Lord, that I might b_____ on him?

4

V. 37 And Jesus said unto him, Thou hast both s_____ h_____, and it is he that t_____ w_____ t_____.

5 V.38 And he said, Lord, _____ b_____. And he w_____ h_____.

6 V. 39 And Jesus said, For j_____ I am _____ into this w_____, that they which see not might see; and that they which see might be made blind.

7 V.41 Jesus said unto them, If ye were b_____, ye should have n_____ s_____: but now ye say, We se_____ therefore your s_____ r_____.

Read John
Chapter 10

CHAPTER 10
V. 1-6
Guide

Bearing witness again for the Trinity

pen for sheep

ladder, rope or window, (not the door)

① V.1 Verily, verily, I say unto you

② V. 1 He that entereth *not* by the *door* into the *sheepfold*, but climbeth up some other way, the same is a *thief* and a *robber*.

⑤ V.5 And a *stranger* will they *not follow*, but will *flee* from him: for they know not the voice of strangers.

John 8:47 He that is of God heareth God's words: ye therefore hear them not, because ye are not of God.

Acts 20:28 Take heed therefore unto yourselves, and to all the *flock*, over the which the Holy Ghost hath made you *overseers*, to feed the church of God, which he hath purchased with his own blood.

Acts 20:29 For I know this, that after my departing shall grievous wolves enter in among you, not sparing the flock.

Door

John 8:47 He that is of God heareth God's words: ye therefore hear them not, because ye are not of God.

③ V.2 But he that entereth in by the *door* is the *shepherd* of the sheep.

④ V.3 To him the porter openeth; and the sheep hear his voice: and he *calleth* his *own* sheep by name, *and leadeth them out.*
V.4 And when he putteth forth his own sheep, he goeth before them, and the sheep *follow* him: for they *know* his voice.

CHAPTER 10
V. 1-6
Notes

1 V.1
V _____, _____, _____ unto you

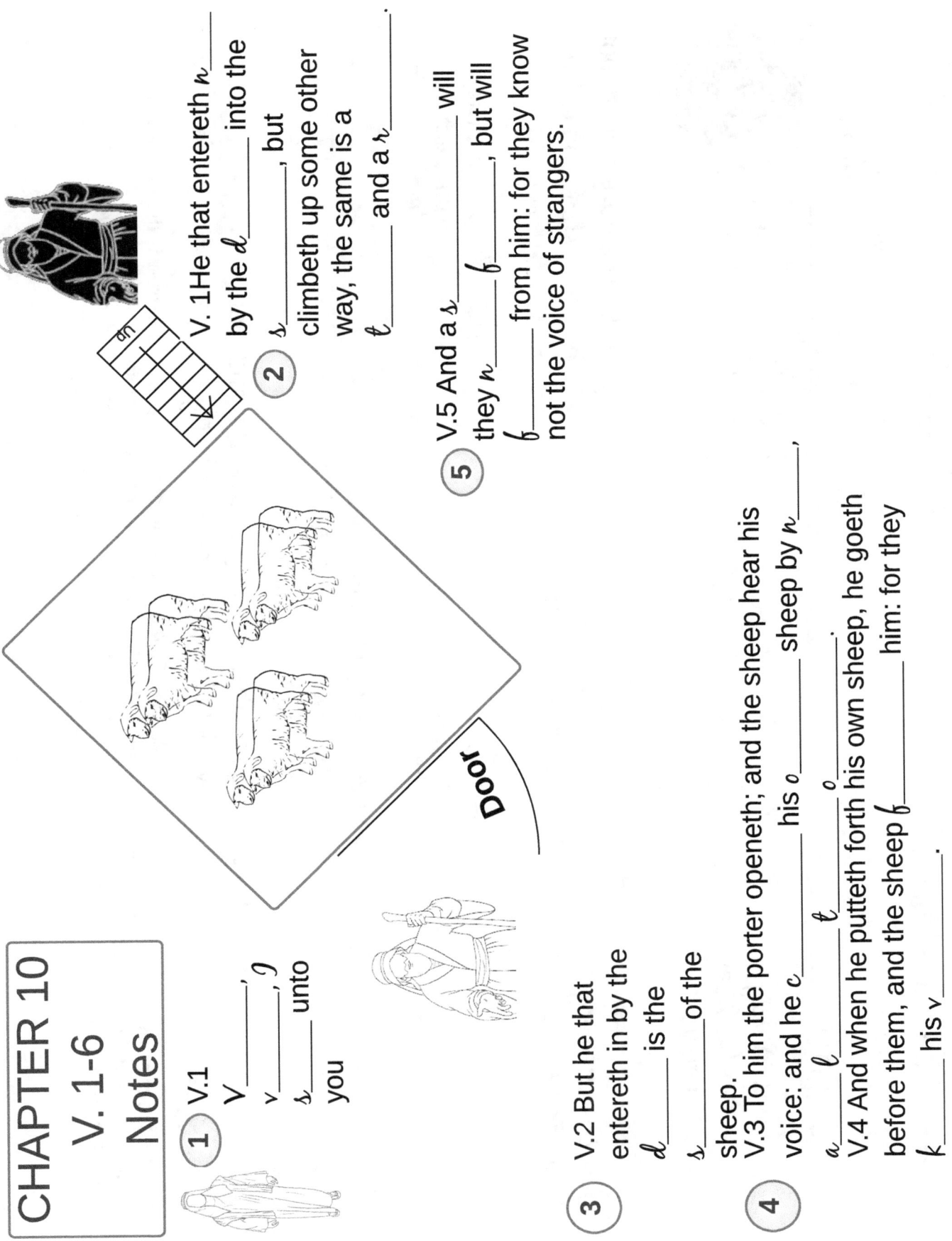

2 V. 1He that entereth n_____ into the
by the d_____ but
climbeth up some other
way, the same is a
t_____ and a r_____ .

3 V.2 But he that
entereth in by the
d_____ is the
s_____ of the
sheep.
V.3 To him the porter openeth; and the sheep hear his
voice: and he c_____ his o_____ l_____ t_____ o_____ .
4 V.4 And when he putteth forth his own sheep, he goeth
before them, and the sheep f_____ him: for they
k_____ his v_____ .

Door

5 V.5 And a s_____ will
they n_____ f_____ , but will
f_____ from him: for they know
not the voice of strangers.

CHAPTER 10
V. 7-10
Guide

Bearing witness again of heavenly things

1 V.7 Verily, verily, I say unto you

Jesus is the only way to heaven.

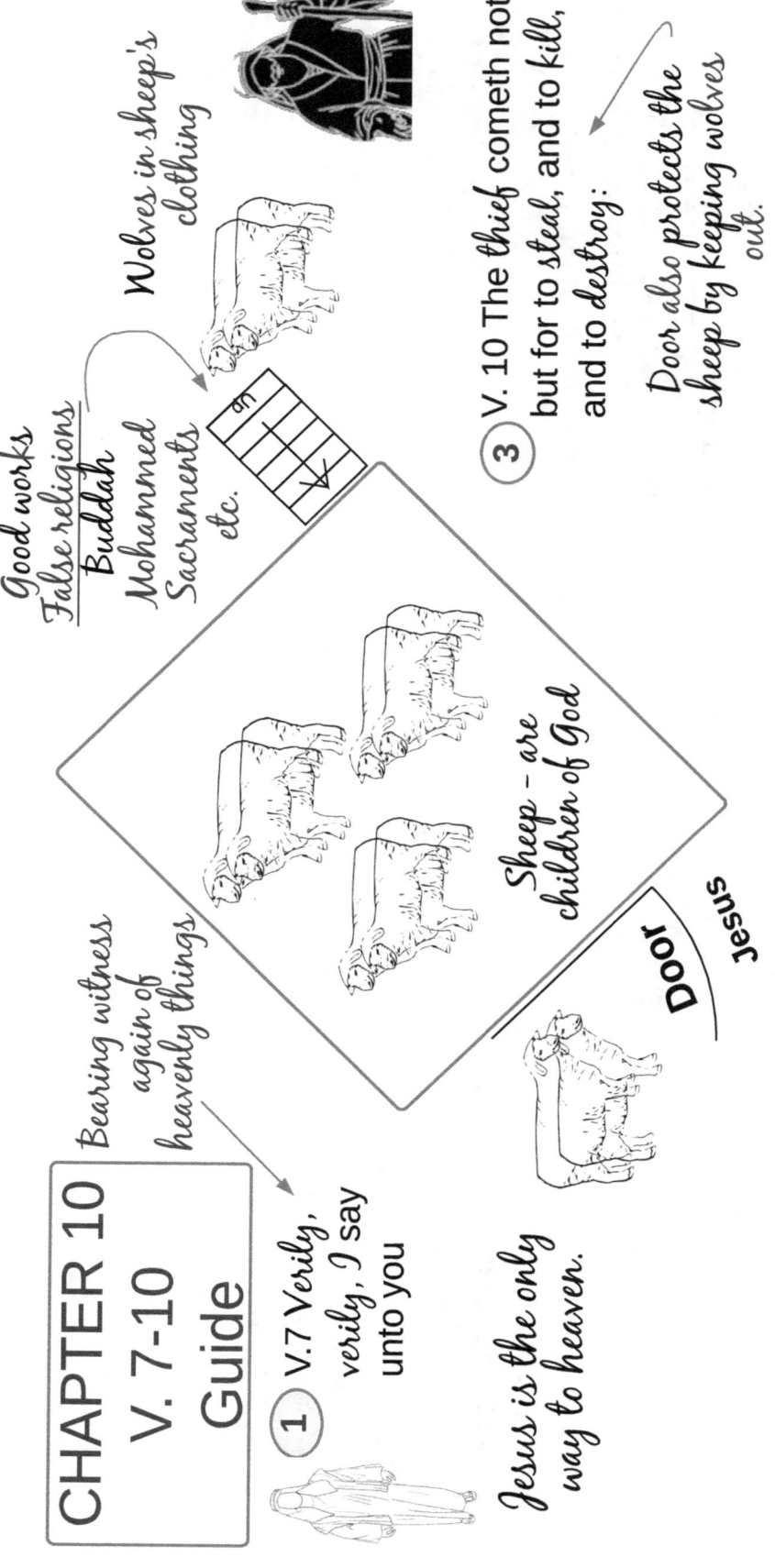

Good works
False religions
Buddah
Mohammed
Sacraments
etc.

Wolves in sheep's clothing

Sheep – are children of God

Door

Jesus

3 V. 10 The thief cometh not, but for to steal, and to kill, and to destroy:

Door also protects the sheep by keeping wolves out.

2 V.9 I am the *door*: by me if any man enter in, he shall be *saved*, and shall go in and out, and find *pasture*.

4 V.10 I am come that they might have *life*, and that they might have it more *abundantly*.

Jesus is the door

John 14:6 Jesus saith unto him, <u>I am the way,</u> the truth, and the life: no man cometh unto the Father, but by me.

Matthew 7:14 Because strait is the gate, and narrow is the way, which leadeth unto life, and few there be that find it.
Matthew 7:15 Beware of false prophets, which come to you in sheep's clothing, but inwardly they are ravening wolves.

CHAPTER 10
V. 7-10
Notes

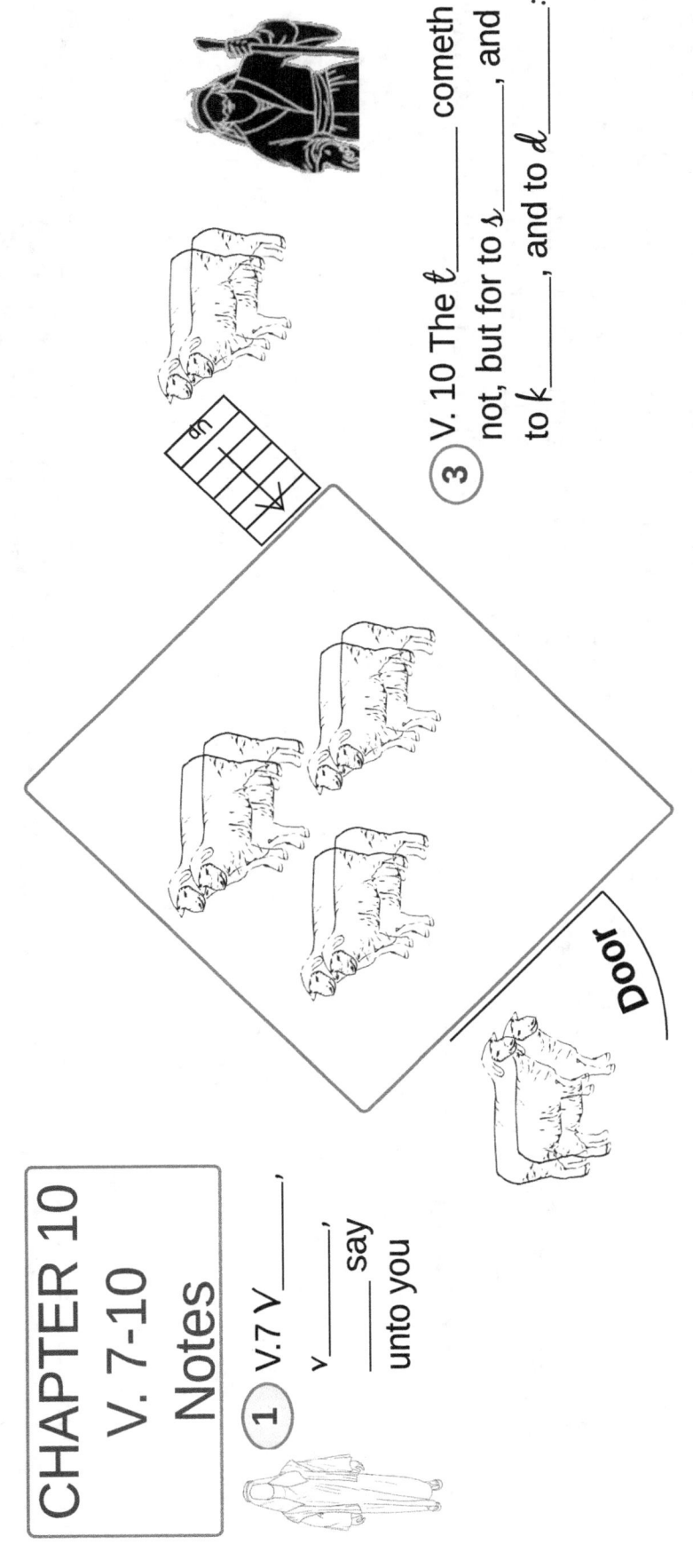

(1) V.7 V_____,
v_____, say _____ unto you

(3) V. 10 The t_____ cometh not, but for to s_____, and to k_____, and to d_____ :

(2) V.9 I am the d_____ : by me if any man enter in, he shall be s_____, and shall go in and out, and find p_____.

(4) V.10 I am come that they might have l_____, and that they might have it more a_____.

Door

CHAPTER 10
V. 11-17
Guide

Jesus

This fold (Israel)

Wolves in sheeps clothing. Not really sheep *False Prophet*

Door *Jesus*

Sheep - are children of God

(1) V. 11 I am the *good shepherd*: the good shepherd *giveth his life* for the sheep.

(3) V:14 I am the good shepherd, and *know my sheep, and am known of mine.*
V:15 As the Father knoweth me, even so know I the Father: and I *lay down* my life for the sheep.
Father gave Him the sheep.

(5) V:17 Therefore doth my *Father love me, because I lay down my life,* that I might *take it again.*

(2) V.12 But he that is an *hireling*, and not the shepherd, whose own the sheep are not, seeth the wolf coming, and *leaveth* the sheep, and fleeth: and the wolf catcheth them, and *scattereth* the sheep.
V.13 The hireling fleeth, because he is an hireling, and *careth not* for the sheep.
(Not a true shepherd (not called by God to preach). He is in it for the money.)
gentiles-anyone that is not a Jew

(Gentiles-the other fold)

V:16 And *other sheep* I have, which are not of this fold: them also I must bring, and they shall hear

(4) my voice; and there shall be *one fold,* and one *shepherd.*

Ezekiel 34:23 And I will set up <u>one shepherd</u> over them, and he shall feed them, even my <u>servant David</u>: he shall feed them, and he shall be their shepherd.

John 6:39 And this is the Father's will which hath sent me, that of all which he hath given me I should lose nothing, but should <u>raise it up again</u> at the last day.

CHAPTER 10
V. 11-17
Notes

Jesus

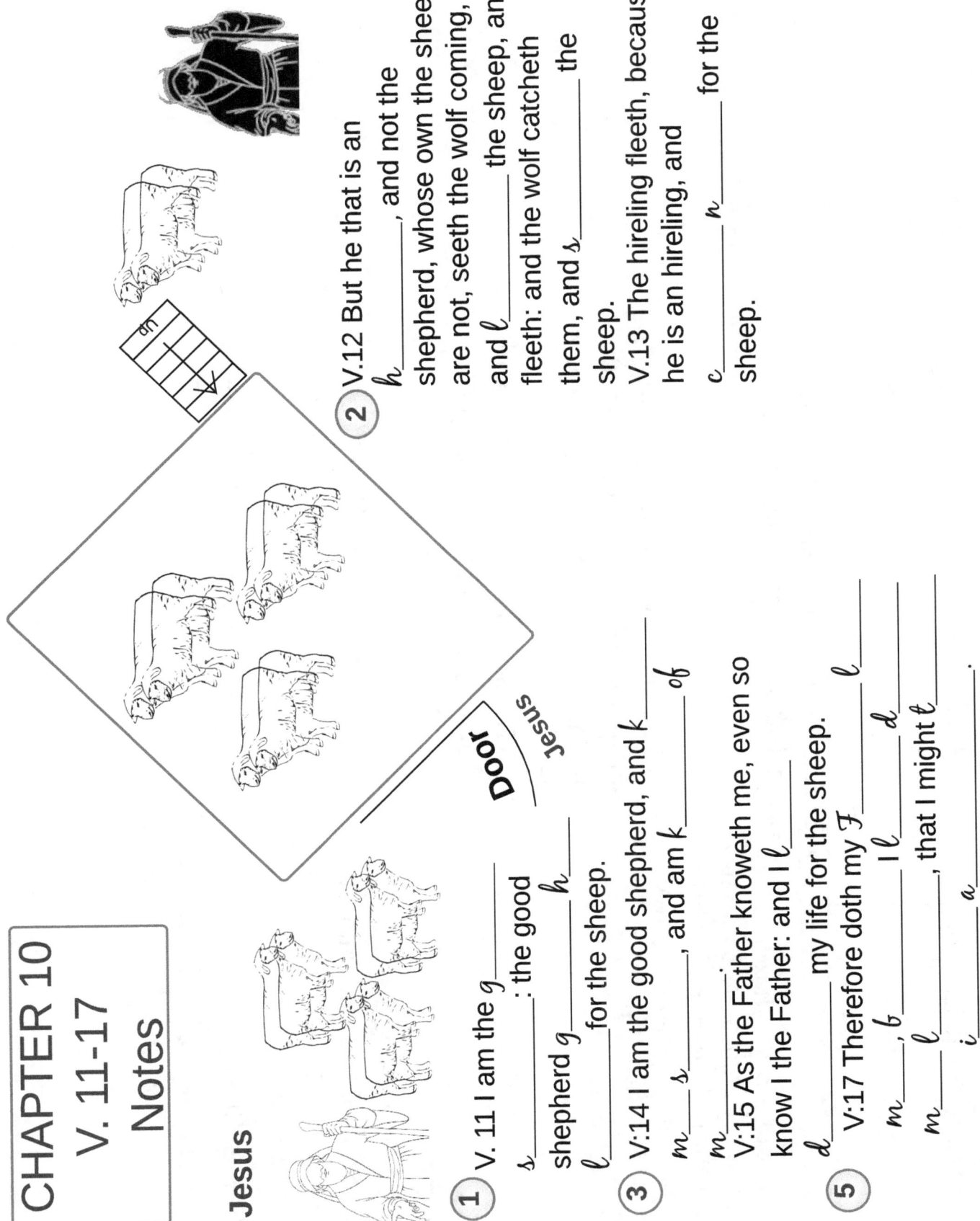

Door

Jesus

(1) V. 11 I am the g_____: the good
s_____ shepherd g_____ h_____
l_____ for the sheep.

(2) V.12 But he that is an
h_____, and not the
shepherd, whose own the sheep
are not, seeth the wolf coming,
and l_____ the sheep, and
fleeth: and the wolf catcheth
them, and s_____ the
sheep.
V.13 The hireling fleeth, because
he is an hireling, and
c_____ n_____ for the
sheep.

(3) V:14 I am the good shepherd, and k_____
m_____ s_____, and am k_____ of
m_____.
V:15 As the Father knoweth me, even so
know I the Father: and I l_____
d_____ my life for the sheep.

(5) V:17 Therefore doth my F_____ l_____
m_____, b_____ I l_____ d_____
m_____ l_____, that I might t_____
i_____ a_____.

CHAPTER 10
V. 22-26
Guide

Called Hanukkah today, Festival of Lights. Not a feast instituted by God in the Old Testament but became a Jewish holiday.

① V.22 And it was at Jerusalem the *feast* of the *dedication*, and it was winter.

Solomon's Porch

③ V.25 Jesus answered them, *I told you, and ye believed not*: the *works* that I do in my Father's name, they *bear witness of* me.

V.26 But *ye believe not*, because ye are *not of my sheep*, as I said unto you.

Calls Himself the Shepherd again.

② V.24 Then came the *Jews* round about him, and said unto him, How long dost thou make us to doubt? If thou be the Christ, *tell us plainly.*

They refuse to believe His works eventhough only God could do them.

Map:
Mediterranean Sea
Tyre
Damascus
Caesarea Philippi
Canatha
Galilee
Dion
Raphana
Capernum · Sea of Galilee
Hippos · R. Yarmuk
Nazareth · Gadara · Gerasa
Scythopolis · Pella · R. Jabbok
Joppa · Philadelphia
Jerusalem
Judea · R. Arnon
Dead Sea
Beersheba

THE DECAPOLIS

CHAPTER 10
V. 22-26
Notes

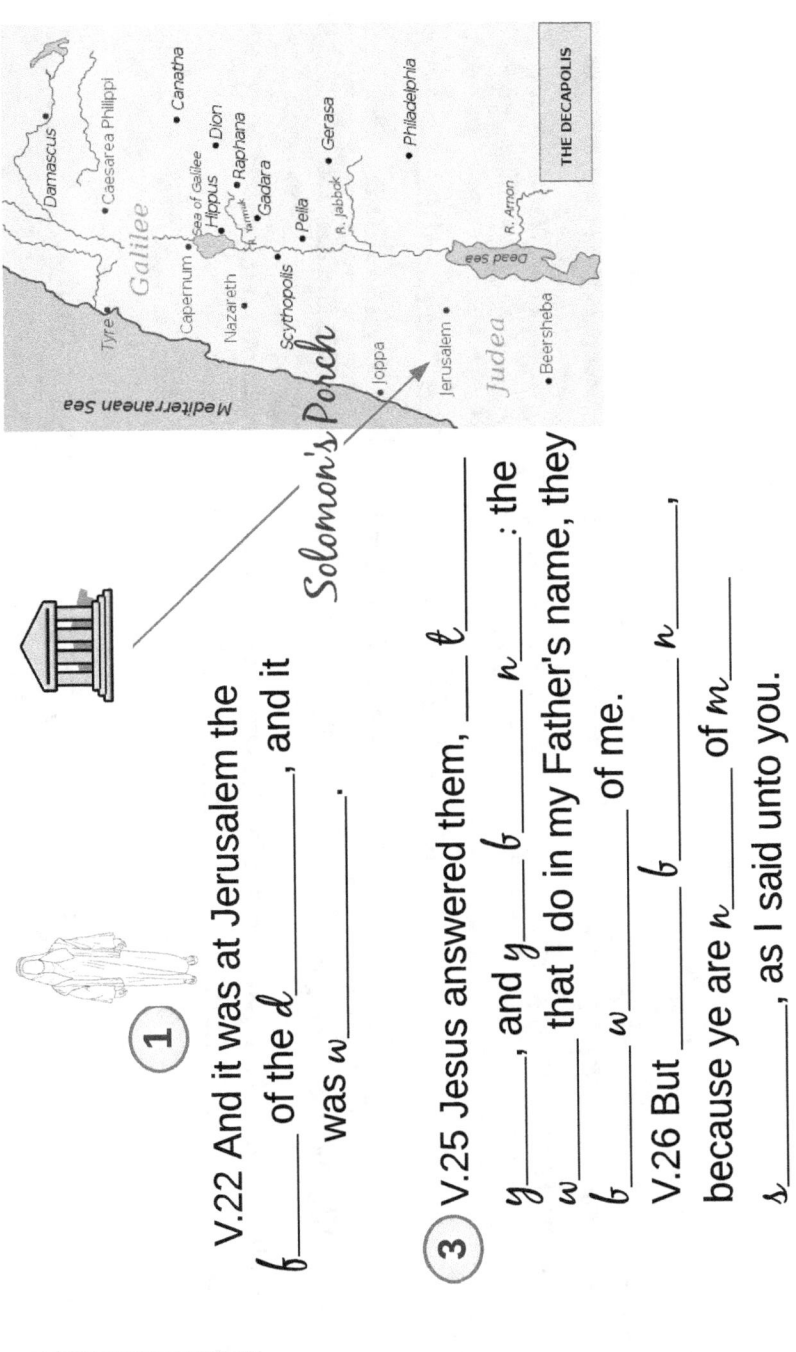

Solomon's Porch

THE DECAPOLIS

1 V.22 And it was at Jerusalem the
f_____ of the d_____, and it
was w_____ .

3 V.25 Jesus answered them, I t_____
y_____, and y_____ b_____ n_____ : the
w_____ b_____ that I do in my Father's name, they
w_____ of me.

V.26 But n_____ ,
because ye are n_____ of m_____
s_____ , as I said unto you.

2 V.24 Then came the J_____ round
about him, and said unto him, How
long dost thou make us to doubt? If
thou be the Christ, t_____ u_____

p_____ .

CHAPTER 10
V. 18-21
Guide

Matthew 27:50 Jesus, when he had cried again with a loud voice, <u>yielded up</u> the ghost.

When Jesus died on the cross, He willingly laid down His life. He gave up the ghost it was not taken from Him.

Resurrection

(to raise from the dead.)

① V.18 No man *taketh* it from me, but I lay it down of *myself.* I have power to lay it down, and I have power to take it again. This commandment have I *received* of my Father.

They just heard Jesus say, I will never die unless, I die willingly. Then I will rise again. That is hard for them to believe.

V.20 And *many* of them said, He *hath* a *devil,* and is mad; why hear ye him?

Do you hear that Shepherds voice?

③

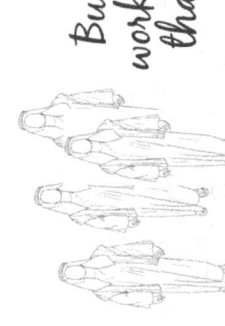

But He has the works as a witness that He is true.

④ V.21 *Others* said, These are *not* the words of him that hath a *devil.* Can a devil open the eyes of the blind?

John 5:36 But I have greater witness than that of John: for the works which the Father hath given me to finish, <u>the same works that I do, bear witness of me, that the Father hath sent me.</u>

② V.19 There was a *division* therefore again *among* the *Jews* for these sayings.

CHAPTER 10
V. 18-21
Notes

1 V.18 N___ m___ t___ it from me, but I lay it down of m___. I have power to l___ i___ d___, and I have power to t___ i___ a___ of m___ F___. This commandment have I r___.

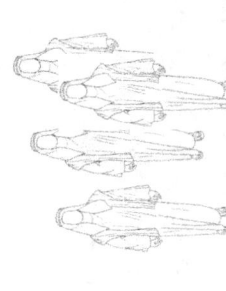

3

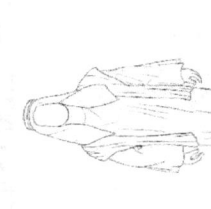

V.20 And m___ of them said, He h___ a d___ and is mad; why hear ye him?

2 V.19 There was a d___ therefore again a___ the J___ for these sayings.

4 V.21 O___ said, These are the words of him that hath a d___. Can a devil open the eyes of the blind?

CHAPTER 10
V. 27-33
Guide

(1)

V.27 My sheep hear my voice, and I know them, and they follow me:

Ezekiel 34:30 Thus shall they know that I the LORD their God am with them, and that they, even the house of Israel, are my people, saith the Lord GOD.
Ezekiel 34:31 And ye my flock, the flock of my pasture, are men, and I am your God, saith the Lord GOD.

Jesus makes Himself equal to God. when He says He is the Shepherd of Israel.

I am your God, saith the Lord GOD.

God calls Himself the Shepherd of Israel

John 17:11 And now I am no more in the world, but these are in the world, and I come to thee. Holy Father, keep through thine own name those whom thou hast given me, that they may be one, as we are.

While Jesus was in the world, He kept all and lost none. After He went back to heaven, we are kept by the Father and He is greater than all.

John 17:21 That they all may be one: as thou, Father, art in me, and I in thee, that they also may be one in us: that the world may believe that thou hast sent me.

(3) John 10:33 The Jews answered him, saying, For a good work we stone thee not; *but for blasphemy; and because that thou, being a man, makest thyself God.*

---

(2) V.28 And I give unto them *eternal life; and they shall never perish, neither shall any man pluck them out of my hand.*
V.29 My Father, which gave them me, is greater than all; and no man is able to pluck them out of my Father's hand.
V.30 I and my Father are one.

My hand

My Father's hand

Sheep

**1 John 2:22 Who is a liar but he that denieth that Jesus is the Christ? He is antichrist, that denieth the Father and the Son.
1 John 2:23 Whosoever denieth the Son, the same hath not the Father: he that acknowledgeth the Son hath the Father also.**

You cannot have the Father without the Son.

Does not say also acknowledgeth the Father. Says hath the Father also,

---

John 1:18 ... the only begotten Son, which is in the bosom of the Father, he hath declared him.

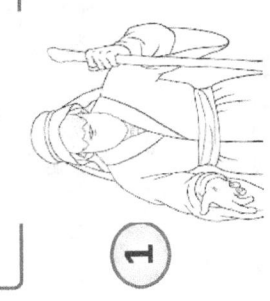

1

V.27 M_____ s_____ hear m_____ v_____, and I know them, and they follow me:

2

Sheep

V.28 And I give unto them e_____ l_____; and they shall n_____ p_____, neither shall any man p_____ them out of m_____ h_____.

V.29 My F_____, which g_____ t_____ m_____, is g_____ than all; and n_____ m_____ is able to p_____ t_____ out of my F_____ h_____.

V.30 _____ and m_____ F_____ are o_____.

3

V.33 The Jews answered him, saying, For a good work we stone thee not; but b_____ b_____; and because that thou, being m_____ t_____ g_____.

CHAPTER 10
V. 34-36
Guide

John 10:33 The Jews answered him, saying, For a good work we stone thee not: but for blasphemy; and because that thou, being a man, makest thyself God.

Direct quote from Psalm 82:6

Genesis 3:5 For God doth know that in the day ye eat thereof, then your eyes shall be opened, and ye shall be as gods, knowing good and evil.

V.34 Jesus answered them, Is it not written in your law, I said, Ye are gods?

Psalm 82:1 God standeth in the congregation of the mighty; he judgeth among the gods.

the gods are judging unjustly

Psalm 82:2 How long will ye judge unjustly, and accept the persons of the wicked? Selah.

Psalm 82:3 Defend the poor and fatherless: do justice to the afflicted and needy.
Psalm 82:4 Deliver the poor and needy: rid them out of the hand of the wicked.
Psalm 82:5 They know not, neither will they understand; they walk on in darkness: all the foundations of the earth are out of course.
Psalm 82:6 I have said, Ye are gods; and all of you are children of the most High.

In the Garden of Eden when man ate of the tree of knowledge

V.35 If he called them gods, unto whom the word of God came, and the scripture cannot be broken;
V.36 Say ye of him, whom the Father hath sanctified, and sent into the world, Thou blasphemest; because I said, I am the Son of God?

set apart

Jesus quotes Psalms 82 to remind them even though they are gods, they will be judged of God for judging unjustly. He is asking, "How can you say it is blasphemy to call Myself, the Son of God when the Father hath sanctified and sent me into the world?"

The Jews were not offended that Jesus was a good man and had been sent from God. His good works, John the Baptist and fulfillment of prophecies already established this was truth. Today, is the same as the past; the world is not offended by the man Jesus. It is the doctrine Jesus is God that is offensive.

CHAPTER 10

V. 34-36
Notes

John 10:33 The Jews answered him, saying, For a good work we stone thee not: but for blasphemy; and because that thou, being a man, makest thyself God.

V.34 Jesus answered them, Is it not written in your law, _____ said, Y_____ a_____ g_____ ?

V.35 If he called them g_____ , unto w_____ the w_____ of g_____ c_____ , and the s_____ cannot be b_____ ;

V.36 Say ye of him, whom the Father hath s_____ , and s_____ into the world, Thou b_____ ; because I said, I am the S_____ of g_____ ?

V. 37 If I do not the works of my Father, believe me not.
V.38 But if I do, though ye believe not me, believe the works: that ye may know, and believe, that the Father is in me, and I in him.

The works not only testify that Jesus was a man sent from God but that the Father is in Him.

If Jesus was not the Son of God but claimed to be so, He would be a liar and of his father the devil. Such a man would be guilty of blasphemy and not be able to do the works of God.

But Jesus does testify that He is the Son of God and God gives evidence that statement is true because of the works that God does through Him. For this reason, they should believe the works.

John 1:18 No man hath seen God at any time, the only begotten Son, which is in the bosom of the Father, he hath declared him. (Jesus is the Son of God)

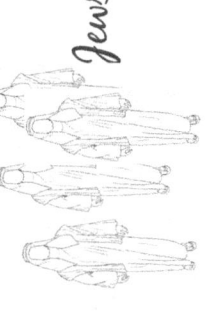

Jesus

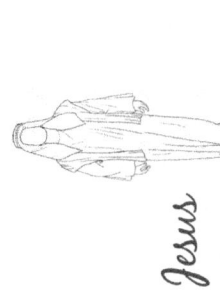

Jews

V. 37 If I d____ n____ the w____
of my Father, b____ m____

n____.

V.38 But if I do, though ye believe not
me, b____ the____

w____: that ye may know, and

b____, that the F____

i____ i____ m____, a____

i____ h____.

Read John
Chapter 11

CHAPTER 11
V. 1-15
Guide

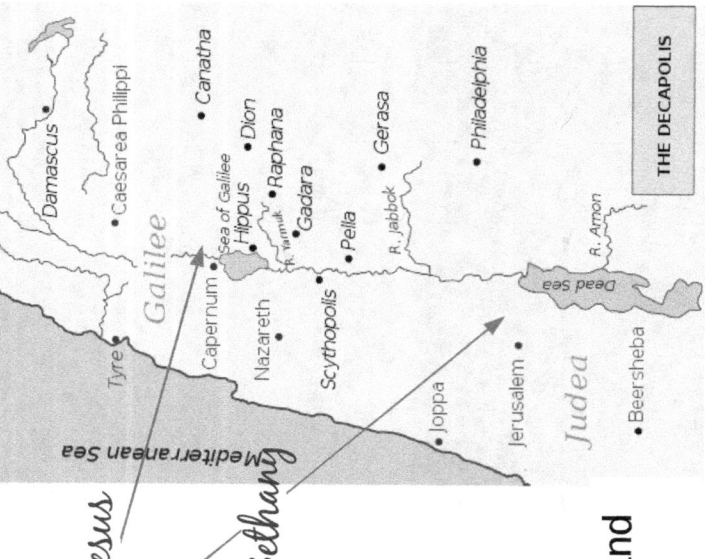

THE DECAPOLIS

① V.1 Now a certain man was sick, named *Lazarus* of *Bethany* the town of *Mary* and her sister *Martha*.

a specific man

John 14:21 He that hath <u>my commandments, and keepeth them</u>, he it is that loveth me: and he that loveth me shall be loved of <u>my Father, and I will love him, and will manifest myself to him.</u>

② V.3 Lord, behold, he whom thou *lovest* is sick

③ V.4 When Jesus heard that, he said, This sickness is *not unto death,* but for the *glory of God,* that the *Son of God* might be *glorified* thereby.

④ V.5 Now Jesus loved *Martha, and her sister, and Lazarus.*

⑤ V.6...he abode two days still in the same place where he was.

⑥ V.9 Jesus answered, Are there not twelve hours in the day? If any man *walk in the day,* he stumbleth not, because he seeth the light of this world.

He time is limited and he must do this miracle while He is here in the world so believers can see His works and not stumble. After the Light of the World is gone, it will be easier for believers to stumble at His works. He will not be intimated by the Jews.

⑦ V.14 Then said Jesus unto them plainly, *Lazarus is dead.*

V.15 And I am glad for your sakes that I was not there, to the intent ye may believe; nevertheless let us go unto him.

Just like the blind man that was born blind, so the works of God could be made manifest in him. John 9:3

God so loved the world but some have a special place in His heart.

Jesus

Bethany

CHAPTER 11
V. 1-15
Notes

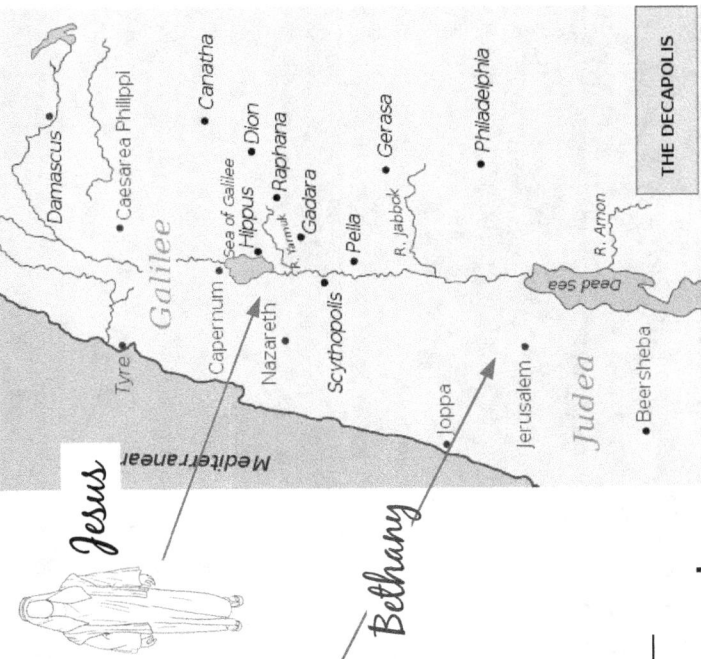

THE DECAPOLIS

Jesus

Bethany

---

1 V.1 Now a c_____ man
was sick, named
L_____ the town
of B_____ and her sister
of M_____ and her sister
M_____ .

2 V.3 Lord, behold, he
whom thou
l_____ is sick

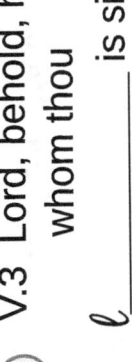

3 V.4 When Jesus heard
that, he said, This sickness
is n_____ unto d_____, but
for the g_____ of G_____,
that the S_____ of G_____
might be g_____
thereby.

4 V. 5 Now Jesus l_____
M_____, and h_____ s_____,
and L_____ .

5 V6...he abode t_____ d_____ still in
the same place where he was.

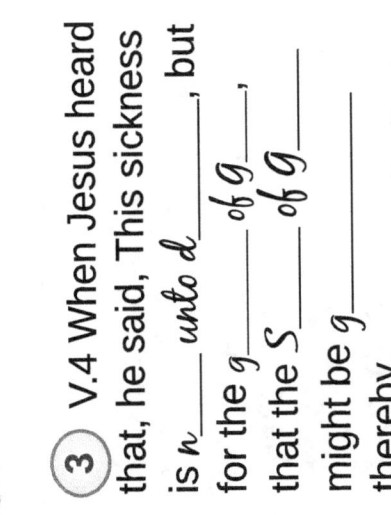

8 V.9 Jesus answered, Are there
not t_____ h_____ in the
day? If any man walk in the day,
he stumbleth not, because he
seeth the light of this world.

7 V.14 Then said Jesus unto them
p_____, L_____, is
V.15 And I am glad for your sakes
that I was not there, to the i_____ ;
y_____ m_____ b_____
nevertheless let us go unto him.

CHAPTER 11
V. 16-27
Guide

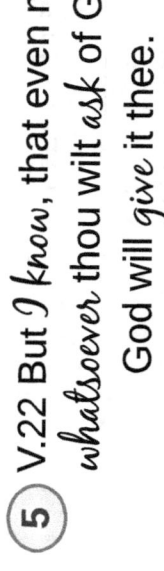

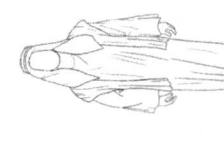

① V.19 And many of the Jews came to Martha and Mary, to comfort them concerning their brother.

② V.20 Then *Martha*, as soon as she heard that Jesus was coming, went and met him:

③ V.20...but *Mary* sat still in the house.

Bethany

Mary

④ V.21 Then said *Martha* unto Jesus, Lord, *if thou hadst been here, my brother had not died.*

⑤ V.22 But *I know, that even now, whatsoever thou wilt ask* of God, God will give it thee.

⑥ V.23 Jesus saith unto her, Thy brother shall rise again.

⑦ V.24 *Martha* saith unto him, I know that he shall rise again in the resurrection at the last day.

⑧ V.25 Jesus said unto her, *I am the resurrection, and the life:* he that believeth in me, though he were dead, yet shall he live:
V.26 And *whosoever liveth* and believeth in me shall never die. Believest thou this?
(spiritually) Believer's never die they go to be present with the Lord. (Heaven).

I am the resurrection, and the life. The blind man lived in darkness, Jesus was the light. Lazarus is dead, he needed life. Jesus is the resurrection and the life.

Jews

⑨ V.27 *She* saith unto him, Yea, Lord: *I believe that thou art the Christ, the Son of God,* which should come into the world.

John 5:29 And shall come forth; they that have done good, <u>unto the resurrection of life:</u> and they that have done evil, unto the resurrection of damnation.

On the last day, all souls will be reunited with their bodies and judged.

15 furlongs is about 2 miles

furlong =1/8 Mile

THE DECAPOLIS

CHAPTER 11
V. 16-27
Notes

2 V.20 Then M_____, as soon as she heard that Jesus was coming, went and met him:

5 V.22 But _____ now, w_____ thou wilt a_____ k_____, that even of God, God will g_____ it thee.

7 V.24 M_____ saith unto him, I know that he shall rise again in the r_____ l_____ d_____.

9 V.27 S_____ saith unto him, Yea, Lord: _____ b_____ that thou art the C_____, the S_____ of G_____, which should come into the world.

3 V.20...but M_____ sat still in the house.

Bethany

1 V.19 And many of the J_____ came to Martha and Mary, to c_____ them concerning their brother.

4 V.21 Then said M_____ unto Jesus, Lord, if t_____ hadst been h_____, my b_____ had n_____ d_____.

6 V.23 Jesus saith unto her, Thy brother s_____ r_____ a_____.

8 V.25 Jesus said unto her, _____ a_____ the l_____: he that believeth in me, though h_____ w_____ d_____, yet shall he l_____: V.26 And w_____ l_____ and believeth in me shall n_____ d_____. Believest thou this?

15 furlongs is about 2 miles
furlong =1/8 Mile

THE DECAPOLIS

CHAPTER 11
V. 28-37
Guide

Disciples

Jesus

Mary

Martha

1 V.28 Mary her sister...
V.29 As soon as she heard that, she arose quickly, and came unto him.

2 V.32 Then when Mary was come where Jesus was, and saw him, she fell down at his feet, saying unto him, Lord, if thou hadst been here, my brother had not died.

3 V.33 When Jesus therefore saw her weeping, and the Jews also weeping which came with her, he groaned in the spirit, and was troubled.

Revelation 21:4 And God shall wipe away all tears from their eyes; and there shall be no more death, neither sorrow, nor crying, neither shall there be any more pain: for the former things are passed away.

4 V.35 Jesus wept.

This verse is short and sweet. But the world could not contain the volumes that could be written of these 2 words. Jesus weeps with us when sorrows come our way. This is a result of His love for us. This love is so powerful that He paid the great price for our redemption.

5 V.36 Then said the Jews, Behold how he loved him!
V.37 And some of them said, Could not this man, which opened the eyes of the blind, have caused that even this man should not have died?

Jews

Bethany

THE DECAPOLIS

Mediterranean Sea
Galilee
Tyre
Capernum
Nazareth
Sea of Galilee
Hippos
R. Yarmuk
Raphana
Gadara
Pella
Scythopolis
R. Jabbok
Gerasa
Damascus
Caesarea Philippi
Canatha
Dion
Joppa
Jerusalem
Judea
Dead Sea
R. Arnon
Philadelphia
Beersheba

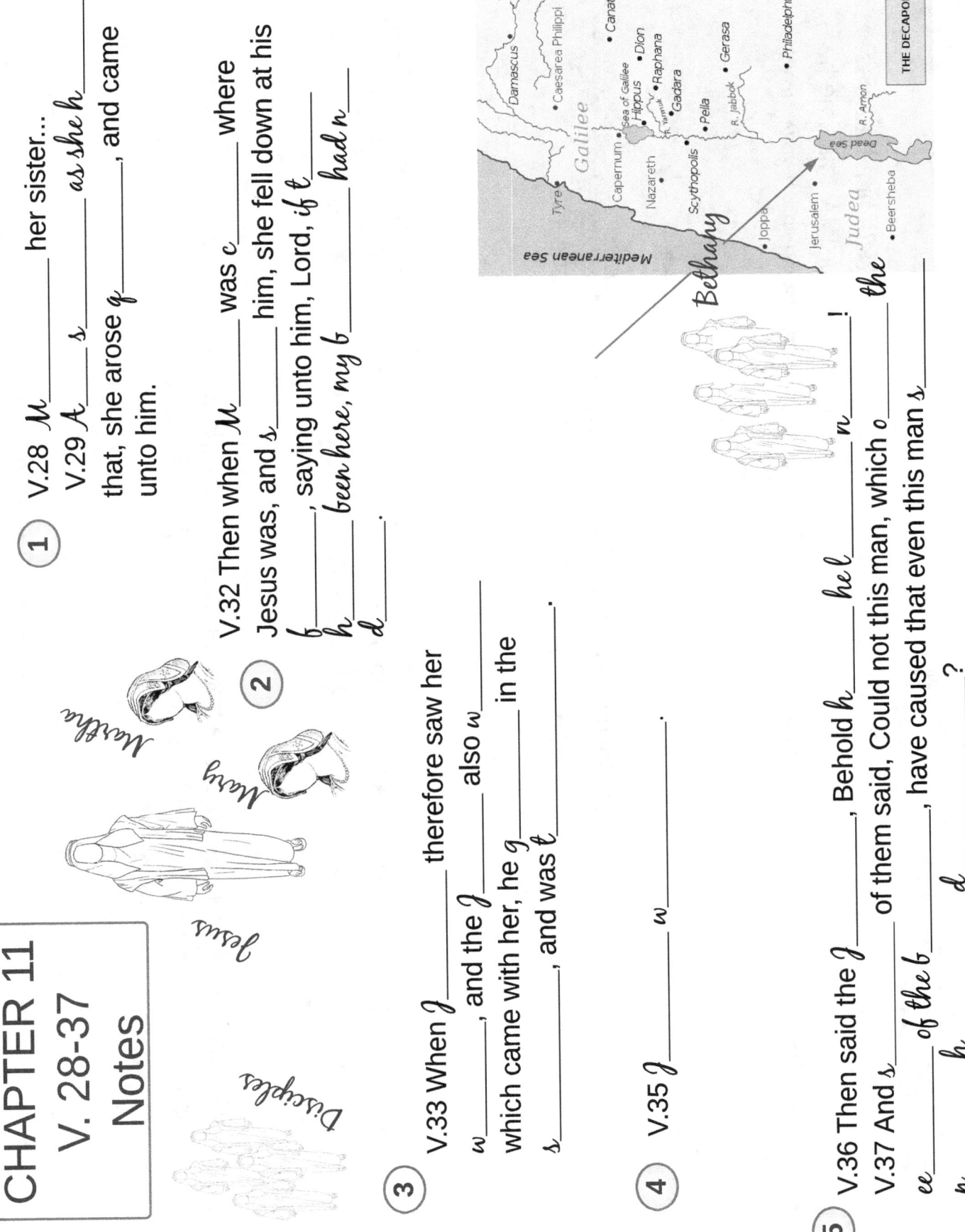

CHAPTER 11
V. 28-37
Notes

1 V.28 M_____ her sister...
V.29 A____ s____ as she h_____
that, she arose q_____, and came
unto him.

2 V.32 Then when M_____ was c_____ where
Jesus was, and s_____ him, she fell down at his
f_____, saying unto him, Lord, if t_____
h_____ been here, my b_____ had n_____
d_____.

3 V.33 When J_____ therefore saw her
w_____, and the J_____ also w_____ in the
s_____, and was t_____.

4 V.35 J_____ w_____.

5 V.36 Then said the J_____, Behold h_____ he l_____
V.37 And s_____ of them said, Could not this man, which o_____ the
ee_____ of the b_____, have caused that even this man s_____
h_____ d_____?

THE DECAPOLIS

Mediterranean Sea
Damascus
Tyre
Caesarea Philippi
Canatha
Galilee
Capernum
Sea of Galilee
Hippus · Dion
Nazareth
Yarmuk · Raphana
Scythopolis · Gadara
Pella
R. Jabbok · Gerasa
Philadelphia
Joppa
Jerusalem
Judea
Bethany
Dead Sea
R. Arnon
· Beersheba

Martha
Mary
Jesus
Disciples

CHAPTER 11
V. 38-42
Guide

Mary and Martha

Disciples

Jews followed Mary. V. 31

2 V.39...*Martha, the sister of him that was dead*, saith unto him, Lord, by this time he *stinketh*: for he hath been dead *four days.*

1 V.38 Jesus therefore again *groaning in himself* cometh to the *grave*. It was a *cave*, and a *stone lay upon it.*

V.39 Jesus said, Take ye away the stone.

3 V.40 Jesus saith unto her, Said I not unto thee, that, if thou wouldest *believe*, thou shouldest see the *glory of God?*

4 V.41 Then they *took away* the stone from the place where the dead was laid. And Jesus *lifted up his eyes*, and said, *Father, I thank thee* that thou hast heard me.
V.42 And I *knew* that thou *hearest* me always: but *because of the people which stand by* I said it, that *they may believe that thou hast sent me* (Another sign to the Jews, that Jesus was sent from God)

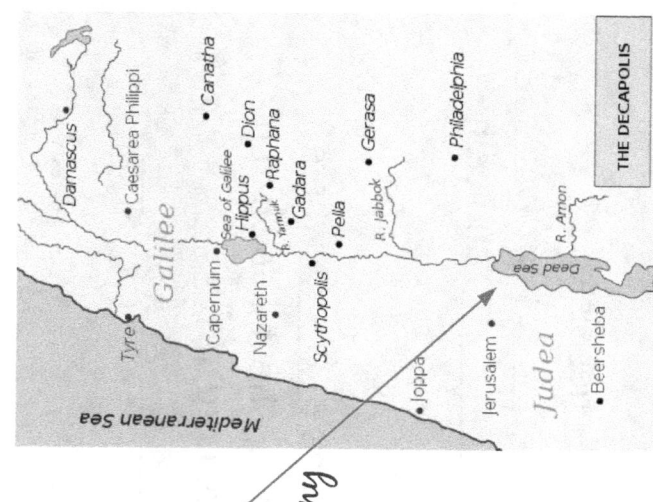

THE DECAPOLIS

Bethany

CHAPTER 11
V. 38-42
Notes

Mary and Martha

Disciples

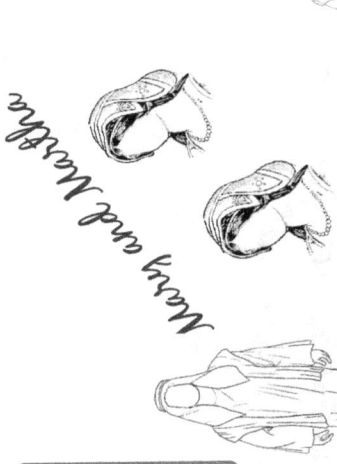

1 V.38 Jesus therefore again g_____ in h_____ cometh to

the g_____. It was a c_____, and a s_____ lay upon it.

V.39 Jesus said, Take ye away the s_____.

2 V.39...M_____, the s_____ of him

that was d_____ saith unto him, Lord,

by this time he s_____: for he hath

been dead f_____ days.

Jews followed Mary. V. 31

3 V.40 Jesus saith unto her, Said I not unto thee,

that, if thou wouldest b_____, thou shouldest

see the g_____ of g_____?

4 V.41 Then they t_____ a_____ the stone from the place where the

dead was laid. And Jesus l_____ u_____ h_____ e_____, and

said, F_____, I t_____ t_____ that thou h_____ me always: but

V.42 And k_____ of the p_____ which stand by I said it, that

b_____ t_____ that t_____ h_____ s_____ m_____.

Bethany

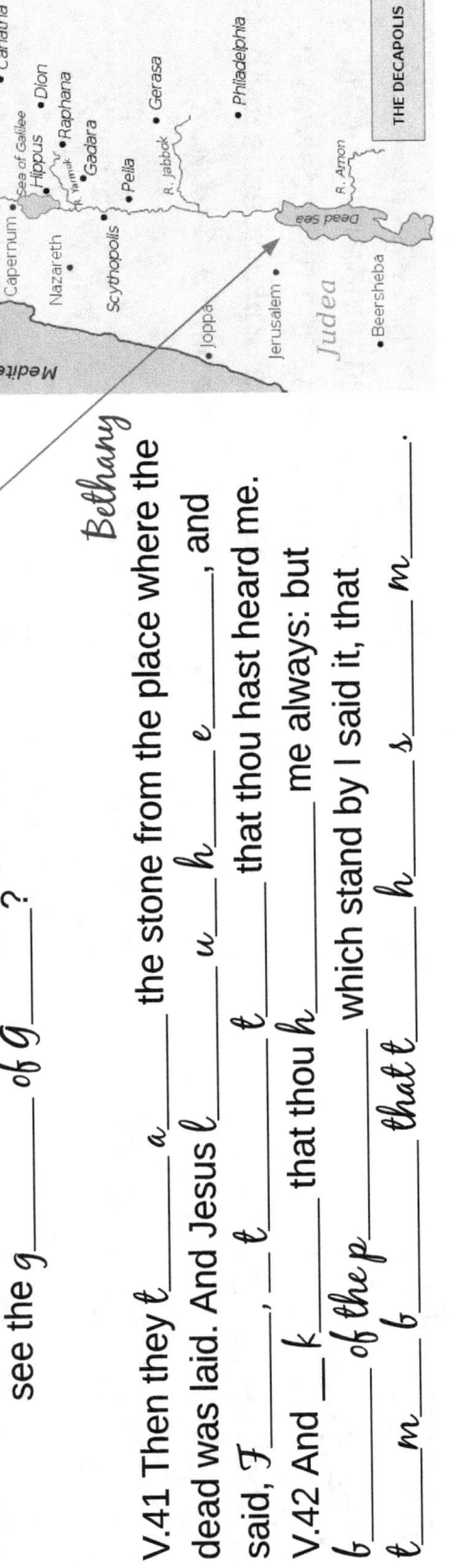

THE DECAPOLIS

CHAPTER 11
V. 43-44
Guide

THE DECAPOLIS

Bethany

2

V.44 And he that was *dead* came *forth*, bound hand and foot with *graveclothes*: and his face was bound about with a *napkin*. Jesus saith unto them, *Loose* him, and *let him go*.

Lazarus

The graveclothes had Lazarus bound hand and foot. He was dead but now he is alive and is no longer in bondage to his clothes. Believers were dead but then alive in the kingdom of God. Since they are dead to the world, they need not be bound any longer to worldly clothing. They are no longer bound to the sins of nakedness and immodesty.

Mary and Martha

Jesus

Jews

Disciples

1

V.43 And when he thus had spoken, he cried with a *loud voice, Lazarus, come forth.*

CHAPTER 11
V. 43-44
Notes

Disciples

Jesus

Mary and Martha

Jesus

Lazarus

▲

(2)

V.44 And he that was d_____
c_____ b_____, bound hand and
foot with g_____: and his face
was bound about with a
n_____. Jesus saith unto them,
L_____ him, and l_____ h_____
g_____.

THE DECAPOLIS

Damascus
• Caesarea Philippi
• Canatha
Galilee
Sea of Galilee • Dion
Hippos • Raphana
Capernaum • Gadara
Nazareth R. Yarmuk • Gerasa
Tyre Scythopolis • Pella
R. Jabbok
• Philadelphia
Dead Sea
Joppa R. Arnon
Judea
Jerusalem
• Beersheba
Mediterranean Sea

Bethany

(1)

V.43 And when he thus had spoken, he cried
with a l_____ v_____,
L_____, c_____ f_____.

CHAPTER 11
V. 45-57
Guide

(1) V.45 Then *many* of the *Jews* which came to Mary, and had *seen* the things which Jesus did, *believed* on him.

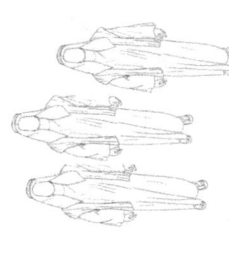

(2) V.46 *But some* of them went *their ways* to the *Pharisees*, and told them what things Jesus had done.

Jesus caused division again

V.47 Then gathered the *chief priests* and the *Pharisees* a council, and said, What do we? for this man doeth *many miracles*.

V.48 If we let him thus alone, all men will believe on him: *and the Romans shall come and take away both our place and nation*.

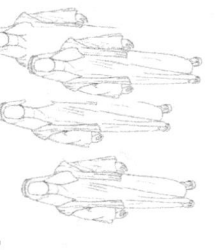

Corrupt politicians and clergy began scheming to protect their power and offices. Sound familiar?

Caiaphas thought He was making a political speech to justify their diabolical plans. What he did not know He was prophesying that the death of Jesus would save not only the Jews but the whole world.

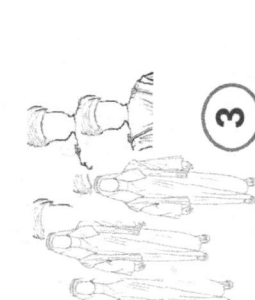

Caiaphas

(4) V.49 And one of them, named *Caiaphas*, being the *high priest* that same year, said unto them, Ye know nothing at all,

(5) V.50 Nor consider that it is *expedient for us*, that *one man should die* for the people, and that *the whole nation perish not*.

V.51 And this spake he not of himself: but being high priest that year, he *prophesied* that Jesus should die for that *nation*;

V.52 And *not* for that *nation only*, but that also he should *gather together in one* the children of God that were *scattered abroad*.(Bring *Gentiles into the fold*)

(6) V.53 Then from that *day* forth they took counsel together for to put him to *death*.

CHAPTER 11
V. 45-57
Notes

1 V.45 Then m_____ of the J_____ which came to Mary, and had s_____ the things which Jesus did, b_____ on him.

2 V.46 B_____ s_____ of them went t_____ w_____ to the P_____, and told them what things Jesus had done.

3

4 V.49 And one of them, named C_____, being the h_____ p_____ that same year, said unto them, Ye know nothing at all,

Caiaphas

5 V.50 Nor consider that it is e_____ f_____ u_____, that o_____ m_____ should die for the people, and that the w_____ n_____ p_____.

V.51 And this spake he not of himself: but being high priest that year, he p_____ that Jesus should die for that n_____;

V.52 And n_____ for that n_____ o_____, but that also he should g_____ together i_____ o_____ the children of God that were s_____ a_____.

V.47 Then gathered the c_____ and the P_____ a_____, and said, What do we? for this man doeth m_____ m_____.

V.48 If we let him thus alone, all men will believe o_____ h_____; and the R_____ s_____ c_____ and t_____ a_____ both o_____ p_____ and n_____.

6 V.53 Then from that d_____ forth they took counsel together for to put him to d_____.

Read John

Chapter 12

CHAPTER 12
V. 1-8
Guide

passover V.1

(1)

Bethany V.1

anointed by Mary *burial for*

(2)

(3) V.2

Jesus **Lazarus** (5) V.2

Martha (served) V.2 (4)

spikenard-very costly aromatic and fragrant

(6) V.2

Judas Iscariot (7) V.4

in charge of carrying the money

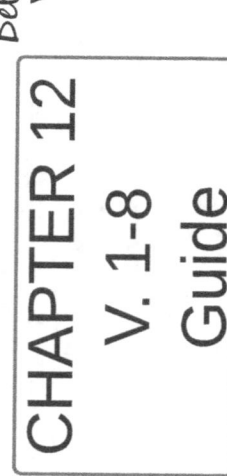

(8) V.5 Why was not this ointment sold for three hundred pence, and given to the poor? V.6 This he said, not that he cared for the poor; but because he was a thief, and had the bag, and bare what was put therein.

V.3 Then took Mary a pound of ointment of spikenard, very costly, and anointed the feet of Jesus, and wiped his feet with her hair: and the house was filled with the odour of the ointment.

V.7 Then said Jesus, Let her alone: against the day of my burying hath she kept this. V.8 For the poor always ye have with you; but me ye have not always.

THE DECAPOLIS

Damascus • Caesarea Philippi • Canatha

Galilee • Dion • Raphana

Tyre • Capernum • Sea of Galilee • Hippus • R. Yarmuk • Gadara • Pella • Gerasa

Nazareth • Scythopolis • R. Jabbok • Philadelphia

Bethany • Joppa

Jerusalem • Judea

Beersheba

Dead Sea • R. Arnon

Mediterranean Sea

CHAPTER 12
V. 1-8
Notes

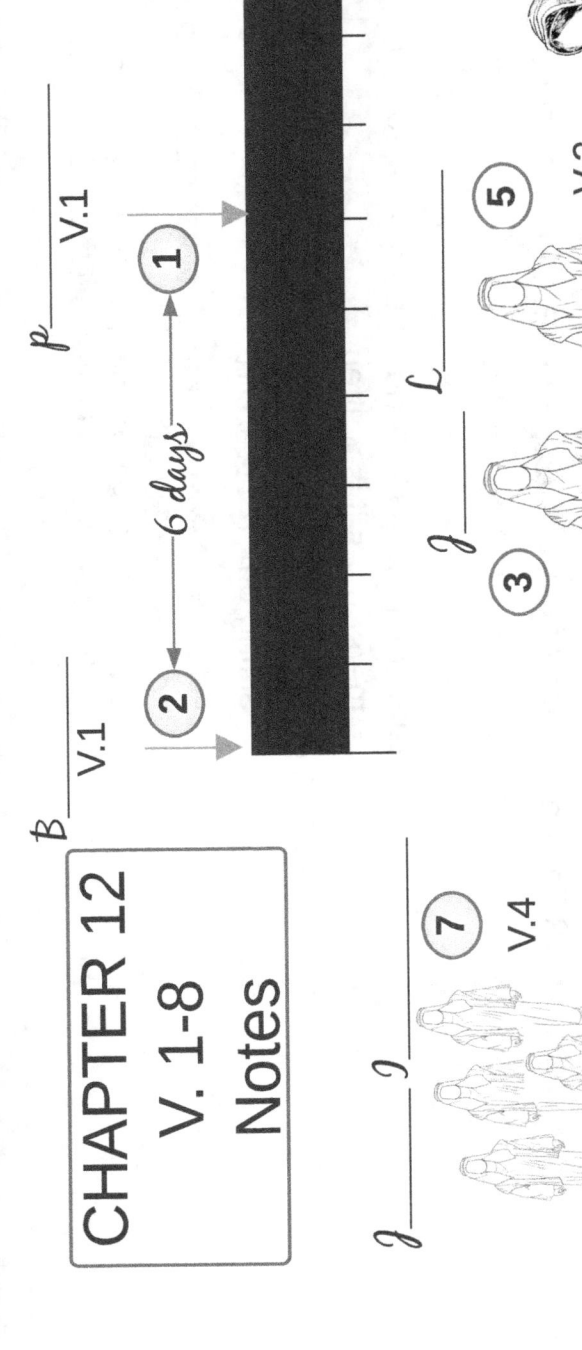

𝓑 _____ V.1

𝓹 _____ V.1

2 ← 6 days → 1

𝓹 _____ V.1

(4) 𝓜 _____ V.2

(5) ℒ _____ V.2

(3) 𝓳 _____ V.2

(7) 𝓳 _____ 𝓳 _____ V.4

(8) V.5 Why was not this ointment 𝓼 _____ for three hundred pence, and 𝓰 _____ 𝓽 _____ 𝓽 _____ ?

V.6 This he said, not that he cared for the poor; but 𝓫 _____ he was a 𝓽 _____, and had the 𝓫 _____, and 𝓫 _____ what was put therein.

V.3 Then took 𝓜 _____ a pound of ointment of 𝓼 _____, 𝓿 _____, and 𝓬 _____ the 𝓪 _____ 𝓫 _____ of Jesus, and 𝔀 _____ his feet with her 𝓱 _____ : and the house was filled with the 𝓸 _____ of the ointment.

(9) v.7 Then said 𝓙 _____, Let her alone: against the day of my 𝓫 _____ hath she kept this. V.8 For the 𝓹 _____ ye have 𝓪 _____ with you; but 𝓶 _____ ye have 𝓷 _____ 𝓪 _____ .

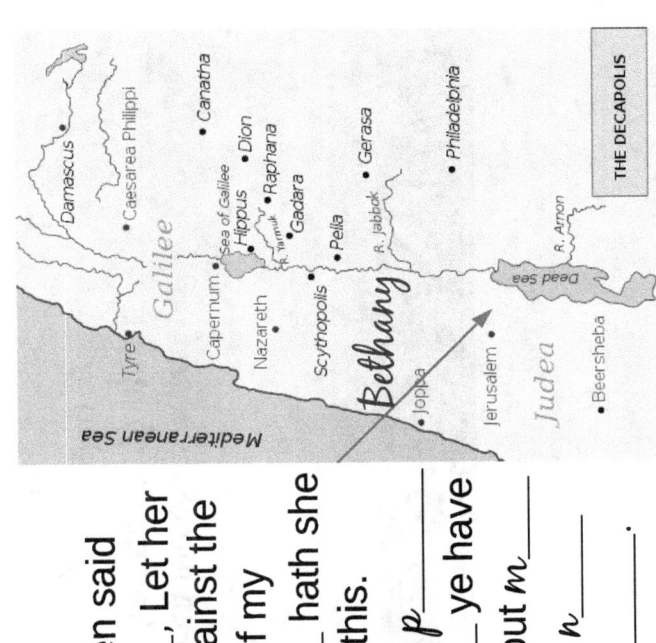

THE DECAPOLIS

CHAPTER 12
V. 9-15
Guide

Triumphal Entry

Bethany

V. 12 the next day ④

passover

THE DECAPOLIS

Map showing: Damascus, Caesarea Philippi, Canatha, Dion, Raphana, Hippos, Gadara, Pella, Gerasa, Philadelphia, Sea of Galilee, Capernum, Nazareth, Scythopolis, Jerusalem, Joppa, Bethany, Beersheba, Tyre, Galilee, Judea, Mediterranean Sea, Dead Sea, R. Jabbok, R. Amon, R. Yarmuk

③ Lazarus

V.10 But the chief priests consulted that they might put *Lazarus* also to *death;*

② Triumphal Entry is also called Palm Sunday.

V.9...but that they might see *Lazarus* also, whom he had raised from the dead.

V.13 Took branches of *palm trees,* and went forth to meet him, and cried, *Hosanna:* Blessed is the *King of Israel that cometh in the name* of the Lord. Donkey (humility)

V.14 And Jesus, when he had found a young ass, sat thereon; as it is written,

V.15 Fear not, *daughter of Sion:* behold, thy *King cometh, sitting on an ass's colt.*

Zechariah 9:9 Rejoice greatly, O daughter of Zion: shout, O daughter of Jerusalem: behold, thy King cometh unto thee: he is just, and having salvation: lowly, and riding upon an ass, and upon a colt the foal of an ass.

① Before Jesus did not tell his brethern He was going up to Jerusalem because it was not time for this prophecy. Now He can go openly. Called the Triumphal Entry.

V.9 *Much* people of the Jews therefore knew that he was there: and they came not for Jesus' sake only,

⑤ "Now" means "Save Now"

Jesus

Jerusalem

Palm Sunday is always celebrated the 1st Sunday before Easter

CHAPTER 12
V. 9-15
Notes

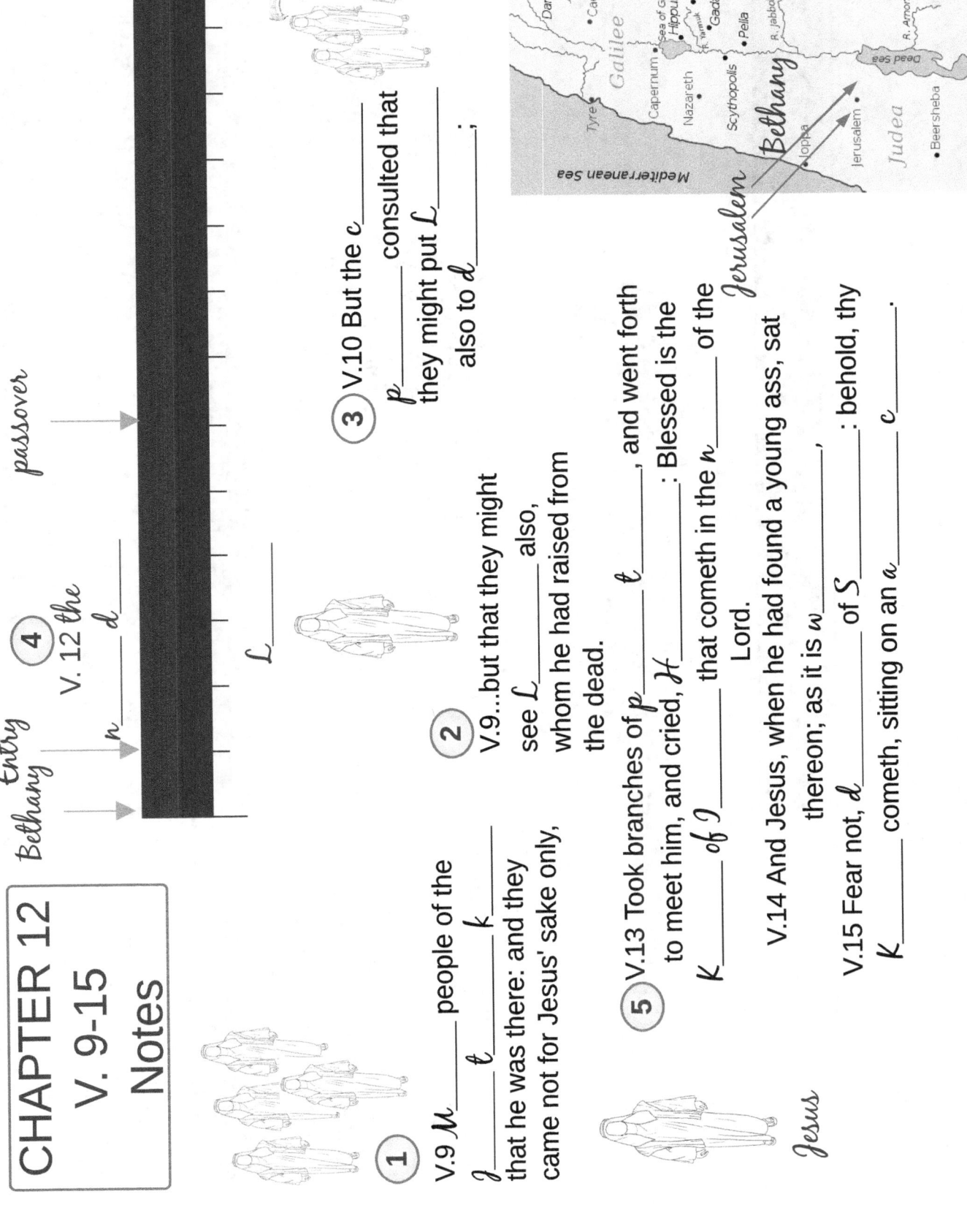

Triumphal Entry

Bethany | passover

1 V.9 M_____ people of the J_____ t_____ k_____ that he was there: and they came not for Jesus' sake only,

2 V.9..but that they might see L_____ also, whom he had raised from the dead.

3 V.10 But the c_____ p_____ consulted that they might put L_____ also to d_____;

4 V. 12 the d_____ n_____ d_____ L_____

5 V.13 Took branches of p_____ t_____, and went forth to meet him, and cried, H_____ of I_____ : Blessed is the n_____ that cometh in the n_____ of the Lord.

V.14 And Jesus, when he had found a young ass, sat thereon; as it is w_____,

V.15 Fear not, d_____ of S_____ : behold, thy k_____ cometh, sitting on an a_____ c_____.

Jesus

THE DECAPOLIS

CHAPTER 12
V. 16-23
Guide

Triumphal
Entry

Bethany

passover

Lazarus

1

V.17 The *people* therefore that was with him *when* he called Lazarus out of his grave, and raised him from the dead, bare record.

Jews that were at Mary and Martha's house that followed to grave of Lazarus.

2

Because the people bare record, others believed

V.18 For this cause the people also met *him*, for that they heard that he had done this miracle.

Perceived could not prevail against the works of God but because of hard hearts could not perceive Jesus was the prophesied Messiah. Matt. 13:14

3

V.19 The *Pharisees* therefore said among themselves, *Perceive* ye how ye prevail *nothing?* behold, the world is gone after him.

Types of people
1. He whom received the miracle.
2. Jews who saw the miracle and believed
3. Jews who heard the miracle and believed.
4. Jews who did not believe.
5. Gentiles who were seeking

4

Gentiles

V.20 And there were certain *Greeks* among them that came up to worship at the feast:

Bringing the Gentiles into the fold

5

V.23 And Jesus answered them, saying, The *hour* is come, that the *Son of man* should be glorified. *hour (time)*

CHAPTER 12
V. 16-23
Notes

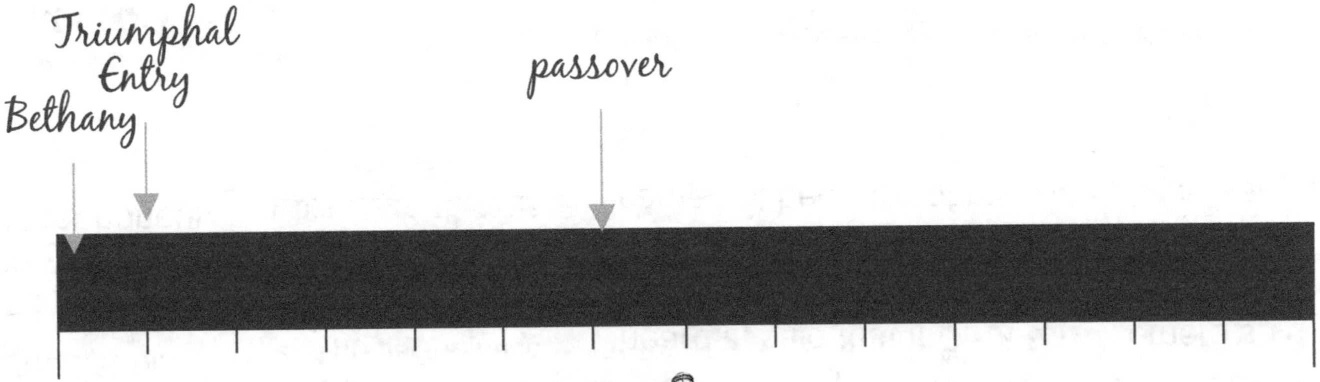

Triumphal Entry
Bethany

passover

Lazarus

1

V.17 The p_____
therefore that was with
him w_____ he
c_____ L_____ out
of his g_____, and
raised him from the
dead, b_____ r_____.

2

V.18 For this
c_____ the people
also met h_____, for
that they h_____
that he had done this
m_____.

3

V.19 The P_____
therefore said among
themselves,
P_____ ye how ye
p_____ ? behold, the
n_____ world is gone after him.

4

Gentiles

V.20 And there were
certain G_____
among them that
came up to worship
at the feast:

CHAPTER 12
V. 24-30
Guide

Triumphal Entry

Bethany

passover

seed

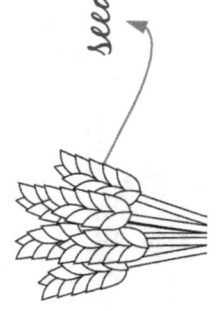

1 V.23 And Jesus answered them, saying, The hour is come, that the Son of man should be glorified.

(hour means time)

2 V.24 Verily, verily, I say unto you, Except a corn of wheat fall into the ground and die, it abideth alone: but if it die, it bringeth forth much fruit.

Jesus must die on the cross so that the world could have eternal life.

3 V.26 If any man serve me, let him follow me; and where I am, there shall also my servant be: if any man serve me, him will my Father honour.

John 14:3 And if I go and prepare a place for you, I will come again, and receive you unto myself; <u>that where I am, there ye may be also.</u>

4 V.27 Now is my soul troubled;

Jesus had emotions the same as us. He was dreading the crucifixion but was obedient to the Father.

As the son of Mary, he is the son of Adam (man). The son of man, will receive a glorified body at the resurrection.

A corn of wheat is glorified when it falls to the ground and sprouts into a plant that gives life to many seeds.

5 V.28 Father, glorify thy name. Then came there a voice from heaven, saying, I have both glorified it, and will glorify it again.
V.29 The people therefore, that stood by, and heard it, said that it thundered: others said, An angel spake to him.
V.30 Jesus answered and said, This voice came not because of me, but for your sakes.

Jesus tarried while Lazarus was dead for their sakes that they may believe. God spake from heaven for the sakes of the people.

CHAPTER 12
V. 24-30
Notes

passover

Triumphal
Entry

Bethany

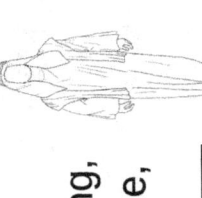

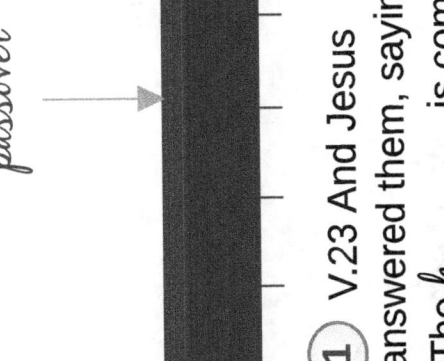

seed

(1) V.23 And Jesus answered them, saying, The h_____ is come, that the S_____ of m_____ should be g_____.

(2) V.24 V_____, v_____, s_____ of w_____, Except a c_____ fall into the ground and d_____, it abideth a_____: but if it die, it bringeth forth m_____ f_____.

(3) V.26 If any man serve me, let him follow me; and w_____ a_____ m_____, t_____ s_____ a_____ s_____ b_____: if any man serve me, him will my Father honour.

(4) V.27 Now is my s_____ t_____;

(5) V.28 Father, glorify thy name. Then came there a v_____ f_____ h_____, saying, I have both glorified it, and will glorify it again.
V.29 The people therefore, that stood by, and heard it, said that it t_____ others said, An angel spake to him.
V.30 Jesus answered and said, This voice came not because of me, but f_____ y_____ s_____.

CHAPTER 12
V. 31-37
Guide

Triumphal
Entry

Bethany

passover

crucified

1 Jesus did not come to judge the world, nevertheless, it will be judged

V.31 Now is the judgment of this world: now shall the prince of this world be cast out. *devil*

2 V.32 And I, if I be *lifted up* from the earth, will draw all men unto me.

V.33 This he said, signifying what *death* he should die.

Old Testament

3 V.34 The people answered him, We have heard out of the *law* that *Christ abideth for ever*: and how sayest thou, The Son of man must be lifted up? *who is this Son of man?*

Jesus was speaking of His own death, they expected Him to set up an eternal kingdom at that time.

The people were expecting a king like David that would save them from the military rule of the Romans and restore their kingdom. They were disappointed he came riding in on an ass speaking of His own death

4 V.37 But though he had done so many miracles before them, yet they *believed not on him:*

They did not believe His words and also refused to believe the works of the Father. They were blind.

CHAPTER 12
V. 31-37
Notes

Triumphal
Entry
Bethany

Passover

1

V.31 Now is the _____ of this world:
j_____ now shall the p_____ of
t_____ w_____
be cast out.

2

V.32 And I, if I be l_____ u_____
from the earth, will draw all men unto
me.
V.33 This he said, signifying what
d_____ he should die.

3

V.34 The people answered him, We have
heard out of the l_____ that C_____
a_____ b_____ e_____ : and
how sayest thou, The Son of man must
be lifted up? w_____ is this S_____ of
m_____ ?

4

V.37 But though he had done so
m_____ m_____ before
them, yet they b_____
n_____ on him:

CHAPTER 12
V. 38-41
Guide

Greek – Esaias
Hebrew – Isaiah

Jewish Nation

V.38 That the saying of Esaias the prophet might be fulfilled, which he spake, Lord, who hath believed our report? and to whom hath the arm of the Lord been revealed?
V.39 Therefore they could not believe, because that Esaias said again,
V.40 He hath blinded their eyes, and hardened their heart; that they should not see with their eyes, nor understand with their heart, and be converted, and I should heal them.
V.41 These things said Esaias, when he saw his glory, and spake of him.

emulation means rivalry here

Isaiah 6:9 And he said, Go, and tell this people, Hear ye indeed, but understand not: and see ye indeed, but perceive not.
Isaiah 6:10 Make the heart of this people fat, and make their ears heavy, and shut their eyes; lest they see with their eyes, and hear with their ears, and understand with their heart, and convert, and be healed.

are in darkness

Why did God blind the nation of Israel?

Romans 11:11 I say then, Have they stumbled that they should fall? God forbid: but rather through their fall salvation is come unto the Gentiles, for to provoke them to jealousy.
Romans 11:12 Now if the fall of them be the riches of the world, and the diminishing of them the riches of the Gentiles; how much more their fulness?
Romans 11:13 For I speak to you Gentiles, inasmuch as I am the apostle of the Gentiles, I magnify mine office:
Romans 11:14 If by any means I may provoke to emulation them which are my flesh, and might save some of them.
(Paul was an Israelite and was an apostle to the Gentiles. He was hoping to provoke his people with jealousy.)
Romans 11:15 For if the casting away of them be the reconciling of the world, what shall the receiving of them be, but life from the dead?

The nation of Israel was stiffnecked and rebellious. To provoke them to jealousy, God blinded them while He brought the Gentiles into the fold. When He receives them back, Jews and Gentiles would become one fold and all be saved. That is the wisdom of God.

CHAPTER 12
V. 38-41
Notes

Why did God blind the nation of Israel?

V.38 That the saying of E_____ the prophet might be fulfilled, which he spake, Lord, who hath believed our report? and to whom hath the arm of the Lord been revealed?

V.39 Therefore they could not believe, because that Esaias said again,

V.40 He hath b_____ t_____ e_____, and h_____ t_____ h_____; that they should not s_____ w_____ t_____ e_____, nor u_____ w_____ t_____ h_____, and be c_____, and h_____ t_____ h_____ s_____.

V.41 These things said E_____, when he saw his glory, and spake of him.

CHAPTER 12
V. 42-46
Guide

Though the nation was blinded, individuals still have the opportunity to believe.

(1) V.42 *Nevertheless* among the *chief rulers* also many *believed* on him; but because of the Pharisees they did not confess him, lest they should be put out of the synagogue:

V.43 For they *loved the praise of men* more than the praise of *God*.

(2) V.44 Jesus cried and said, He that *believeth* on me, *believeth not* on me, *but* on him that *sent* me.

You cannot believe in Jesus, the Son of God, withouth believing He was sent by God, the Father.

and

You cannot believe on the Father, God of Abraham, Isaac and Jacob, without believing on Jesus Christ, the Son of God.

John 2:23 Whosoever denieth the Son, the same hath not the Father: he that acknowledgeth the Son hath the Father also.

(3) V.45 And he that *seeth me* seeth him that *sent* me.

John 14:6 Jesus saith unto him, I am the way, the truth, and the life: no man cometh unto the Father, but by me.

John 14:7 If ye had known me, ye should have known my Father also: <u>and from henceforth ye know him, and have seen him.</u>

(4) V.46 I am come a *light* into the world, that whosoever *believeth* on me should *not* abide in *darkness.*

John 8:12 Then spake Jesus again unto them, saying, I am the light of the world: <u>he that followeth me shall not walk in darkness, but shall have the light of life.</u>

John 3:20 For every one that <u>doeth evil hateth the light, neither cometh to the light, lest his deeds should be reproved.</u>

John 3:21 But he that doeth truth cometh to the light, that his deeds may be made manifest, that they are wrought in God.

CHAPTER 12

V. 42-46

Notes

1 V.42 N_____ among the c_____ r_____ also m_____ b_____ on him; but because of the Pharisees they did not confess him, lest they should be put out of the synagogue:

V.43 For they l_____ the p_____ of m_____ more than the praise of G_____.

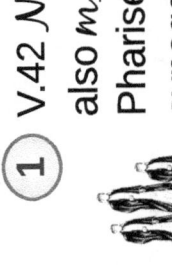

2 V.44 Jesus cried and said, He that b_____ on m_____, b_____ n_____ on me, b_____ on him that s_____ m_____.

3 V.45 And he that s_____ m_____ seeth him that s_____ me.

4 V.46 I am come a l_____ into the world, that whosoever b_____ on me should n_____ abide in d_____.

CHAPTER 12
V. 47-50
Guide

1

V.47 And if any man hear my words, and believe not, I judge him not: for I came not to judge the world, but to save the world.

John 3:17 For God sent not his Son into the world to condemn the world; but that the world through him might be saved.

Great White Throne Judgement

2

V:48 He that rejecteth me, and receiveth not my words, hath one that judgeth him: *the word* that I have spoken, the same shall *judge* him in the *last day*

John 3:18 He that believeth on him is not condemned: but he that believeth not is condemned already, because he hath not believed in the name of the only begotten Son of God.

Jesus did not come to condemn the world. It was already condemned. He came to save the world.

3

V.49 For I have *not spoken of myself*; but the Father which sent me, he gave me a *commandment*, what I should say, and what I should speak.

John 3:11 Verily, verily, I say unto thee, We speak that we do know, and testify that we have seen; and ye receive not our witness.

Wherever the words Verily, verily, I say are used the subject is of the Father, heaven, or eternal life.

The plural we is referring to the Father, Son and Holy Spirit

4

V.50 And I know that his commandment is life everlasting: whatsoever I speak therefore, even as the Father said unto me, so I speak.

This is a commandment God gave to Jesus to speak.

John 3:16 For God so loved the world, that he gave his only begotten Son, that whosoever believeth in him should not perish, but have everlasting life.

CHAPTER 12
V. 47-50
Notes

1 V.47 And if any man hear my words, and believe not, I judge him not: for I came not to judge the world, but to s_____ t_____ w_____.

2

V:48 He that rejecteth me, and receiveth not my words, hath one that judgeth him: t_____ w_____ that I have spoken, the same shall j_____ him in the l_____ d_____.

3

V.49 For I have n_____ s_____ of m_____; but the Father which sent me, he gave me a c_____ what I should say, and what I should speak.

4

V.50 And I know that his c_____ is life e_____; whatsoever I speak therefore, e_____ a_____ t_____ F_____ s_____ u_____ m_____, so I speak.

Read John
Chapter 13

CHAPTER 13
V. 1-5
Guide

Triumphal Entry

Bethany

2 V.2 And supper being ended

Passover

Last Supper

V.1 (1) Jesus

(3) V.2 Judas Iscariot

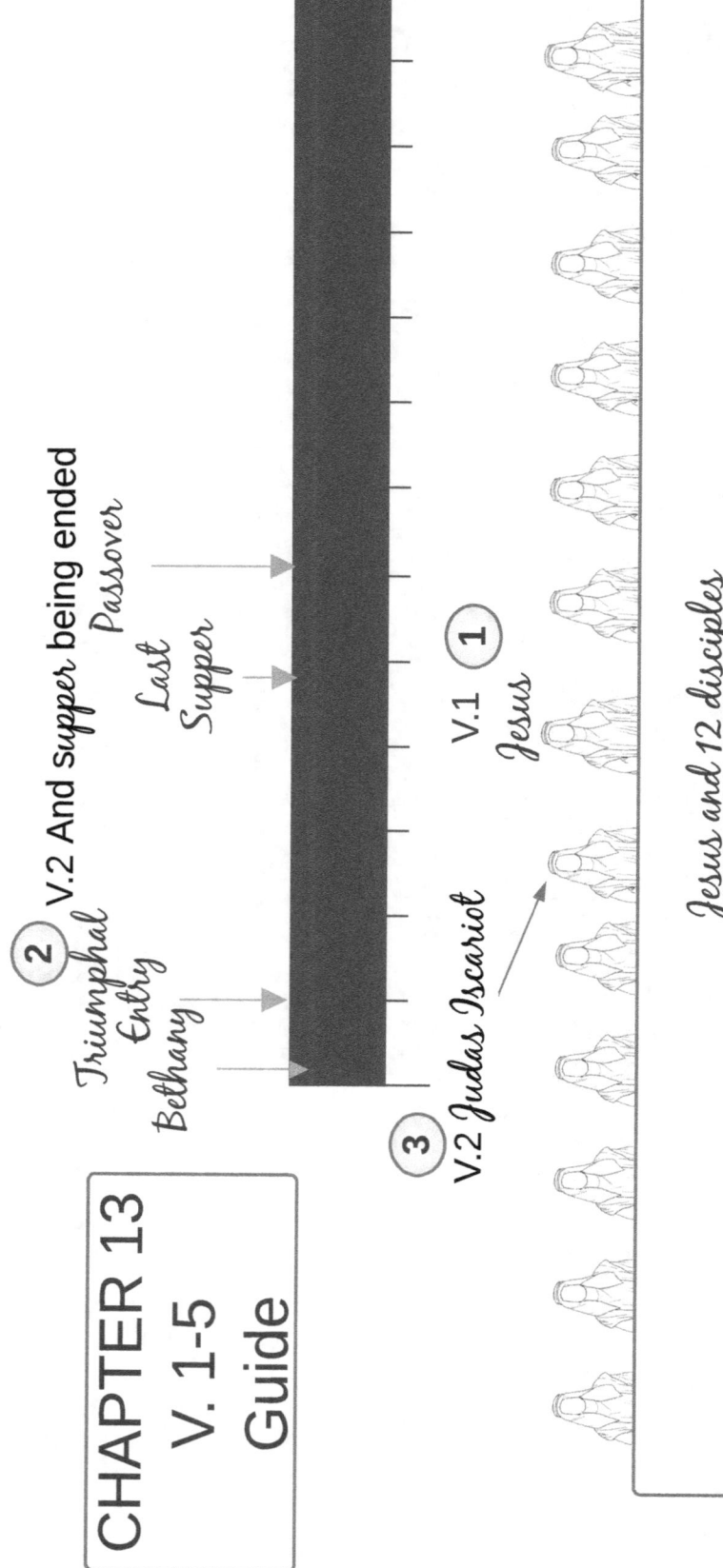

Jesus and 12 disciples

V.4 He riseth from supper, and *laid aside* his *garments*; and took a *towel*, and *girded himself.*
V.5 After that he poureth water into a bason, and began to *wash* the *disciples' feet*, and to wipe them with the towel wherewith he was girded.

The fact that it's even mentioned that Jesus laid aside His garments and girded Himself with a towel makes it significant. His outward appearance reflected a humble servant with humility. Do not think that appearances don't matter for man looketh on the outside. It is important enough that man looketh on the outside. Jesus changed His garments.

Outward appearance matters.

1Samuel 16:7 But the LORD said unto Samuel, Look not on his countenance, or on the height of his stature; because I have refused him: for the LORD seeth not as man seeth; for man looketh on the outward appearance, but the LORD looketh on the heart.

CHAPTER 13
V. 1-5
Notes

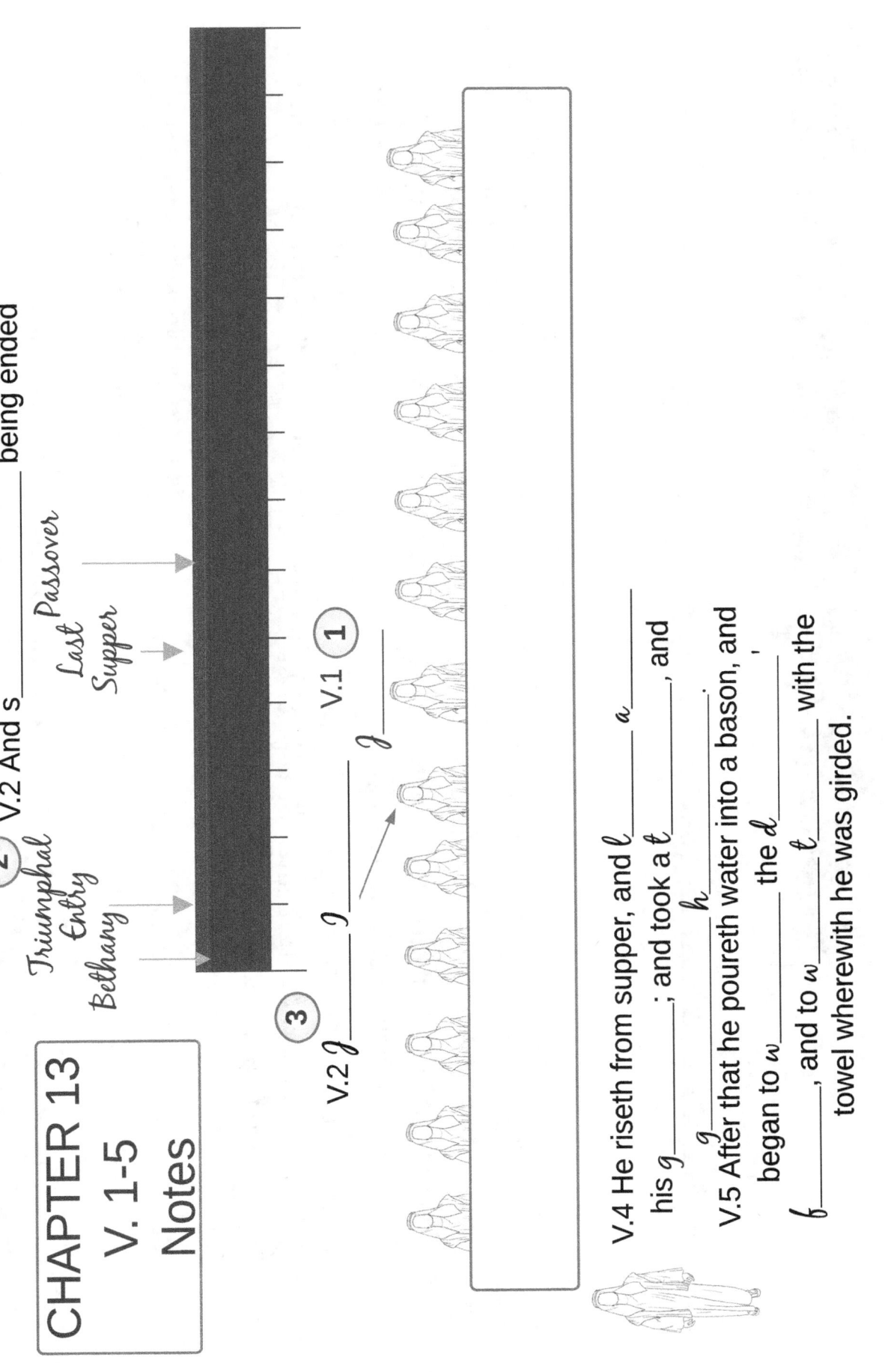

2 V.2 And s _____ being ended

Triumphal Entry
Bethany

Last Passover
Supper

V.1 ① _____

3 _____ J

V.2 J _____

V.4 He riseth from supper, and l _____ a _____
his g _____; and took a t _____, and
h _____.

V.5 After that he poureth water into a bason, and
began to w _____ the d _____ t _____ with the
f _____, and to w _____ t _____ with the
towel wherewith he was girded.

CHAPTER 13
V. 6-10
Guide

Triumphal Entry
Bethany

Last Passover Supper

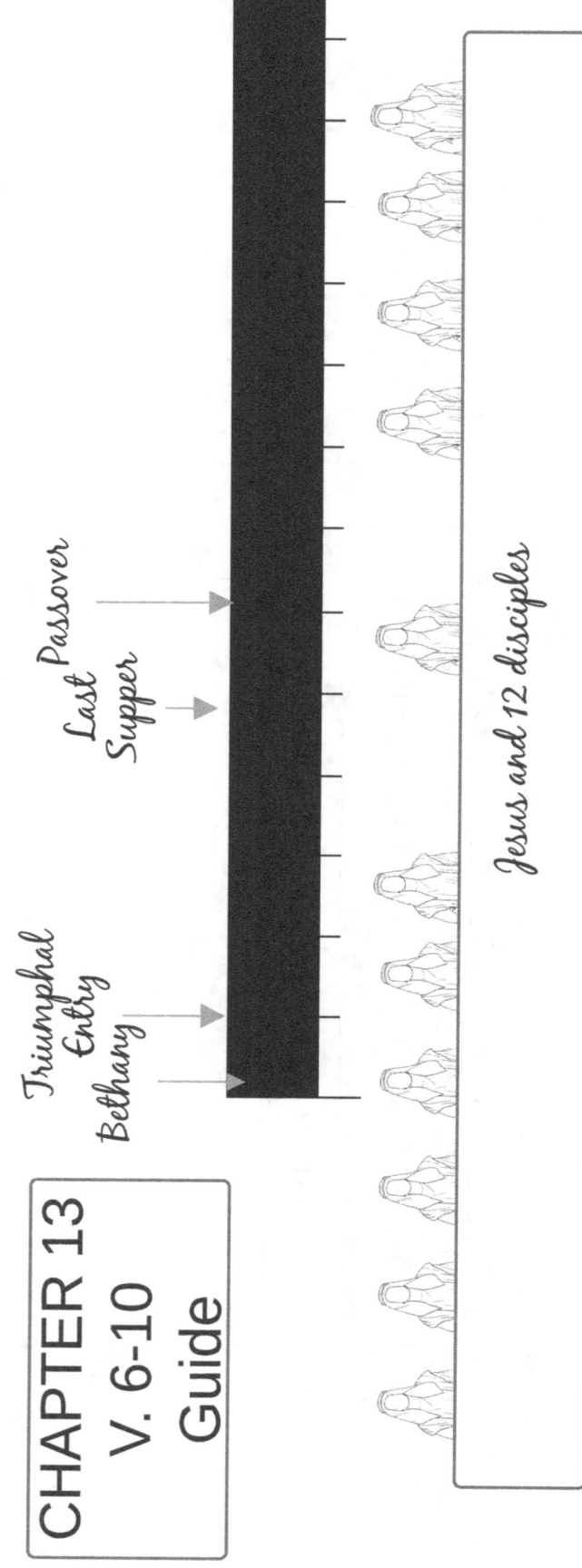

Jesus and 12 disciples

(1) Didn't understand why Jesus would become a servant to him.

V6 ...Peter saith unto him, Lord, dost thou wash my feet?

Peter's humility

(4) V. 8 Thou shalt *never* wash my feet.

(6) V.9 Lord, not my feet only, but also my hands and my head.

(2) V.7 Jesus

After Jesus has risen, they will know how much more he became a servant and loved them.

(3) V.7 ...What I do thou knowest not now; but thou shalt know hereafter.

(5) V. 8 ... If I wash thee not, thou hast no part with me.

Just as Jesus was a servant who washed their feet, He will be their servant by washing with the regeneration of the Holy Ghost. (A disciple) (saved.)

(7) V.10 Jesus saith to him, He that is *washed* needeth not save to wash his feet, but is *clean every whit:* and ye are

→ clean, but not all. → (disciples)

(except) → (saved) (Judas not saved.)

→ clean, but not all.

always clean all over

Titus 3:5 Not by works of righteousness which we have done, but according to his mercy he saved us, **by the washing of regeneration, and renewing of the Holy Ghost:**

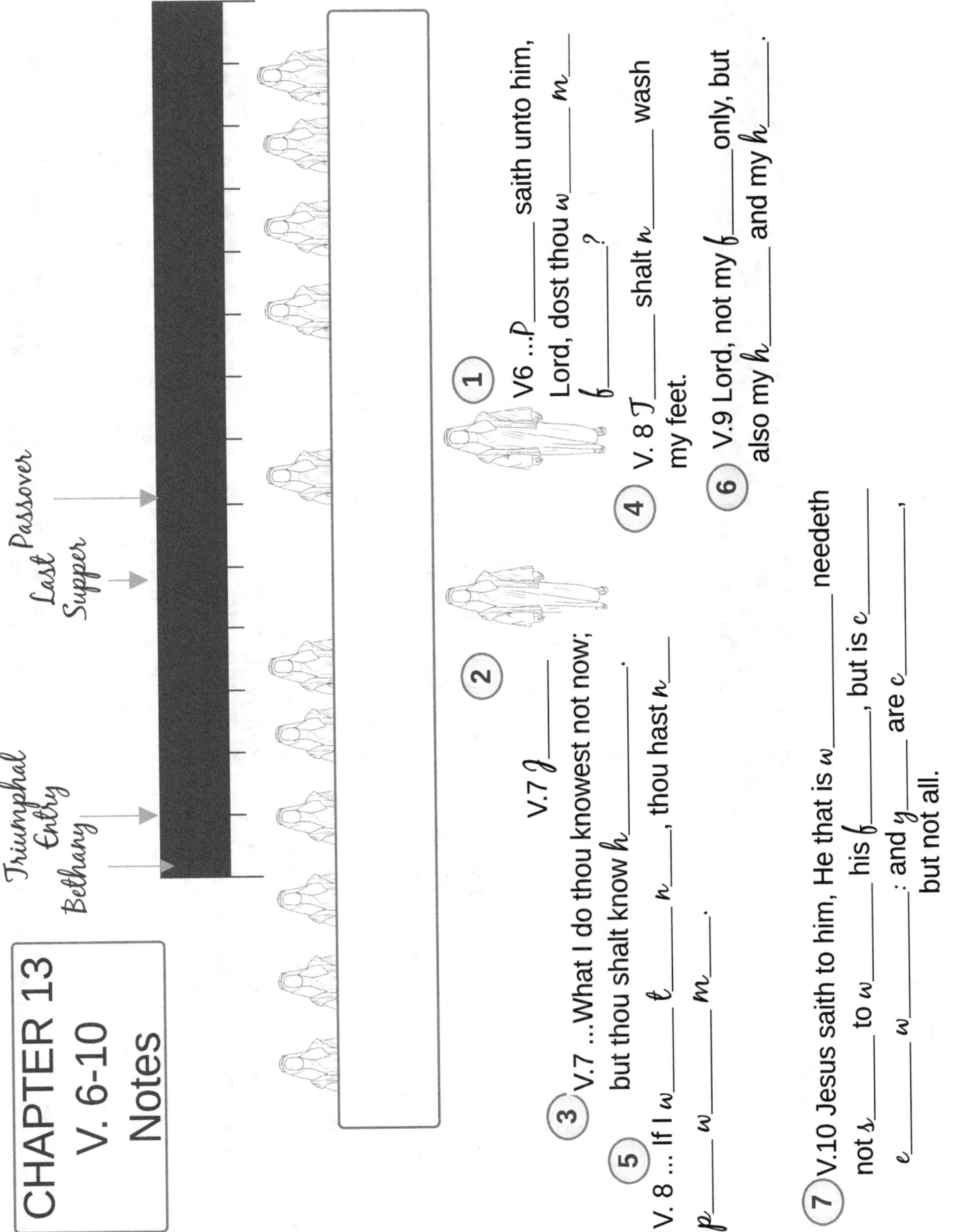

CHAPTER 13
V. 6-10
Notes

Triumphal Entry
Bethany
Last Supper
Passover

1 V6 ...P_____ saith unto him,
Lord, dost thou w_____ m_____
f_____?

2 V.7 J_____

3 V.7 ...What I do thou knowest not now;
but thou shalt know h_____.

V. 8 ... If I w_____ t_____ n_____, thou hast n_____
p_____ w_____ m_____.

4 V. 8 J_____ shalt n_____ wash
my feet.

6 V.9 Lord, not my f_____ only, but
also my h_____ and my h_____.

7 V.10 Jesus saith to him, He that is w_____ needeth
not s_____ to w_____ his f_____, but is c_____
w_____; and y_____ are c_____,
but not all.

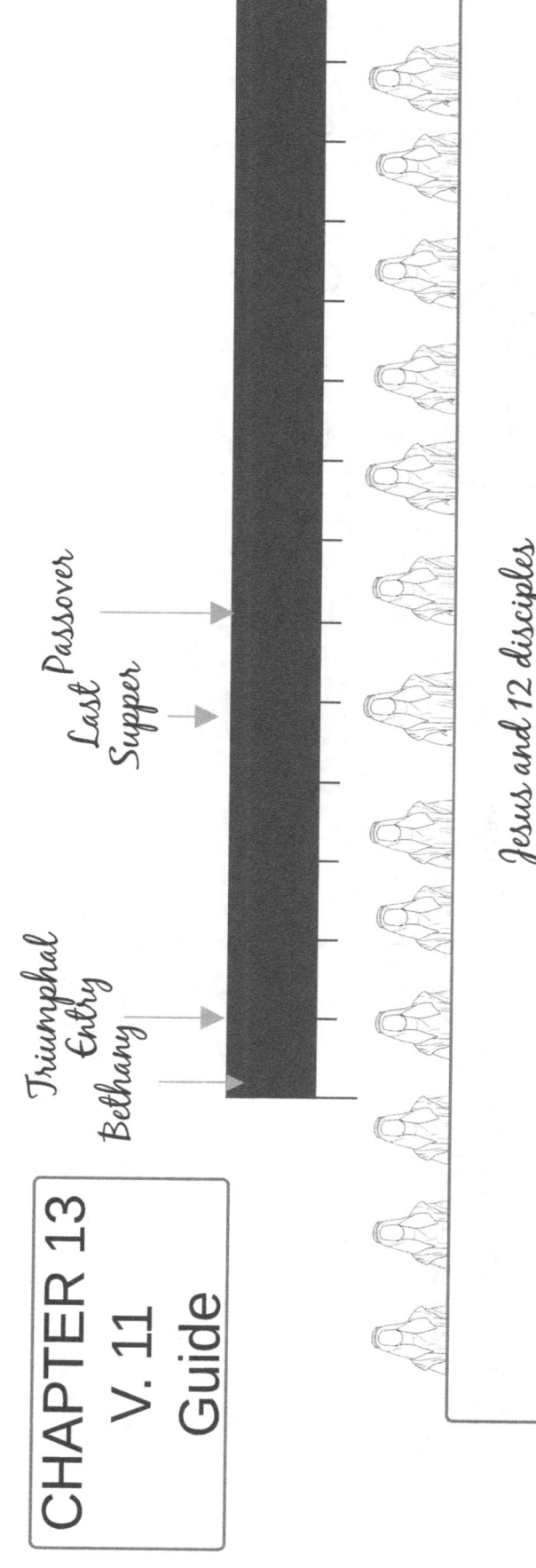

CHAPTER 13
V. 11
Guide

Triumphal
Entry

Bethany

Last Passover
Supper

Jesus and 12 disciples

V.13 Ye call me *Master* and *Lord*: and ye say well; for so *I am*.

V.14 If I then, your Lord and Master, have *washed your feet*; ye also ought to *wash one another's feet*. (Literally as a good work for them) — Literally washed their feet. *Not speaking spiritually.*

V.15 For I have given you an example, that ye should *do as I have done to you.*

V.16 *Verily, verily, I say unto you,* The servant is not greater than his lord; neither he that is sent greater than he that sent him. ("sent from heaven", hence the witness Verily, verily, I)

V.17 If ye know these things, *happy are ye if ye do them.*

In Biblical times, people walked wherever they went. They wore sandals and their feet got dirty and tired. It was a nice gesture for a guest to be able to wash their feet upon entering. Washing their feet is only an example of how to serve them or a good work. Today, we should look for other ways to serve one another.

1Timothy 5:10 Well reported of **for good works**; if she have brought up children; if she have lodged strangers, if she **have washed the saints' feet,** → *We should serve others by doing good works for them*

Luke 7:44 And he turned to the woman, and said unto Simon, Seest thou this woman? I entered into thine house, **thou gavest me no water for my feet:** but she hath **washed my feet with tears,** and wiped them with the hairs of her head.

CHAPTER 13
V. 11-17
Notes

Triumphal
Entry
Bethany

Last Passover
Supper

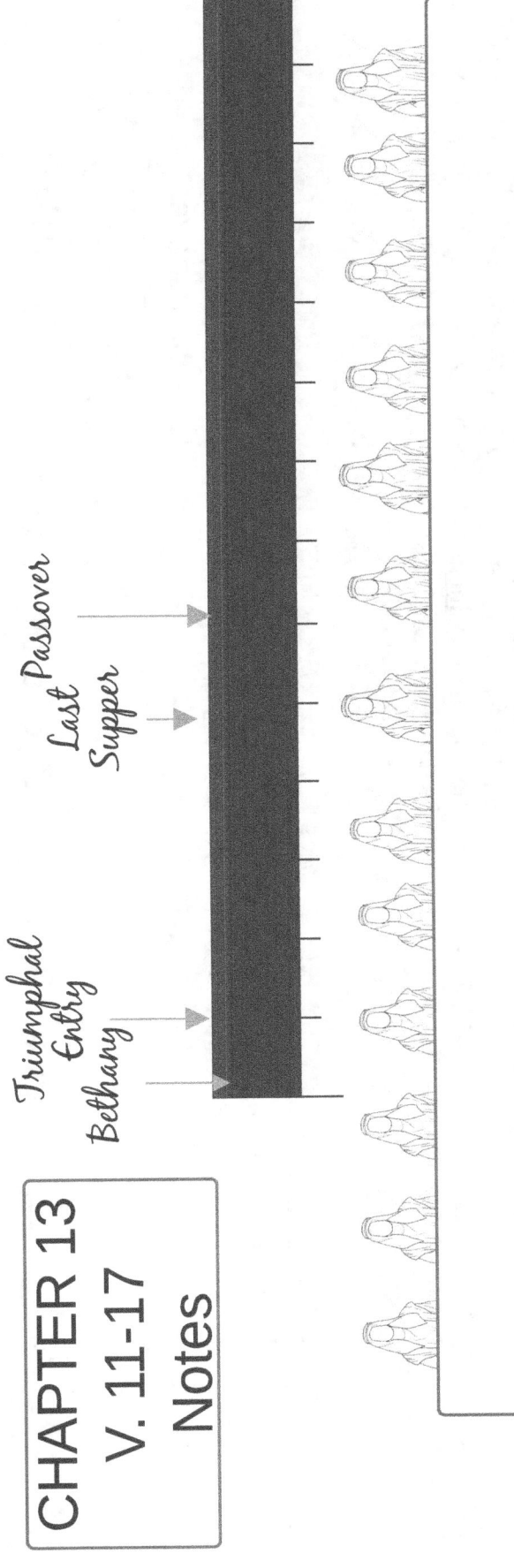

V.13 Ye call me M_____ and L_____ : and ye say well; for so ___a___ .

V.14 If I then, your Lord and Master, have w_____ y_____ f_____ ; ye also ought to

w_____ o_____ a_____ f_____ .

V.15 For I have given you a___ e_____ , that ye should d___ a___ h___ to you.

V.16 V_____ , v_____ , s_____ unto you, The servant is not greater than

his lord; neither he that is sent greater than he that s___ h_____ .

V.17 If ye know these things, h_____ are y_____ if ye do them.

CHAPTER 13
V. 18-21
Guide

Triumphal Entry
Bethany

Last Passover
Supper

Prophecy

Jesus and 12 disciples

Jesus

Judas Iscariot

(1)

V.18 I speak not of you all: I know whom I have chosen: but that the scripture may be fulfilled, He that eateth bread with me hath lifted up his heel against me.

Genesis 3:15 And I will put enmity between thee and the woman, and between thy seed and her seed; it shall bruise thy head, and thou shalt bruise his heel.

God is talking to the serpent (Satan). The seed of Satan and the seed of Eve shall be enemies. The serpent shall bruise the heel of the Saviour but the Saviour shall bruise the head of the serpent's seed. You kill a serpent by "bruising" it's head.

Psalm 41:9 Yea, mine own familiar friend, in whom I trusted, which did eat of my bread, hath lifted up his heel against me.

(2)

V.19 Now I tell you before it come, that, when it is come to pass, ye may believe that I am he.

Prophecy is given to us so that we may believe that Jesus is the Saviour. Prophecy is more important than history.

Witness Jesus was sent from the Father

(3)

V.20 Verily, verily, I say unto you, He that receiveth whomsoever I send receiveth me; and he that receiveth me receiveth him that sent me.

Prophecy from the Father

(4)

V.21, Verily, verily, I say unto you, that one of you shall betray me.

CHAPTER 13
V. 18-21
Notes

Bethany

Triumphal Entry

Last Supper

Passover

Jesus

Jesus and 12 disciples

1. V.18 I speak n_____ of you a_____: I know whom I have chosen: but that the s_____ may be f_____, He that e_____ b_____ with m_____ hath lifted up his h_____ a_____ m_____.

2. V.19 Now I tell you b_____ it come, that, when it is come to pass, ye m_____ b_____ that I am he.

3. V.20 V_____, v_____, I s_____ unto you, He that receiveth whomsoever I send receiveth me; and he that receiveth me receiveth him that s_____ m_____.

4. V.21, V_____, v_____, I s_____ unto you, that one of you shall betray me.

CHAPTER 13
V. 22-30
Guide

Triumphal
Entry
Bethany

Last Passover
Supper

Jesus and 12 disciples

1 V.23 Now there was leaning on Jesus' bosom one of his disciples, whom Jesus loved.

John is known as the disciple "whom Jesus loved" but the only place in the scriptures where he is called that is in the Book of John. John wrote that of himself. We should all feel that way "I am the one that Jesus loves!".

2 V.26 Jesus answered, He it is, to whom I shall give a sop, when I have dipped it. And when he had dipped the sop, he gave it to Judas Iscariot, the son of Simon.

someone's son (somewhere there's a broken hearted father)

V.27 And after the sop Satan entered into him. Then said Jesus unto him, That thou doest, do quickly.

V.28 Now no man at the table knew for what intent he spake this unto him.

3 V.29 For some of them thought, because Judas had the bag, that Jesus had said unto him, Buy those things that we have need of against the feast; or, that he should give something to the poor.

money

Would they have tried to stop him from betraying their Lord?

V.30 He then having received the sop went immediately out: and it was night.

Ephesians 6:12 For we wrestle not against flesh and blood, but against principalities, against powers, against the rulers of the darkness of this world, against spiritual wickedness in high places.

CHAPTER 13
V. 22-30
Notes

Triumphal
Entry
Bethany

Last Passover
Supper

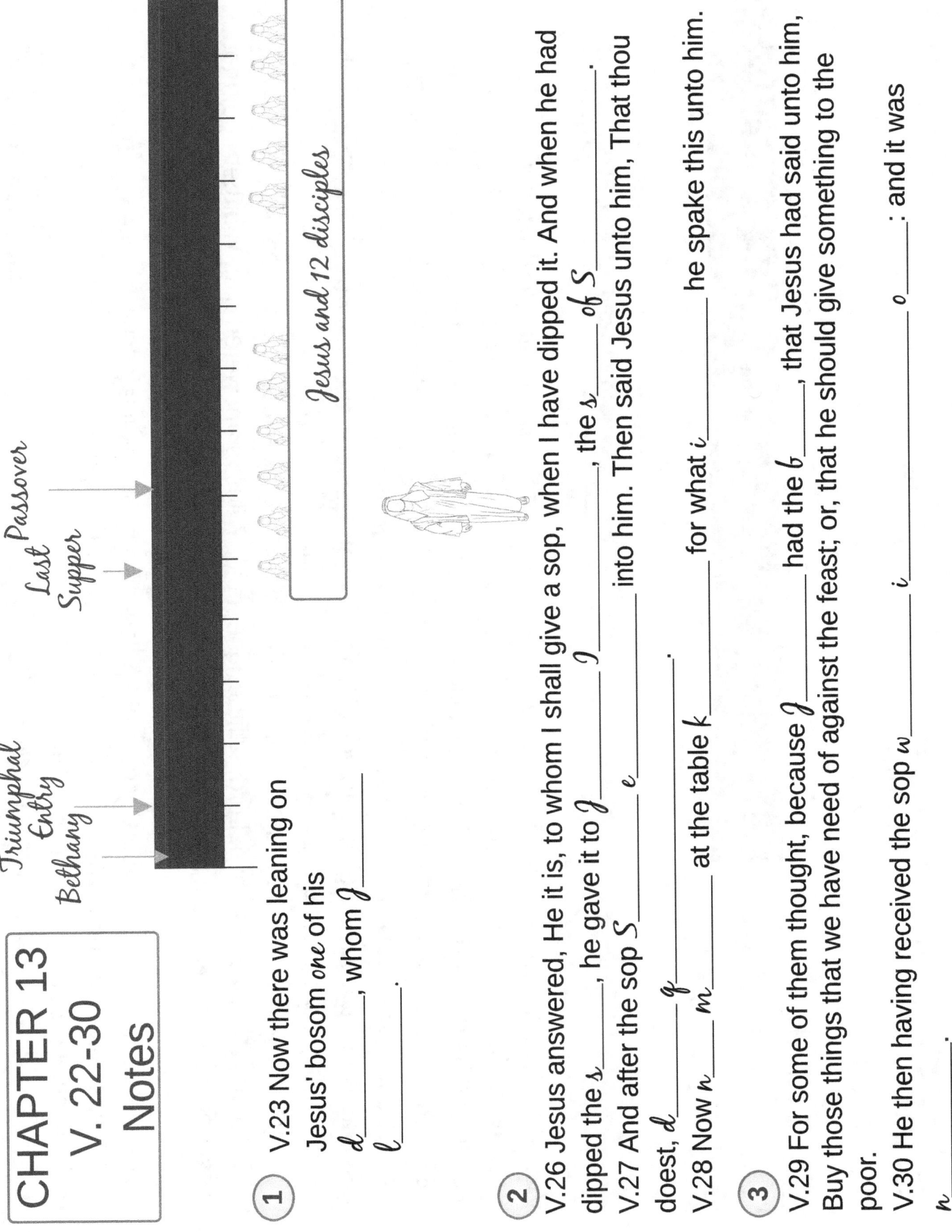

Jesus and 12 disciples

(1) V.23 Now there was leaning on Jesus' bosom *one* of his
d_____, whom J_____
l_____.

(2) V.26 Jesus answered, He it is, to whom I shall give a sop, when I have dipped it. And when he had dipped the s_____, he gave it to J_____, the s_____ of S_____.
V.27 And after the sop S_____ e_____ into him. Then said Jesus unto him, That thou doest, d_____ q_____.
V.28 Now n_____ m_____ at the table k_____ for what i_____ he spake this unto him.

(3) V.29 For some of them thought, because J_____ had the b_____, that Jesus had said unto him, Buy those things that we have need of against the feast; or, that he should give something to the poor.
V.30 He then having received the sop w_____ i_____ o_____: and it was
n_____.

CHAPTER 13
V. 31-38
Guide

Triumphal
Entry
Bethany

Last Passover
Supper

Jesus and 12 disciples

V.31 Therefore, when he was gone out, Jesus said, Now is the Son of man glorified, and God is glorified in him. (Will become the only man who has risen from the dead and receive a glorified body)

V.32 If God be glorified in him, God shall also glorify him in himself, and shall straightway glorify him.

V.33 Little children, yet a little while I am with you. Ye shall seek me: and as I said unto the Jews, Whither I go, ye cannot come; so now I say to you. (He is going to heaven)

V.34 A new commandment I give unto you, That ye love one another; as I have loved you, that ye also love one another. (Gave an example of good works by washing their feet)

V.35 By this shall all men know that ye are my disciples, if ye have love one to another.

V.36 Simon Peter said unto him, Lord, whither goest thou? Jesus answered him, Whither I go, thou canst not follow me now; but thou shalt follow me afterwards. Peter thought he was willing to die for Him and go with Him to heaven now.

V.37 Peter said unto him, Lord, why cannot I follow thee now? I will lay down my life for thy sake.

V.38 Jesus answered him, Wilt thou lay down thy life for my sake? Verily, verily, I say unto thee, The cock shall not crow, till thou hast denied me thrice. Only someone from heaven could know this

Cocks (Roosters) crow very early in the day.

CHAPTER 13
V. 31-38
Notes

Triumphal
Entry
Bethany

Last
Supper

Passover

Jesus and 12 disciples

V.31 Therefore, when he was gone out, Jesus said, Now is the S_____ of m_____ g_____, and g_____ is g_____ in him.

V.32 If God be glorified in him, God shall also glorify him in himself, and shall s_____ glorify him.

V.33 L_____ c_____, yet a little while I am with you. Ye shall s_____ m_____; and as I said unto the Jews, Whither I go, y_____ c_____ c_____; so now I say to you.

V.34 A n_____ c_____ I give unto you, That ye love one another; as h_____ l_____ g_____, that ye also l_____ on a_____.

V.35 By this shall a_____ m_____ k_____ that ye are my d_____, if ye have love one to another.

V.36 Simon P_____ said unto him, Lord, whither goest thou? Jesus answered him, Whither I go, thou canst not follow me n_____; but thou shalt follow me a_____.

V.37 Peter said unto him, Lord, why cannot I follow thee now? _w_____ lay down my life for t_____ s_____.

V.38 Jesus answered him, Wilt thou lay down thy life for my sake? V_____, v_____, s_____, unto thee, The c_____ shall n_____ c_____, till thou hast d_____ m_____ t_____.

Read John Chapter 14

CHAPTER 14
V. 1-3
Guide

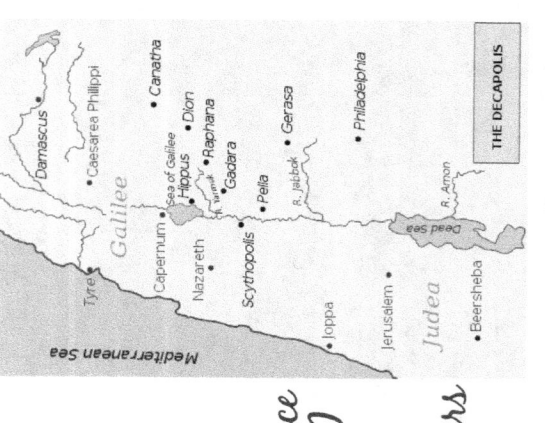

1 V.1 Let not your heart be troubled: ye believe in God, believe also in me.

As they see Him die, though they believe in God, they may begin to loose faith in Him.

2 V.2 In my Father's house are many mansions: <u>if it were not so,</u> I would have told you. I go to prepare a place for you. *Disciples were already expecting a place to dwell in heaven. If it were not so I would have told you.*

in heaven

The Old Testament temple was a pattern of heaven. Inside the temple were chambers for the priests dwell.

1Kings 6:5 And against the wall of the house he built chambers round about, against the walls of the house round about, <u>both of the temple and of the oracle: and he made chambers round about:</u>

Jeremiah 35:2 Go unto the house of the Rechabites,... and bring them into the <u>house of the LORD,</u> <u>into one of the chambers,</u> and give them wine to drink.

Jeremiah 35:4 And I brought them into the <u>house of the LORD,</u> into <u>the chamber of the sons of Hanan,</u> the son of Igdaliah, a man of God, which was <u>by the chamber of the princes,</u> which was <u>above the chamber of Maaseiah the son of Shallum,</u> the keeper of the door:

Jesus called the temple, "My Father's house"

John 2:15 And when he had made a scourge of small cords, he drove them all <u>out of the temple,</u> and the sheep, and the oxen; and poured out the changers' money, and overthrew the tables;
John 2:16 And said unto them that sold doves, Take these things hence; make not <u>my Father's house</u> an house of merchandise.

3 V.3 And if I go and prepare a place for you, *I will come again,* and receive you unto myself; that where I am, *there ye may be also.*

2 Corinthians 5:8 We are confident, I say, and willing rather to be <u>absent from the body,</u> and to be <u>present with the Lord.</u>

CHAPTER 14
V. 1-3
Notes

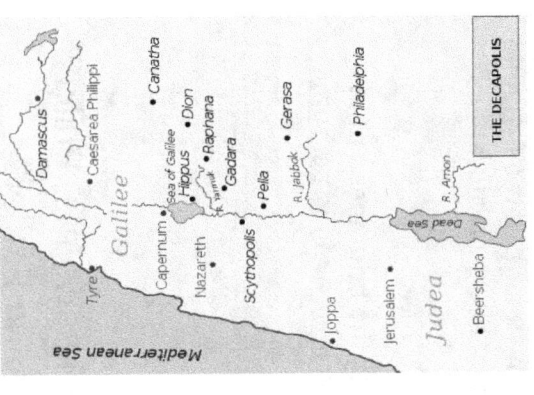

THE DECAPOLIS

1 V.1 Let not your heart be troubled: ye believe in God, b_____ also i_____ m_____.

2 V.2 In m_____ F_____ h_____ are m_____ m_____ b_____ : if it were not so, I would have told you. I go to prepare a p_____ g_____ .

3 V.3 And if I go and prepare a place for you, ____ w____ c____ a_____, and receive you unto myself; that where I am, t____ y____ m____ be a____ .

CHAPTER 14
V. 4-9
Guide

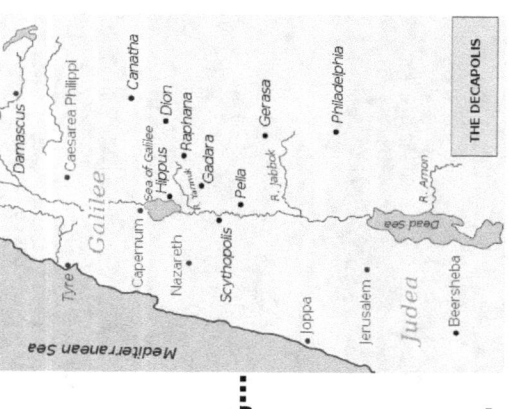

THE DECAPOLIS

1

V.6 Jesus saith unto him, I am *the way, the truth,* and *the life*: no man cometh unto the Father, but by me.

Jesus is the Word.

John 1:14 And the Word was made flesh, and dwelt among us,...

(way) **Psalm 119:105 Thy <u>word</u> is a lamp unto my feet, and a light unto my path.**

(truth) **John 17:17 Sanctify them through thy truth: thy <u>word</u> is truth.**

(life) **John 6:63 ...the <u>words</u> that I speak unto you, they are spirit, and they <u>are life</u>.**

2

V.7 If ye had known me, ye should have known *my Father* also: and from henceforth ye know him, and *have seen him.*

God is a Spirit. He is invisible. No one has ever seen Him but we can see His express image. Jesus is the image, more explicitly, the express image of His person. Express image is not merely an image it is an image of that which could not otherwise be seen.

Colossians 1:15 Who is the image of the <u>invisible</u> God, the firstborn of every creature:

Hebrews 1:3 Who being the brightness of his glory, and the <u>express image of his person.</u>

3

V.9 Jesus saith unto him, Have I been so long time with you, and yet hast thou not known me, Philip? he that hath *seen me hath seen the Father*; and how sayest thou then, Shew us the Father?

CHAPTER 14
V. 4-9
Notes

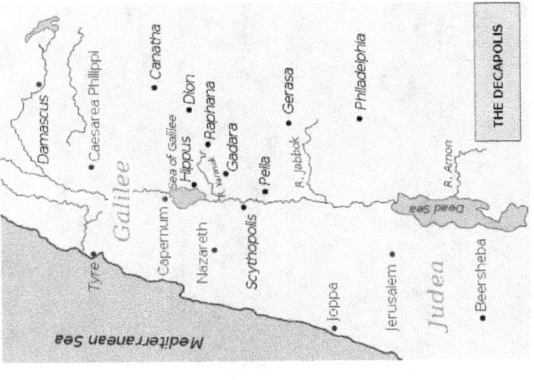

THE DECAPOLIS

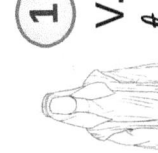

1

V.6 Jesus saith unto him, I am *the* w_____ , *the*
t_____ , and *the* l_____ : no man
cometh unto the Father, but by me.

2

V.7 If ye had known me, ye should have known *m*_____
also: and from henceforth ye know him, and
*F*_____ s_____ h_____ .

3

V.9 Jesus saith unto him, Have I been so long time with you, and yet hast thou not known me, Philip?
he that hath s_____ *m*_____ hath s_____ *the* F_____ ; and how sayest thou then, Shew us the
Father?

CHAPTER 14
V. 10-11
Guide

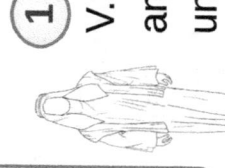

1

V.10 Believest thou not that I am in the Father, and the Father in me? the *words* that I speak unto you I speak not of myself: but the Father that dwelleth in me, <u>he doeth the</u> *works*.

V.11 Believe me that I am in the Father, and the Father in me: or else *believe me* for the very *works' sakes*.

Jesus Speaks the Words and The Father does the Works

Words (Jesus)

John 5:8 Jesus *saith* unto him, Rise, take up thy bed, and walk.

John 9:11...and *saith* unto me, Go to the pool of Siloam, and wash:

John 11:43 And when he thus had spoken, he *cried* with a loud *voice*, Lazarus, come forth.

Works (the Father)

John 5:9 And immediately the man *was made* whole, and took up his bed

John 9:11...and I went and washed, and I *received* sight.

John 11:44 And he that was dead *came forth*

2

V.11 Believe me that I am in the Father, and the Father in me: or else *believe me* for the very *works' sake*.

CHAPTER 14
V. 10-11
Notes

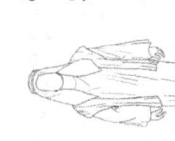
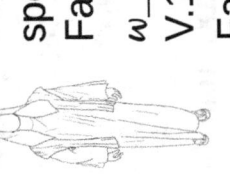

(1) V.10 Believest thou not that I am in the Father, and the Father in me? the w_____ that I speak unto you I speak not of myself: but the Father that dwelleth in me, <u>he doeth the</u> w_____.

V.11 Believe me that I am in the Father, and the Father in me: or else b_____ m_____ for the very w_____'s_____.

Jesus Speaks the Words and The Father does the Works

Words (Jesus)

John 5:8 Jesus s_____ unto him, Rise, take up thy bed, and walk.

John 9:11…and s_____ unto me, Go to the pool of Siloam, and wash:

John 11:43 And when he thus had spoken, he c_____ with a loud voice, Lazarus, come forth.

Works (the Father)

John 5:9 And immediately the man w_____ m_____ whole, and took up his bed

John 9:11…and I went and washed, and I r_____ sight.

John 11:44 And he that w_____ d_____ came forth

(2) V.11 Believe me that I am in the Father, and the Father in me: or else b_____ m_____ for the very w_____ s_____.

CHAPTER 14
V. 12-24
Guide

(1) V.13 And whatsoever ye shall ask in my name, that will I do, that the Father may be glorified in the Son.

V.14 If ye shall ask any thing in my name, I will do it.

V.15 If ye love me, keep my commandments.

John 5:2 By this we know that we love the children of God, when we love God, and keep his commandments.

John 5:3 For this is the love of God, that we keep his commandments: and his commandments are not grievous.

— how to love God or the loving of God

V.16 And I will pray the Father, and he shall give you another Comforter, that he may abide with you for ever;

17 Even the Spirit of truth; whom the world cannot receive, because it seeth him not, neither knoweth him: but ye know him; for he dwelleth with you, and shall be in you.

John 14:18 I will not leave you comfortless: I will come to you.

John 14:19 Yet a little while, and the world seeth me no more; but ye see me: because I live, ye shall live also.

John 14:20 At that day ye shall know that I am in my Father, and ye in me, and I in you.

John 14:21 He that hath my commandments, and keepeth them, he it is that loveth me: and he that loveth me shall be loved of my Father, and I will love him, and will manifest myself to him.

John 14:22 Judas saith unto him, not Iscariot, Lord, how is it that thou wilt manifest thyself unto us, and not unto the world?

John 14:23 Jesus answered and said unto him, If a man love me, he will keep my words: and my Father will love him, and we will come unto him, and make our abode with him.

John 14:24 He that loveth me not keepeth not my sayings: and the word which ye hear is not mine, but the Father's which sent me.

CHAPTER 14
V. 12-24
Notes

V.13 And w_____ ye shall ask in my name, that will I do, that the F____ m____ be g_____ in the Son.

V.14 If ye shall ask a____ in m___ n____, I will do it.

V.15 If ye l____ m___, keep my c_____.

V.16 And I will pray the Father, and he shall give you a_____ C_____, that he may abide with you f___ e____;

V.17 E____ the S____ of t____; whom the world cannot receive, because it seeth him not, neither knoweth him: but ye know him; for he d_____ with you, and s____ be i___ y____.

V.18 I will not leave you c_____: I will come to you.

V.19 Yet a little while, and the world seeth me no more; but ye see me: b_____ I l____, y___ s_____ l____ a____.

V.20 At that day ye shall know that I am i___ m___ F_____, and y___ i___ m____, and ___ i___ y___.

V.21 He that hath my c_____, and k____ them, he it is that l_____ m_____: and he that loveth me shall be loved of my Father, and I will love him, and will m_____ m____ to him.

V.22 Judas saith unto him, not Iscariot, Lord, how is it that thou wilt manifest thyself unto us, and n_____ unto the w_____?

V.23 Jesus answered and said unto him, If a man l____ m____, he will k____ m___ w____: and my Father will l____ h_____, and we will come unto him, and make our a_____ with h_____.

V. 24 He that l_____ m____ not k____ n___ m____ s_____: and the word which ye hear is not mine, but the Father's which sent me.

Read John Chapter 15

CHAPTER 15
V. 1-6
Guide

5 V.3 Now ye are *clean* through the *word* which I have spoken unto you.

...even as Christ also loved the church, and gave himself for it;
Ephesians 5:26 That he might <u>sanctify and cleanse it</u> with the washing of water by the <u>word</u>.

Galatians 5:22-23 But the <u>fruit of the Spirit</u> is love, joy, peace, longsuffering, gentleness, goodness, faith, Meekness, temperance:

purge means to make clean.
trials—thru the fire
V.2 every branch that *beareth fruit*, he *purgeth* it, that it may bring forth more fruit.

4 V. 1 Father is the husbandman.

gardener–planted the vine (sent Jesus to Earth because He takes pleasure in the fruit.)

fruit

Believer (Church)

The Holy Spirit

—The Holy Spirit

speaking of fellowship

3 V.2 Every branch *in me* that beareth *not fruit* he *taketh away*

Ephesians 5:9 (For the fruit of the Spirit is in all goodness and righteousness and truth;)
Ephesians 5:11 And have <u>no fellowship</u> with the <u>unfruitful works of darkness</u>, but rather reprove them.

no fruit

6 V.6

If *a man abide not in me*, he is cast forth *as a branch, and is withered; and men gather them, and cast them into the fire,* and they are burned.

men gather them (no Divine protection)

1 V.1 I am the *true vine* —The Holy Spirit

Jesus is the (true) body that casts the (pattern) shadow. He is not the shadow or pattern.

John 15:1 I am the <u>true vine</u>.

Hebrews 8:2 ....<u>true tabernacle</u>, which the Lord pitched, and not man.

John 1:9 That was the <u>true Light</u>

John 6:32...the <u>true bread from heaven</u>.

Colossians 2:17 Which are a <u>shadow of things</u> to come; but the <u>body</u> is of Christ.

Body of Christ	Shadow
bread from heaven	manna
Temple	Old Testament tabernacle
Christ on the cross	Brzen Serpent

2 V. 1 Father is the husbandman.

CHAPTER 15
V. 1-6
Notes

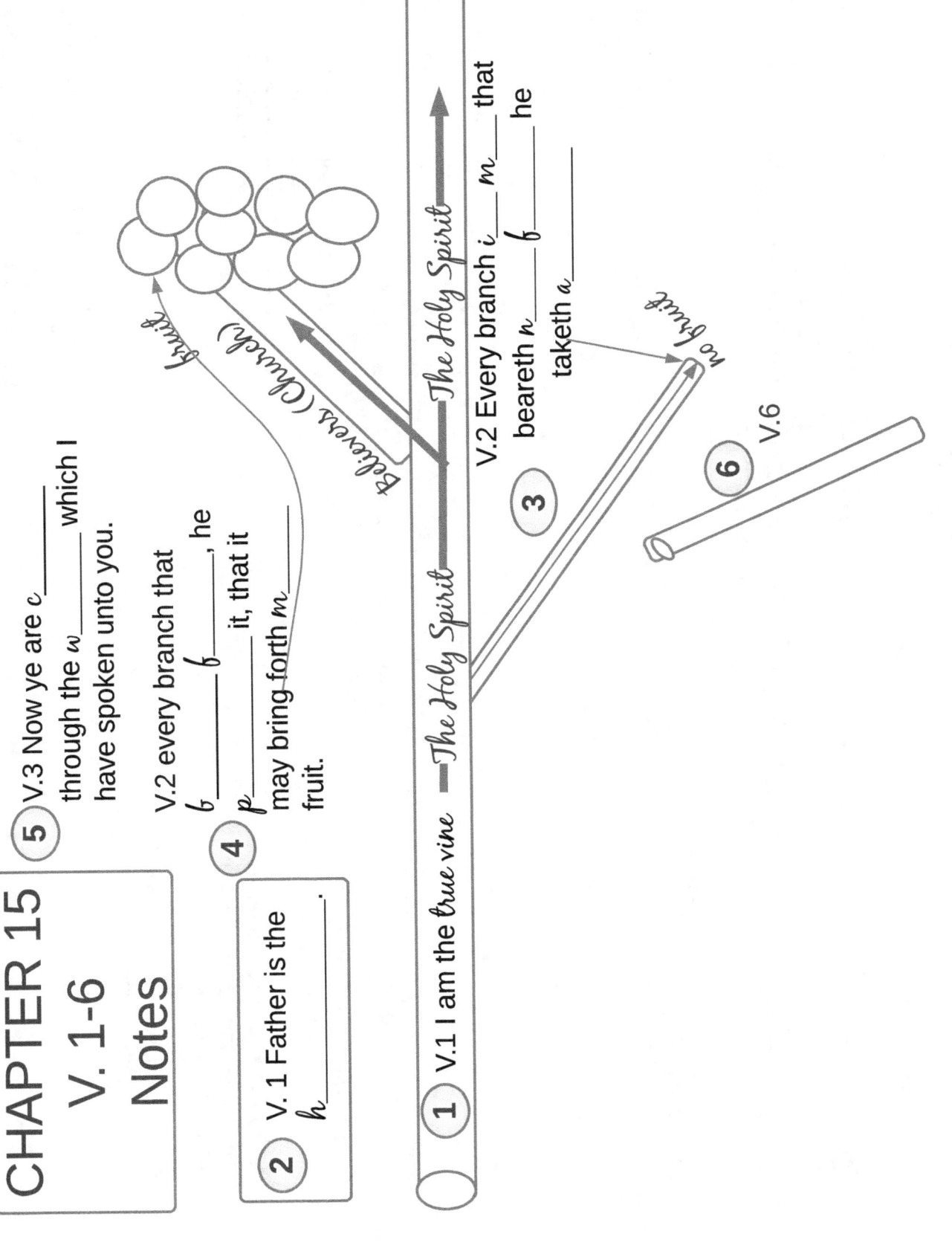

5 V.3 Now ye are c_____ which I
through the w_____
have spoken unto you.

V.2 every branch that
b_____ f_____, he
p_____ it, that it
may bring forth m_____
fruit.

4

2 V. 1 Father is the
h_____.

1 V.1 I am the *true vine* ―*The Holy Spirit*

The Holy Spirit

Believers (Church)

3 V.2 Every branch i___ m___ that
beareth n___ f___ he
taketh a___

no fruit

6 V.6

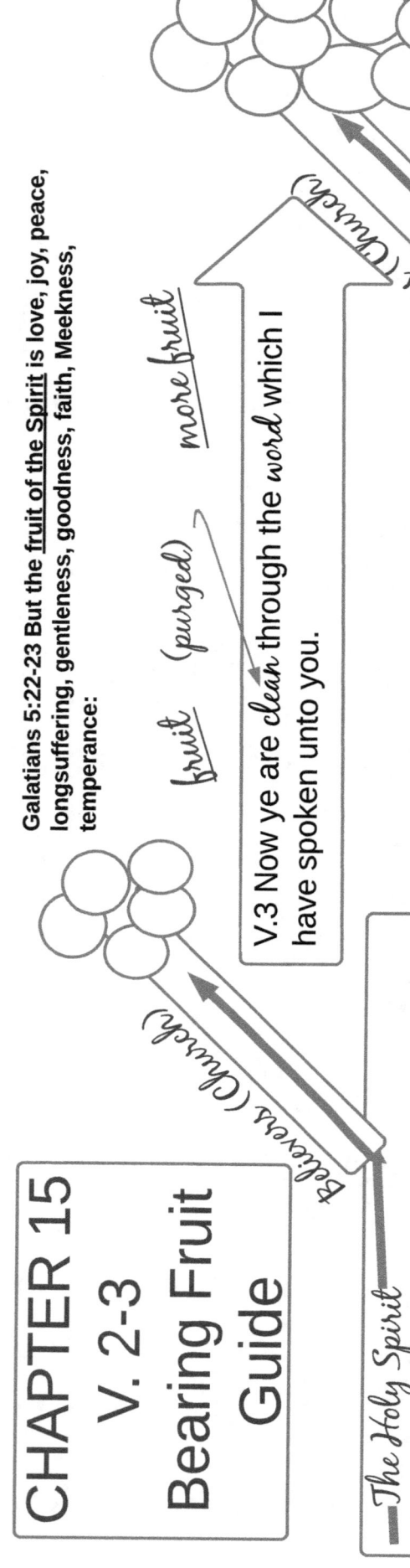

CHAPTER 15
V. 2-3
Bearing Fruit Guide

Galatians 5:22-23 But the <u>fruit</u> of the <u>Spirit</u> is love, joy, peace, longsuffering, gentleness, goodness, faith, Meekness, temperance:

fruit   (purged)   more fruit

V.3 Now ye are *clean* through the *word* which I have spoken unto you.

—The Holy Spirit

Believers (Church)

—The Holy Spirit

Believers (Church)

no fruit

no fellowship

Believers who abides in the world and darkness.

Matthew 13:18 Hear ye therefore the parable of the sower.

...some fell on stony ground and some fell by the wayside

Matthew 13:23 But he that received seed into the good ground is he that heareth the word, and understandeth it; <u>which also beareth fruit,</u> and bringeth forth, some an hundredfold, some sixty, some thirty.

Soulwinning is when the believer who abides in the Holy Spirit plants the seed from the fruit of that abiding...

John 12:24 Verily, verily, I say unto you, Except a corn of wheat fall into the ground and die, it abideth alone: but if it die, <u>it bringeth forth much fruit.</u>

The soulwinner produces much fruit when that seed falls upon good ground, and produces a believer that also bears fruit.

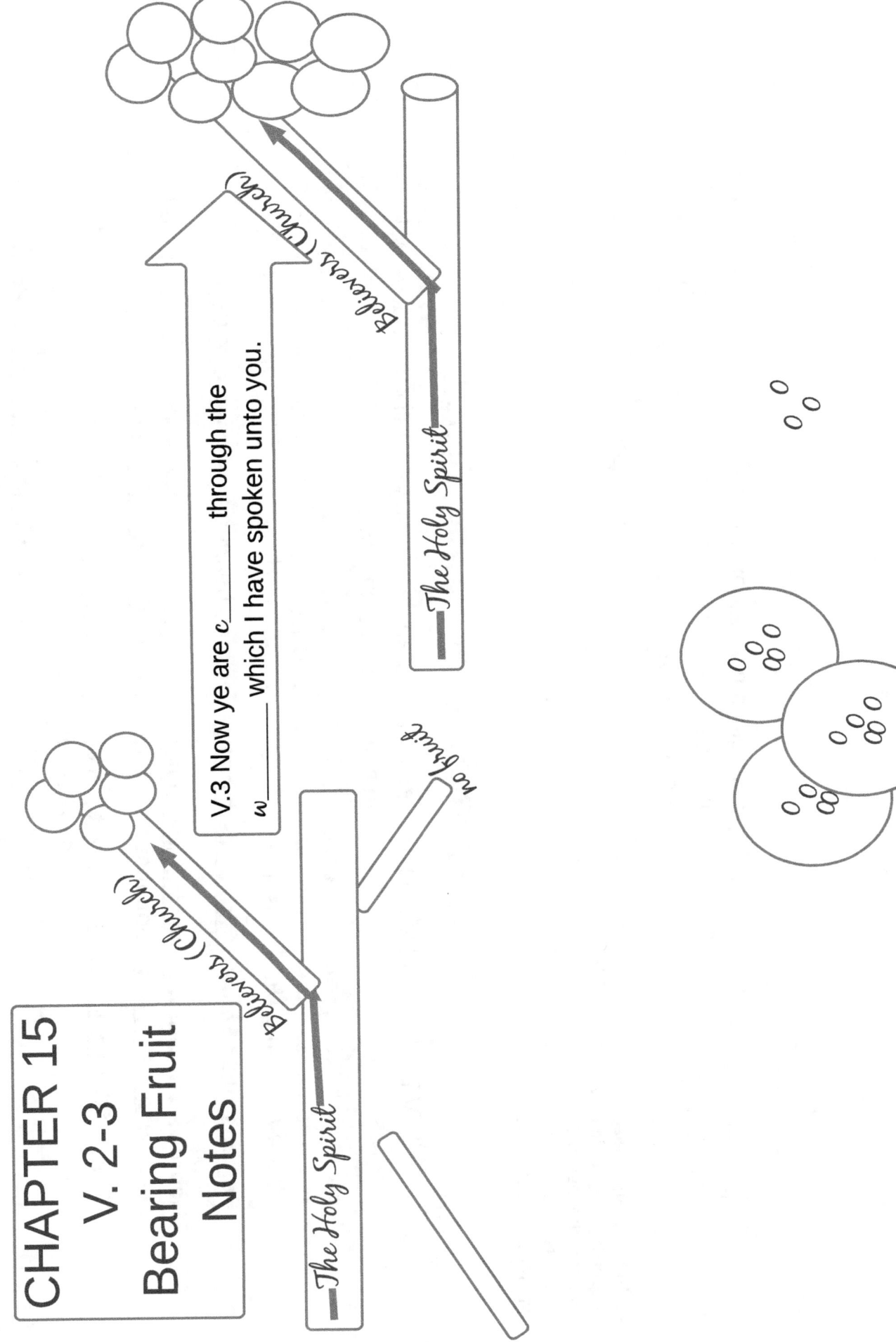

CHAPTER 15
V. 2-3
Bearing Fruit
Notes

Believers (Church)

The Holy Spirit

no fruit

V.3 Now ye are c_____ through the
w_____ which I have spoken unto you.

Believers (Church)

The Holy Spirit

CHAPTER 15
V. 7-8
Guide

Father
(Husbandman)

1 John 2:5 But whoso
keepeth his word, in him
verily is the love of God
perfected: hereby know
we that we are in him.

Abide–rest, dwell or wait patiently. To remain firm.

True Vine

——Words—— ——Words—— ——Words——

Words

Bible Words

(My) Words

② V.8 Herein is my Father glorified,
that ye bear much fruit; so shall
ye be my disciples.

How important is reading your Bible?

① V.7 ⟨If⟩ ye abide in me, and my words abide in you, ye shall ask what ye will,
and it shall be done unto you.

There are conditions to receiving answers to prayer. Not just any believer receives this blessing.
If ye abide in me, and my words abide in you. These words produces faith. Faith that results
in #1 believing that He is and #2 He is a rewarder of those that diligently seek Him.

Romans 10:17 So then faith cometh by hearing, and hearing by the word of God.

Hebrews 11:6 But without faith it is impossible to please him: for he that cometh to God
must believe that he is, and that he is a rewarder of them that diligently seek him.

James 4:3 Ye ask, and receive not, because ye ask amiss, that ye may
consume it upon your lusts.   Asking amiss is from the works of the
flesh not from His Words abiding in you..

CHAPTER 15
V. 7-8
Notes

Father
(Husbandman)

True Vine

Words —— Words —— Words

Believers (Words)

Jesus Words

② V.8 Herein is my Father

g_____, that ye bear

m____ f_____ ; so shall ye

be my d____ .

① V.7 J_____ ye a_____ in me, and m____ w____ abide in you, ye shall

a_____ what ye will, and it shall be d_____ unto you.

CHAPTER 15
V. 9-16
Guide

Father
(Husbandman)

The love of God (loving God or how to love God).

John 5:3 For this is the <u>love of God</u>, that we keep his commandments: and <u>his commandments</u> <u>are not grievous.</u>

Abide in His love through obedience (keeping commandments.)

Love ——— Love ——— Love ——— Love

True Vine

Disobedience

Love Obedience

Love

Blessing Love

The fruit of the Spirit includes joy and peace

(1) V.9 As the Father hath loved me, so have I loved you: *continue ye in my love. (Keep my commandments.)*

(3) V.11 These things have I spoken unto you, *and that my joy might remain in you, and that your joy might be full.*

— *Because we love Him, they are not grievous* *Joy comes from pleasing Him.*

(2) V.10 If ye keep my commandments, ye shall *abide in my love; even as I have kept my Father's commandments, and abide in his love*

(4) V.12 This is my commandment, That ye love one another, as I have loved you.

No greater love than laying down your life for a friend. (Cross)

CHAPTER 15
V. 9-16
Notes

Father
(Husbandman)

(1) V.9 As the Father hath loved me, so have I loved you:
c_____ ye in my love.

(3) V.11 These things have I spoken unto you,
that m___ j____ m____ in you, and that y____
r____ j____ m____ b____ b____.

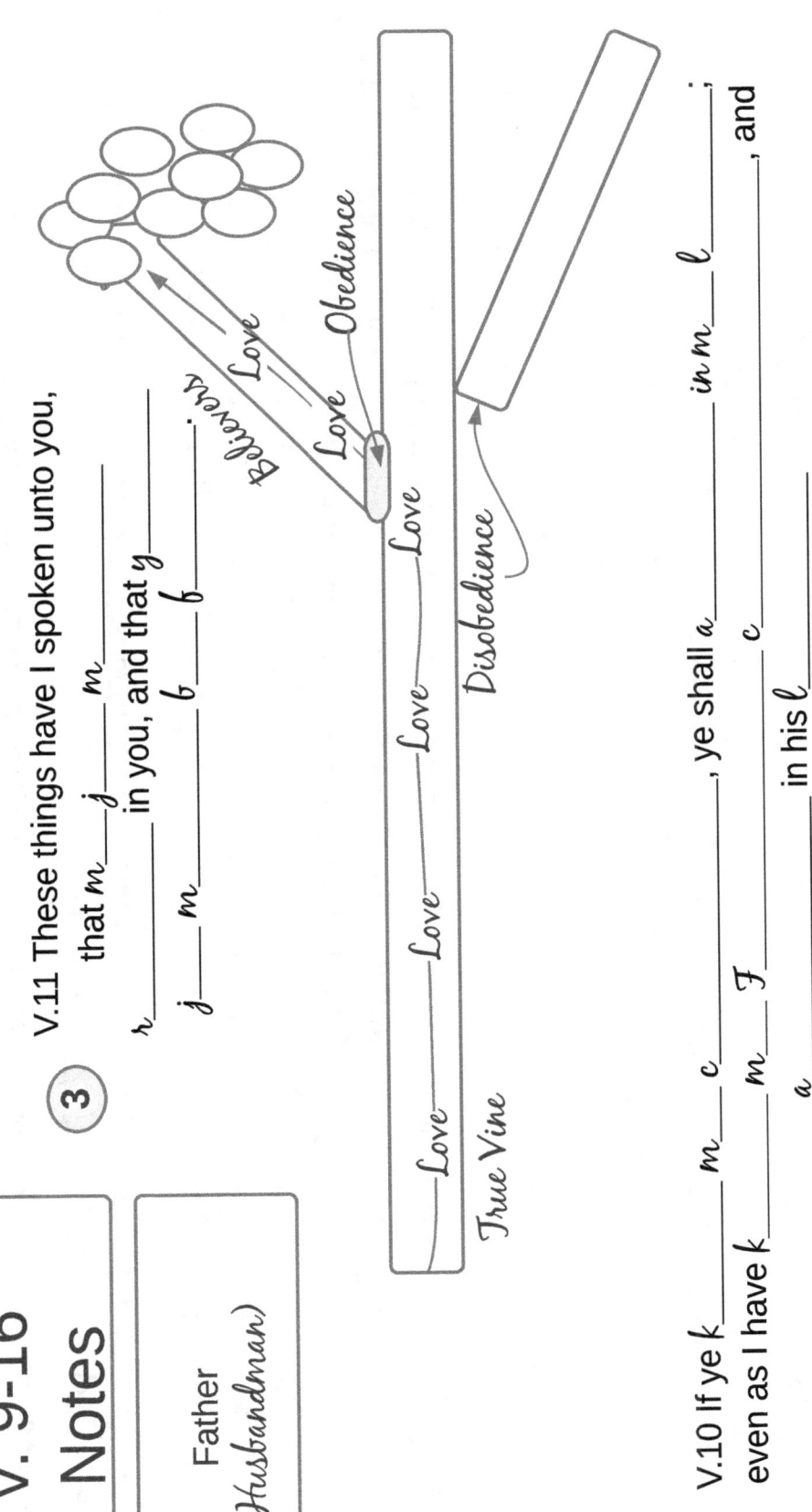

Love — Love — Love — Love
Love

True Vine

Abide Love

Obedience

Disobedience

(2) V.10 If ye k____ m____ c_____, ye shall a____ in m____ l____ ;
even as I have k____ m____ F____ c____
a____ in his l____, and

(4) V.12 This is m____ c_____, That ye l____ o____
a____, as h____ l____ y____.

CHAPTER 15
V. 16
Guide

Father
(Husbandman)

True Vine

Fruit of the Spirit brings joys

Getting ready to go to heaven and doesn't want to leave them sorrowful. He assures them they can still have their petitions granted eventhough He is not on earth.

We can determine whether our fruit remains by keeping His commandments and abiding in His love.

Love — Love — Love — Love

Love

Branches

Love

appointed or prepared

Speaking to his disciples

1. V.16 Ye have not chosen me, but I have chosen you, and ordained you, that ye should go and bring forth fruit, and that your fruit should remain: that whatsoever ye shall ask of the Father in my name, he may give it you.

The Disciples were ordained they should go and bring forth fruit and their fruit would remain. The church multiplied and grew.

The Father loves the Son because He kept the Father's commandments. He will give them their petitions when they ask in the name of His Son.

John 5:14 And this is the confidence that we have in him, that, if we ask any thing ACCORDING TO HIS WILL, he heareth us: (He heareth us if we ask according to His will.)

John 5:15 And IF we know that he hear us, whatsoever we ask, we know that we have the petitions that we desired of him. Because we asked according to His will.

John 15:7 If ye abide in me, and my words abide in you, ye shall ask what ye will, and it shall be done unto you.

James 4:3 Ye ask, and receive not, because ye ask amiss, that ye may consume it upon your lusts.

CHAPTER 15
V. 16
Notes

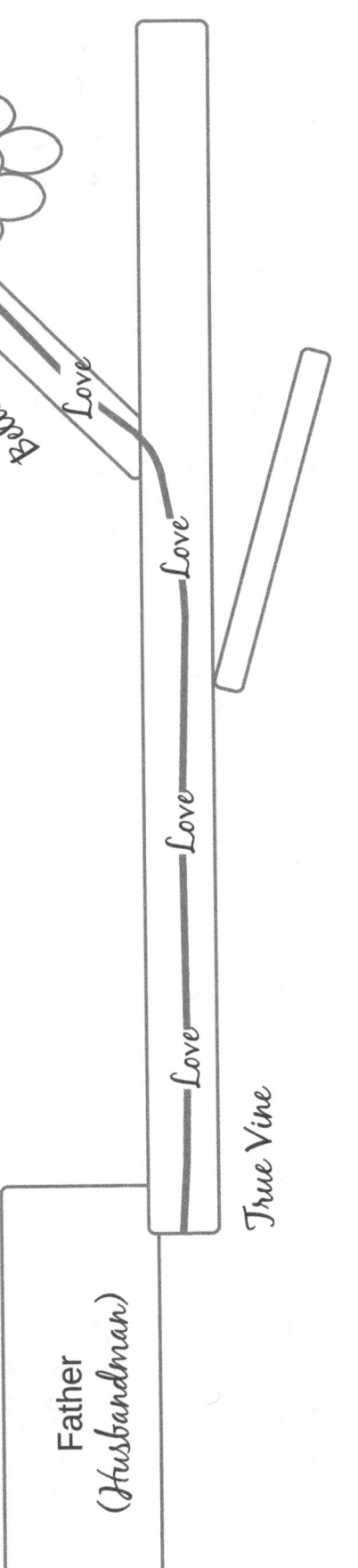

Father (Husbandman)

True Vine

Love

Love

Love

Love

Love

Believers

1. V.16 Ye have not chosen me, but I have chosen you, and ordained you, that ye should _go_ _____ and _b_____ _f_____ fruit, and that _y_____ _f_____ _s_____ _h_____ : that _w_____ ye shall ask of the Father in _m_____ _n_____, he may give it you.

CHAPTER 15
V. 17-24
Guide

He did not say this thing rather these things. so

① V.17 These things I command you, that ye love one another.

He commanded these things, so that we can love one another. These things are abiding in Him, keeping His commandments, abiding in His word and abiding in His love. These things bring forth the Fruits of the Spirit. Without doing these things, we could not love one another and would have works of the flesh.

Galatians 5:15...ye bite and devour one another

Works of the flesh

Galatians 5:19 ...Adultery, fornication, uncleanness, lasciviousness,
Galatians 5:20 Idolatry, witchcraft, hatred, variance, emulations, wrath, strife, seditions, heresies,
Galatians 5:21 Envyings, murders, drunkenness, revellings, and such like:

V.24 If I had not done among them the works which none other man did, they had not had sin: but now have they both seen and hated both me and my Father.

Had they not seen the True Vine, they would not have been condemned for their own fruit.

Matthew 7:18 A good tree cannot bring forth evil fruit, neither can a corrupt tree bring forth good fruit.

works of flesh

Text

works of flesh

work of flesh

works of flesh

Corrupt Tree

Does not know the Husbandman God.
The one who planted the vineyard.

Galatians 5:14... Thou shalt love thy neighbour as thyself

Fruits of The Spirit

Galatians 5:22 But the fruit of the Spirit is love, joy, peace, longsuffering, gentleness, goodness, faith,
Galatians 5:23 Meekness, temperance:

Believers

Holy Spirit

Holy Spirit

Holy Spirit

Holy Spirit

True Vine

V.23 He that hateth me hateth my Father also.

If you hate the True Vine you will hate the Husbandman that chose to plant it.

CHAPTER 15
V. 17-24
Notes

① V.17 These t_____
a_____ I command you, that ye l_____ o_____.

② V.23 He that
h_____ m_____
h_____ m_____
F_____ also.

③ V.24 If I h_____ n_____ among them the works which none other man did, t_____ h_____ n_____ h_____ s_____: but now have they both seen and hated both me and my Father.

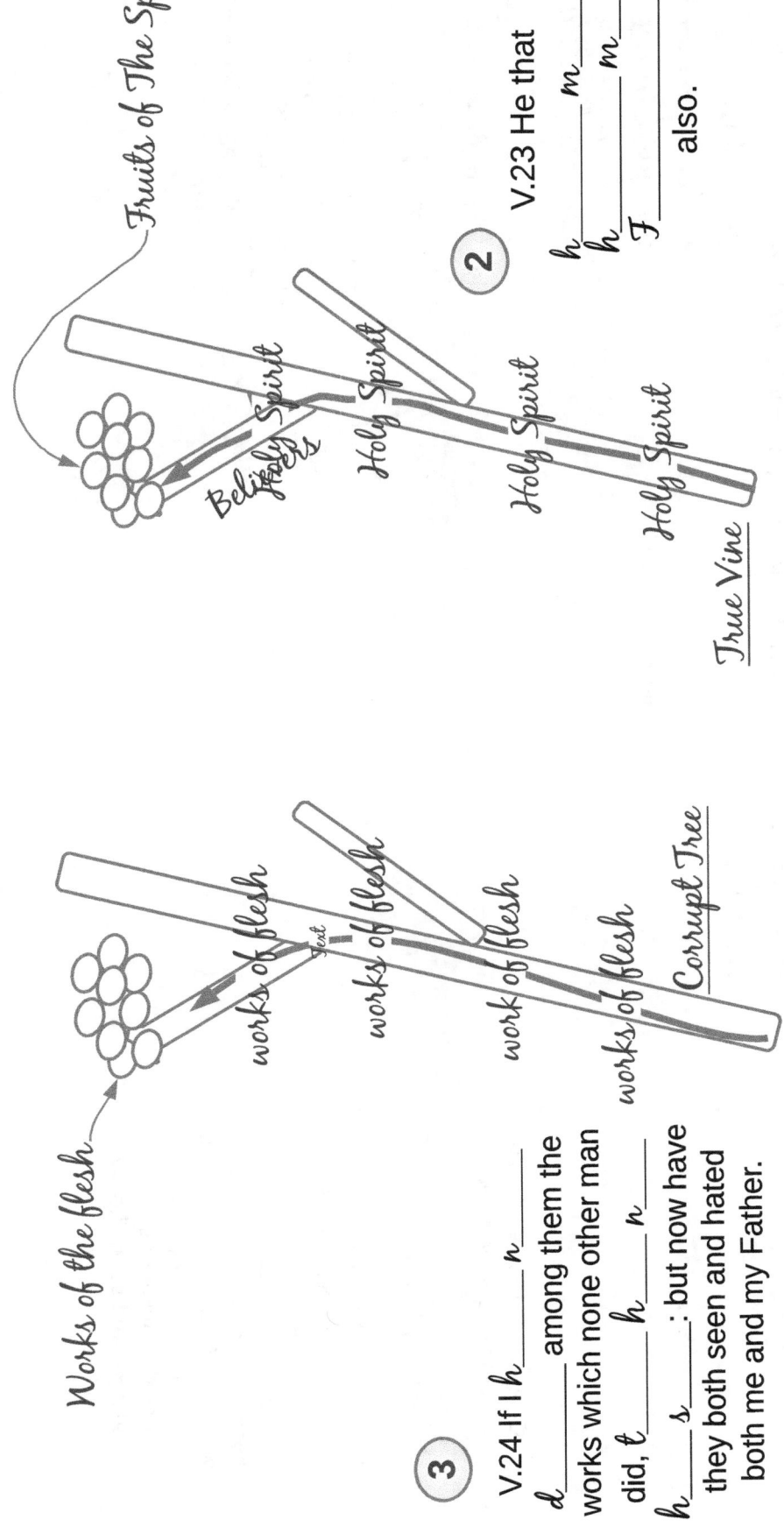

Fruits of The Spirit

Believers

Holy Spirit

Holy Spirit

Holy Spirit

True Vine

Works of the flesh

works of flesh

works of flesh

work of flesh

works of flesh

Corrupt Tree

CHAPTER 15
V. 25-27
Guide

1. John V.25 But this cometh to pass, that the word might be fulfilled that is written in their law, They *hated me* without a cause.

without a cause

Works of the flesh bite and devour one another but Fruit of the Spirit is love thy neighbor. No cause to hate Him.

Galatians 5:14... Thou shalt love thy neighbour as thyself

Fruits of The Spirit

Galatians 5:22 But the fruit of the Spirit is love, joy, peace, longsuffering, gentleness, goodness, faith, Galatians 5:23 Meekness, temperance:

Love
Love
Love
Love

The Flesh

Holy Spirit = Spirit of Truth (Comforter)

Galatians 5:15...ye bite and devour one another

Works of the flesh

Galatians 5:19 ...Adultery, fornication, uncleanness, lasciviousness,
Galatians 5:20 Idolatry, witchcraft, hatred, variance, emulations, wrath, strife, seditions, heresies,
Galatians 5:21 Envyings, murders, drunkenness, revellings, and such like:

2. V.26 But when the *Comforter* is come, whom I will send unto you from the Father, *even the Spirit of truth*, which proceedeth from the Father, he shall *testify* of me: John 15:27 And ye also shall *bear witness*, because ye have been with me from the beginning.

Jesus has many witnesses and testimonies that He is true.

CHAPTER 15

V. 25-27

Notes

1 V. 25 But this cometh to pass, that the word might be fulfilled that is written in their law, They h_____

m_____ w_____ a c_____ .

Works of the flesh

The Flesh

Fruits of The Spirit

Love

Love

Love

Love

Love

2 V.26 But when the C_____ of t_____

the S_____ of me:

t_____ of me:

V.27 And ye also shall b_____ w_____

beginning.

is come, whom I will send unto you from the Father, which proceedeth from the Father, he shall

, because ye have been with me from the

Read John
Chapter 16

CHAPTER 16
V. 1-11
Guide

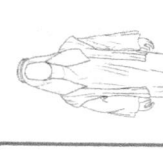

V.1 These things have I spoken unto you, that ye should *not be offended*.

offend means to harm. That you should not be harmed.

V.4 But these things have I told you, that when the time shall come, ye may remember that I told you of them. And these things I said not unto you at the beginning, *because I was with you.*

God gave us His Word so that we can have confidence. Nothing happens that He is not in control of.

V.5 But now I go my way to him that sent me; and none of you asketh me, *Whither goest thou?*

V.6 But because I have said these things unto you, sorrow *hath filled your heart.*

They should be happy for Jesus that He is going home to heaven to be with the Father in glory and we shall receive the Holy Spirit which is expedient for us.

Jesus didn't want them to be sorrowful (profitable)

V.7 Nevertheless I tell you the truth; It is *expedient* for you that I go away: for if I go not away, the *Comforter* will not come unto you; but if I depart, I will send him unto you. (Holy Spirit) *It is more profitable for us that the Holy Spirit dwells within us than for us to see Jesus manifest in the flesh.*

V.8 And when he is come, he will *reprove* the world of *sin*, and of *righteousness, and of judgment:*

reprove—convince of a fault

V.9 Of *sin*, because they believe not on me;

V.10 Of *righteousness*, because I go to my Father, and ye see me no more;

V.11 Of *judgment*, because the *prince of this world* is judged.

Hebrews 10:16 This is the covenant that I will make with them after those days, saith the Lord, I will put my laws into their hearts, and in their minds will I write them;

John 12:31 Now is the judgment of this world: now shall the prince of this world be cast out.

Jesus will no longer speak of righteousness. It will be done through the Holy Spirit.

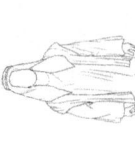

CHAPTER 16
V. 1-11
Notes

V.1 These things have I spoken unto you, that ye should n_____ t_____ o_____.

V.4 But these things have I told you, that when the time shall come, ye may remember that I told you of them. And these things I said not unto you at the beginning, b_____ I w_____ w_____ y_____.

V.5 But now I g_____ m_____ w_____ to h_____ that sent me; and none of you asketh me, W_____ g_____ t_____?

V.6 But because I have said these things unto you, s_____ h_____ f_____ y_____ h_____.

V.7 N_____ I tell you the truth; It is e_____ for you that I go away: for if I go not away, the C_____ will not come unto you; but if I depart, I will send him unto you.

V.8 And when he is come, he will r_____ the world of s_____, and of r_____, and of j_____:

V.9 Of s_____, because they believe not on me;

V.10 Of r_____, because I go to my Father, and ye see me no more;

V.11 Of j_____, because the p_____ of this w_____ is judged.

Mediterranean Sea

Galilee

Damascus
• Caesarea Philippi
• Canatha
Tyre
• Dion
Capernum • Sea of Galilee
Hippus
• Raphana
Nazareth
• Gadara
Scythopolis
• Pella
R. Yarmuk
R. Jabbok
• Gerasa
• Philadelphia
Joppa
Jerusalem •
Judea
• Beersheba
Dead Sea
R. Arnon

THE DECAPOLIS

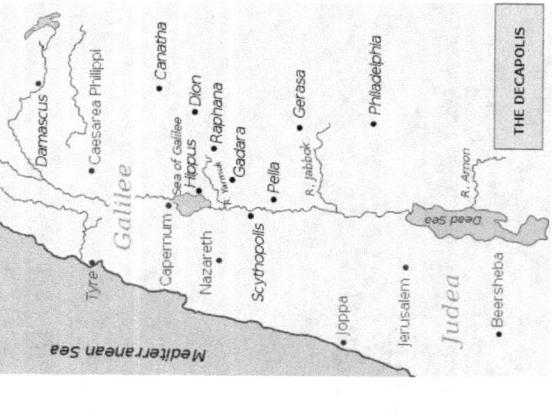

THE DECAPOLIS

hour (time)

Jesus' hour is come that many shall be born again.

CHAPTER 16
V. 12-24
Guide

The Son spoke as the Father commanded, so the Holy Spirit will not speak of Himself.

(Holy Spirit)

V.13 Howbeit when he, the Spirit of truth, is come, he will guide you into all truth: for he shall not speak of himself; but whatsoever he shall hear, that shall he speak: and he will shew you things to come.

(prophecy)

V.14 He shall glorify me: for he shall receive of mine, and shall shew it unto you.

V.15 All things that the Father hath are mine: therefore said I, that he shall take of mine, and shall shew it unto you.

The Holy Spirit receives it from Jesus because all things of the Father is His also.

(Prophecy—Heavenly witness)

John 16:20 Verily, verily, I say unto you, That ye shall weep and lament, but the world shall rejoice: and ye shall be sorrowful, but your sorrow shall be turned into joy. (resurrection)

John 16:21 A woman when she is in travail hath sorrow, because her hour is come: but as soon as she is delivered of the child, she remembereth no more the anguish, for joy that a man is born into the world.

resurrection

John 16:22 And ye now therefore have sorrow: but I will see you again, and your heart shall rejoice, and your joy no man taketh from you. (eternal life)

John 16:23 And in that day ye shall ask me nothing. Verily, verily, I say unto you, Whatsoever ye shall ask the Father in my name, he will give it you. (Father loves the Son)

John 16:24 Hitherto have ye asked nothing in my name: ask, and ye shall receive, that your joy may be full.   Emphasis is that we can ask the Father in Jesus name, so that our prayers are heard while Jesus is away. The Father will hear us through the Holy Spirit.

CHAPTER 16
V. 12-24
Notes

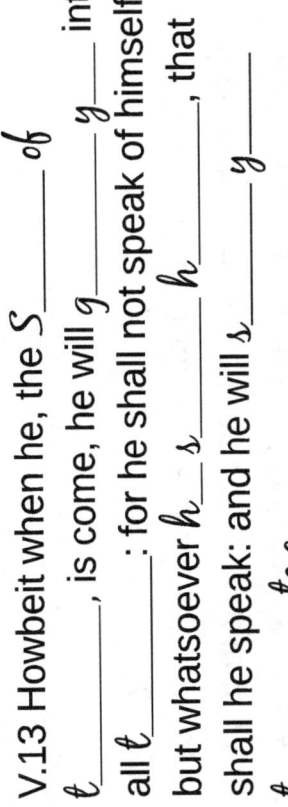

V.13 Howbeit when he, the S_____ of t_____, is come, he will g_____ y_____ into all t_____: for he shall not speak of himself; but whatsoever h____ s____ h_____, that shall he speak: and he will s_____ y_____ t_____ to c_____.

V.14 He shall glorify me: for he shall r_____ of m_____, and shall s_____ it unto you.

V.15 A____ t_____ that the Father hath a____ m_____: therefore said I, that he shall take of mine, and shall shew it unto you.

V.20 V_____, v_____, I s_____ unto you, That ye shall weep and lament, but the world shall rejoice: and ye shall be sorrowful, but your s_____ shall be turned into j_____.

V.21 A woman when she is in t_____ hath s_____, because her h____ is c_____: but as soon as she is delivered of the child, she remembereth no more the anguish, for joy that a man is born into the world.

V.22 And ye n_____ therefore have s_____: but I will see you again, and your heart shall rejoice, and your j_____ n____ m____ t____ from you.

V.23 And in that day ye shall ask me nothing. V_____, v_____, I s_____ unto you, Whatsoever ye shall ask the Father i____ m____ n_____, he will give it you. John 16:24 Hitherto have ye asked nothing in my name: ask, and ye shall receive, that your j_____ may be f_____.

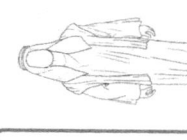

CHAPTER 16
V. 25-33
Guide

V.25 These things have I spoken unto you in proverbs: but the time cometh, when I shall no more speak unto you in proverbs, but I shall *shew you plainly of the Father.*

V.26 At that day ye shall ask in my name: and I say *not unto you, that I will pray the Father* for you:

V.27 For the *Father himself loveth you, because ye have loved me, and have believed that I came out from God.*

V.28 I came forth from the Father, and am come into the world: again, I leave the world, and go to the Father.   *(Told them plainly)*

V.29 His disciples said unto him, Lo, *now speakest thou plainly, and speakest no* proverb. *(Already believed because of the works and now believe the words.)*

      disciples   *Jesus*

V.30 Now *are we sure that thou knowest all things, and needest not that any man should ask thee:* by this we believe that thou camest forth from God.

V.31 Jesus answered them, Do ye now *believe?*

V.32 Behold, the *hour cometh,* yea, is now come, that ye shall be *scattered,* every man to his own, and shall *leave me alone:* and yet I am not alone, because the *Father is with me.*

V.33 These things I have spoken unto you, that in me ye might have *peace.* In the *world* ye shall have *tribulation:* but be of good cheer; *I have overcome the world.*

John 5:5 <u>Who is he that overcometh the world, but he that believeth that Jesus is the Son of God?</u>

CHAPTER 16
V. 25-33
Notes

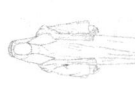

V.25 These things have I spoken unto you in proverbs: but the time cometh, when I shall no more speak unto you in proverbs, but I shall s_____ you p_____ of _the_ F_____.

V.26 At that day ye shall ask in my name: and I say n_____ unto you, that I will _pray_ the F_____ for you:

V.27 For the F_____ himself l_____ y_____, b_____, l_____ m_____, and have b_____ that I c_____ out b_____ g_____.

V.28 I came forth from the Father, and am come into the world: again, I leave the world, and go to the Father.

V.29 His disciples said unto him, Lo, now s_____ thou p_____, and speakest no proverb.

V.30 Now a_____ w_____ s_____ that t_____ k_____ a_____ t_____, and needest not that any man should ask thee: by this we believe that thou camest forth from God.

V.31 Jesus answered them, Do ye now b_____?

V.32 Behold, the h_____ c_____, yea, is now come, that ye shall be s_____, every man to his own, and shall l_____ m_____ a_____: and yet I am not alone, because the F_____ is _with_ m_____.

V.33 These things I have spoken unto you, that in me ye might have p_____. In the w_____ ye shall have t_____; but be of good cheer, _h_____ o_____ _the w_____

Read John
Chapter 17

CHAPTER 17
V. 1-5
Guide

Jesus prays plainly to the Father

V.1 These words spake Jesus, and *lifted up* his eyes to heaven, and said, *Father, the hour is come; glorify thy Son, that thy Son also may glorify thee:*

V.2 As thou hast given him *power over all flesh,*

that he should *give eternal life* to as many as *thou hast given him.* (*Jesus did not give all 12 disciples eternal life. Judas was to betray Him as the scriptures says. So Judas was not given to Jesus by the Father.*)

V.3 And this is *life eternal,* that they might know thee the *only true God,* and *Jesus Christ,* whom thou hast sent.

V.4 I have *glorified thee* on the earth: *I have finished the work* which thou gavest me to do.

V.5 And now, O Father, *glorify thou me* with thine own self with the *glory which I had* with thee before the world was. (*Jesus was with God before the world was created.*)

CHAPTER 17
V. 1-5
Notes

Jesus prays plainly to the Father

V.1 These words spake J_____, and l_____ u_____ his e_____ t_____ h_____, and said, F_____, the h_____ i_____ c_____; g_____ t_____ : g_____; that t_____ S_____ a_____ m_____ g_____ :

V.2 As thou hast given him p_____ o_____ a_____ b_____, to as m_____ e_____ l_____ to as m_____ h_____ a_____ t_____ h_____ g_____ h_____.

V.3 And this is l_____ e_____, that they might know thee the o_____ t_____ g_____, and J_____ C_____, whom thou hast s_____.

V.4 I have g_____ t_____ on the earth: h_____ b_____ the w_____ which thou gavest me to do.

V.5 And now, O Father, g_____ t_____ m_____ with thine own self with the g_____ w_____ h_____ with thee b_____ the w_____ w_____.

CHAPTER 17
V. 6-12
Guide

The Disciples

V.6 I have *manifested thy name* unto the *men* which thou *gavest* me out of the world: thine they were, and *thou gavest them me; and they have kept thy word.* (obedience)

John 15:16 Ye have not chosen me, but I have chosen you, and ordained you, that ye should go and bring forth fruit, and that your fruit should remain: that whatsoever ye shall ask of the Father in my name, he may give it you. *(Speaking to the Disciples)*

V.7 Now they have known that *all things* whatsoever thou hast *given me are of thee.*

V.8 For I have given unto them *the words* which thou *gavest me; and they have received them,* and have *known surely* that I came out from thee, and they have *believed* that thou didst *send me.*

V.9 I pray *for them:* I pray *not for the world,* but for them which thou hast given me; for *they are thine.*

V.10 And all *mine are thine, and thine are mine;* and I am glorified in them.

V.11 And now I am no more in the world, but these are in the world, and I come to thee. Holy Father, *keep* through *thine own name* those whom thou hast given me, that *they may be one, as we are.*

V.12 While I was with them in the world, I kept them in thy name: those that thou gavest me I have kept, and *none of them is lost,* but *the son of perdition; that the scripture might be fulfilled.* *(Judas was the son of perdition)* *Perdition means eternal death.*

CHAPTER 17
V. 6-12
Notes

The Disciples

V.6 I have m_____ t____ n____ unto the m_____ which thou g_____ m_____ out of the world: thine they were, and t____ g____ th_____ me; and they have k____ t____ w____ . (obedience)

V.7 Now they have known that a____ t____ whatsoever thou hast g_____ m_____ are of t_____ .

V.8 For I have given unto them the w_____ which thou g_____ m_____; and they have r_____ t____, and have k____ s_____ that I came out from thee, and they have b_____ thou didst s____ m____ .

V.9 I pray f____ t____ : I pray n____ for the w_____ , but for them which thou hast given me; for t____ are t____ .

V.10 And all m_____ are t____ , and t____ are m_____ ; and I am glorified in them.

V.11 And now I am no more in the world, but these are in the world, and I come to thee. Holy Father, k____ through t____ o____ n____ those whom thou hast given me, that t____ may be o_____ , as w____ a____ .

V.12 While I was with them in the world, I kept them in thy name: those that thou gavest me I have kept, and n_____ of t____ is l_____ , but the s_____ of p_____ ; that the s_____ m_____ be f____ .

V.13 And now come I to thee; and these things I speak in the world, that they might have *my joy fulfilled in themselves.*

V.14 I have given *them thy word;* and *the world hath hated them,* because they are not of the world, even as *I am not of the world.*

disciples

V.15 I pray *not* that thou shouldest take them *out of the world,* but that thou shouldest *keep them from the evil.*

V.16 They are not of the *world,* even as I am not of the *world.*

V.17 *Sanctify* them *through thy truth:* thy *word is truth.* (*Sanctify means to separate, cleanse or make holy*)

V.18 As thou hast *sent me* into the world, even so have I also *sent them* into the world.

V.19 And for *their sakes I sanctify myself,* that they also might be *sanctified through the truth.*

CHAPTER 17
V. 13-19
Notes

V.13 And now come I to thee; and these things I speak in the world, that they might have m_____ j_____ f_____ in t_____.

V.14 I have g_____ t_____ t_____ w_____; and the w_____ hath h_____ t_____, because they are not of the world, even as _____ am n_____ of the w_____. disciples

V.15 I pray not that thou shouldest take them o_____ of the w_____, but that thou shouldest k_____ t_____ f_____ the e_____.

V.16 They are not of the w_____, even as I am not of the w_____.

V.17 S_____ them t_____ thy t_____: thy w_____ is t_____.

V.18 As thou hast s_____ m_____ into the world, even so have I also s_____ t_____ into the world.

V.19 And for t_____ s_____ I s_____ m_____, that they also might be s_____ t_____ the t_____.

CHAPTER 17
V. 20-26
Guide

V. 20 Neither pray I for these alone, but for them also which shall *believe on me through their word;*

all believers   soulwinning

V.21 That *they* all may be one; as thou, *Father, art in me, and I in thee,* that they also may be one in us: that *the world may believe that thou hast sent me.* (God's plan for soulwinning)

V.22 And the *glory which thou gavest me I have given them;* that *they may be one, even as we are one:*

V.23 *I in them, and thou in me,* that they may be made *perfect in one;* and that the *world may know that thou hast sent me, and hast loved them,* as thou hast loved me.

Matthew 5:48 Be ye therefore perfect, even as your Father which is in heaven is perfect.
(Perfect means complete or mature)

V. 24 Father, I will that they also, whom thou hast given me, be with me *where I am;* that they may *behold my glory,* which thou hast given me: for thou *lovedst me before the foundation of the world.*

V.25 O righteous Father, the world hath not known thee: but I have known thee, and these *have known that thou hast sent me.*

V.26 And I have declared unto them thy name, and will declare it: *that the love wherewith thou hast loved me may be in them, and I in them.*

Jesus asked these things of the Father
#1 That all believers and the disciples would be one, with Him and the Father that the world may believe. V.21
#2 That we may be one in the glory that the Father has given Him, so they world may know He was sent .
#3 That we may become perfect (mature) in One
#4 That we may be with Him where He is.

CHAPTER 17
V. 20-26
Notes

all believers

V. 20 Neither pray I for these alone, but for them also which shall b_____ on me t_____
t_____ w_____; (soulwinning)

V.21 That t_____ all may be o_____; as thou, F_____, art i_____ m_____, and i_____
t_____, that they also may be o_____ in u_____: that thou hast that the w_____ m_____ b_____
s_____ m_____.

V.22 And the g_____ which thou gavest me I have g_____ t_____; that t_____ m_____ be
o_____, even as w_____ are o_____:

V.23 i_____ t_____, and t_____ i_____ m_____, that they may be made p_____ in o_____;
and that the w_____ m_____ k_____ that t_____ hast s_____ m_____, and h_____ l_____, as
thou hast l_____ m_____.

V. 24 Father, I will that they also, whom thou hast given me, be with me w_____ a_____; that
they may b_____ m_____ g_____, which thou hast given me: for thou l_____ m_____
b_____ the f_____ of the w_____.

V.25 O righteous Father, the world hath not known thee: but I have known thee, and these h_____
k_____ t_____ h_____ s_____ m_____.

V.26 And I have declared unto them thy name, and will declare it: that the l_____ wherewith thou hast
l_____ me m_____ be i_____ t_____, and i_____ t_____.

Read John
Chapter 18

CHAPTER 18
V. 1-6
Guide

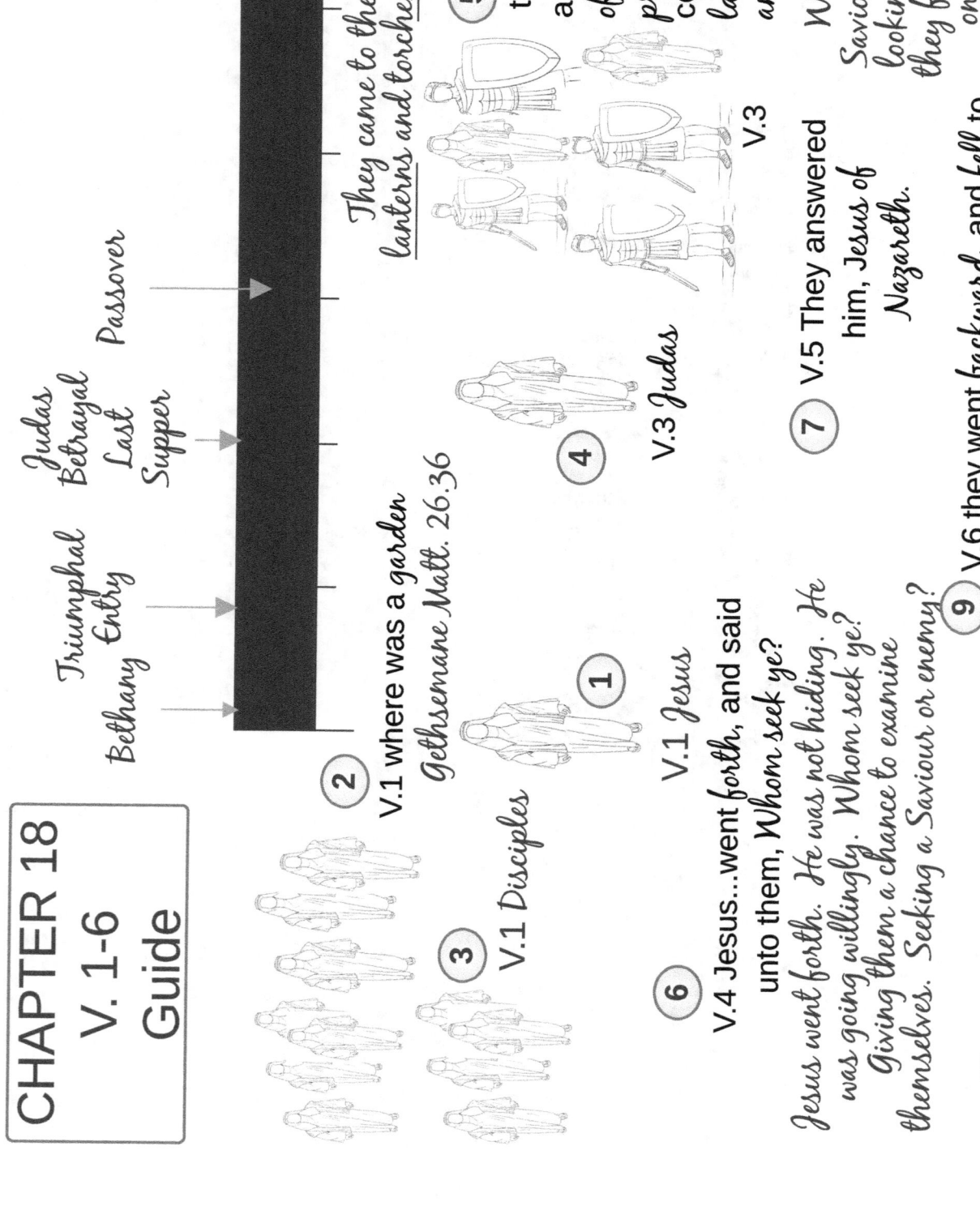

Triumphal Entry
Bethany

Judas
Betrayal
Last
Supper

Passover

2 V.1 where was a garden Gethsemane Matt. 26.36

They came to the True Light with lanterns and torches to light their way.

5 then, having received a band of men and officers from the chief priests and Pharisees, cometh thither with lanterns and torches and weapons.

Were not seeking the Saviour, instead they were looking to capture Him. So they fell backwards and not on their faces before Him…this time.

V.3

4 V.3 Judas

7 V.5 They answered him, Jesus of Nazareth.

9 V.6 they went backward, and fell to the ground.

1 V.1 Jesus

6 V.4 Jesus…went forth, and said unto them, Whom seek ye?

3 V.1 Disciples

Jesus went forth. He was not hiding. He was going willingly. Whom seek ye? Giving them a chance to examine themselves. Seeking a Saviour or enemy?

8 V.6 I am he

CHAPTER 18
V. 1-6
Notes

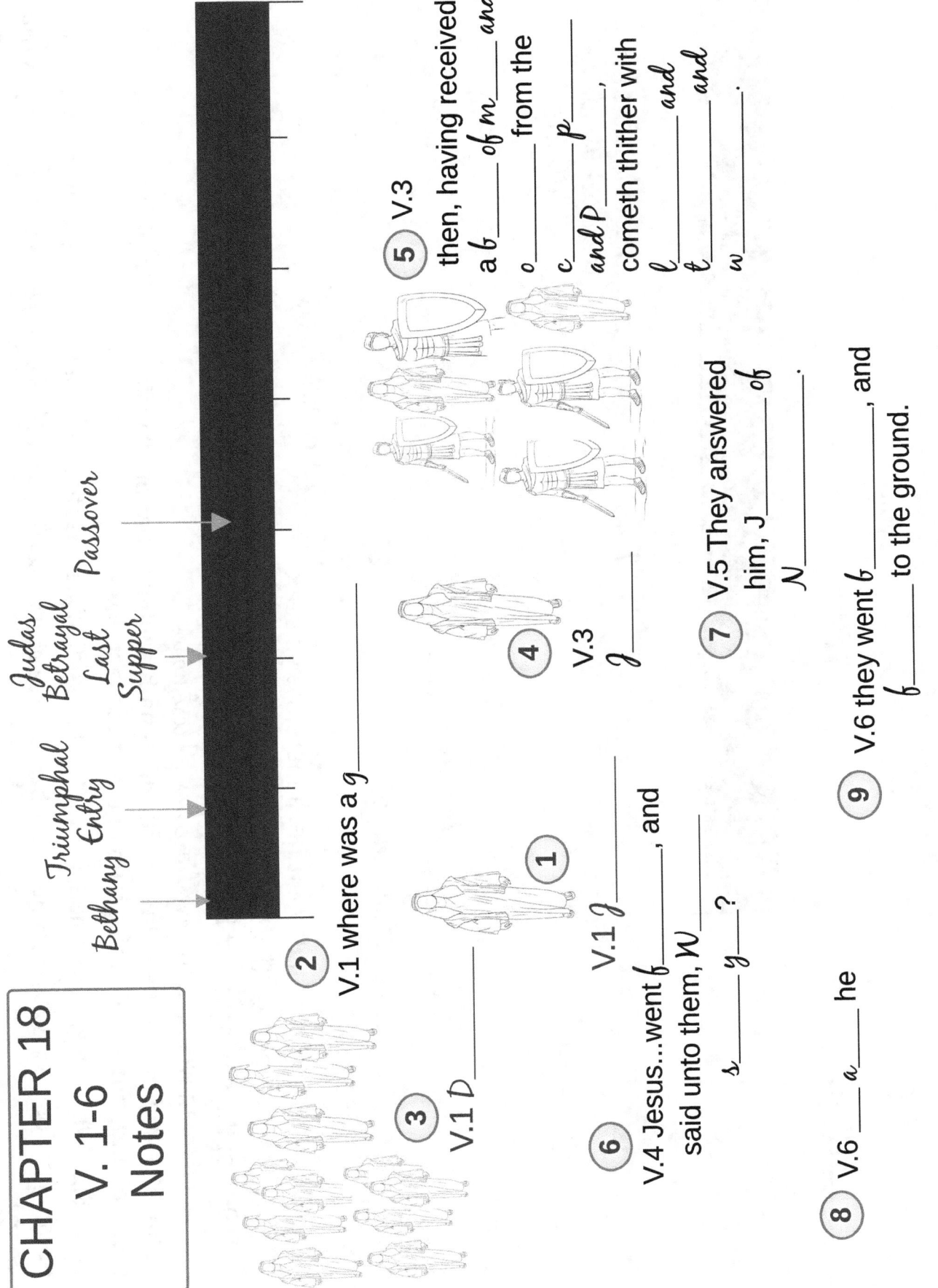

Triumphal Entry
Bethany

Judas
Betrayal
Last
Supper

Passover

2 V.1 where was a g_____

3 V.1 D_____

1 V.1 J_____

6 V.4 Jesus...went f_____, and said unto them, W_____ s_____ y_____?

8 V.6 _____ a_____ he

4 V.3 J_____

5 V.3
then, having received
a b_____ of m_____ and
from the
o_____
c_____ p_____
and P_____, cometh thither with
l_____ and
t_____ and
w_____ .

7 V.5 They answered him, J_____ of N_____ .

9 V.6 they went b_____ , and f_____ to the ground.

CHAPTER 18
V. 7-9
Guide

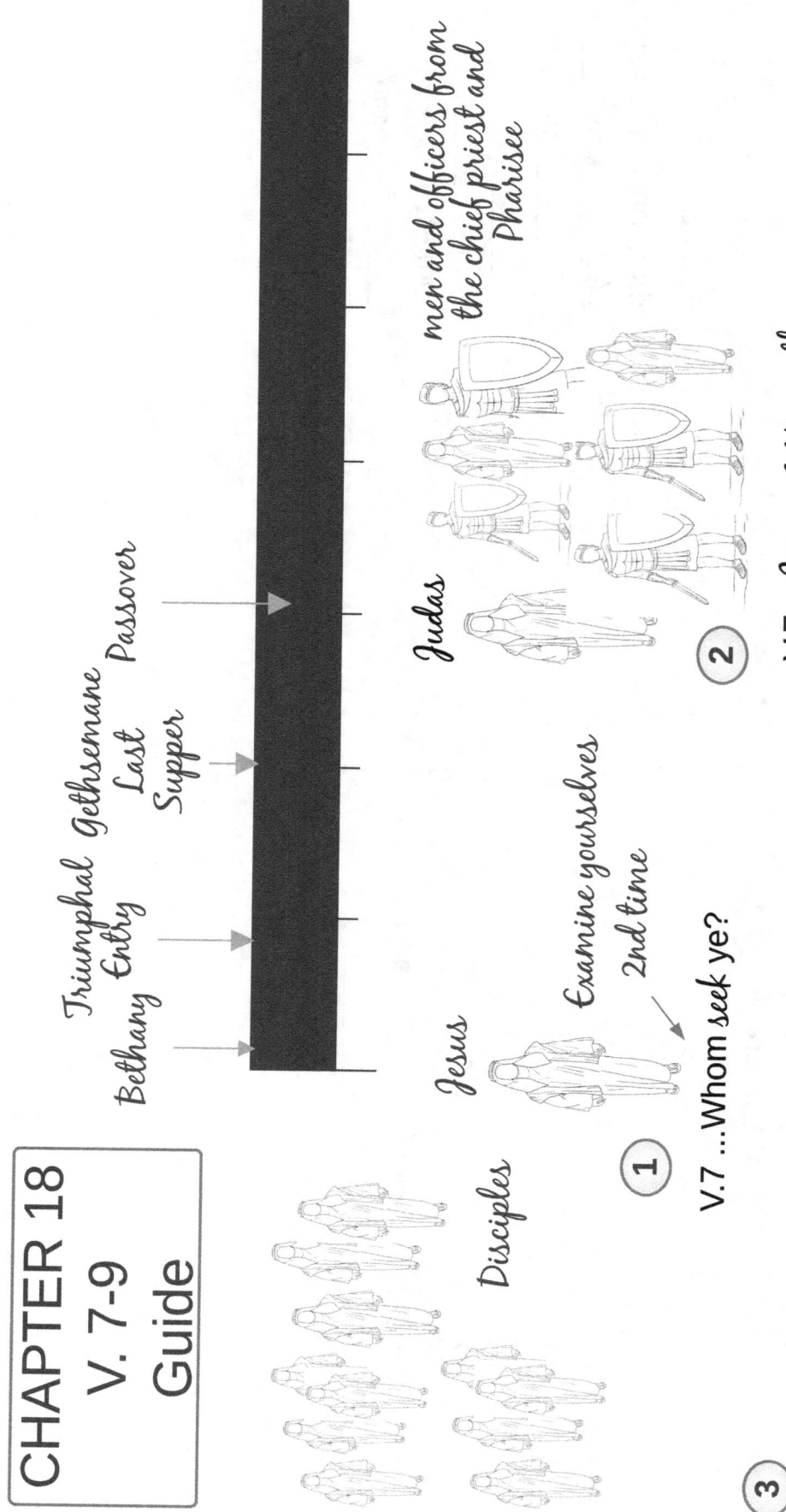

Disciples

Triumphal Gethsemane
Bethany Entry   Last   Passover
                       Supper

Jesus

Examine yourselves
2nd time

(1)

V.7 ...Whom seek ye?

Judas

men and officers from
the chief priest and
Pharisee

(2)   V.7 ...Jesus of Nazareth.

(3) V.8 ... I have told you that I am he: if therefore ye seek
     me, *let these go* their way:

V.9 That the saying might be *fulfilled*, which he spake,
    Of them which thou gavest me have I lost none.

John 6:39 And this is the Father's will which hath sent me, that of all which he hath given me I should lose nothing, but should raise it up again at the last day.

John 6:12 When they were filled, he said unto his disciples, Gather up the fragments that remain, that nothing be lost. *(Jesus looses nothing! Spiritually or physically, even the fragments at the feeding of the 5000)*

CHAPTER 18
V. 7-9
Notes

Bethany Triumphal Gethsemane Last Passover
Entry Supper

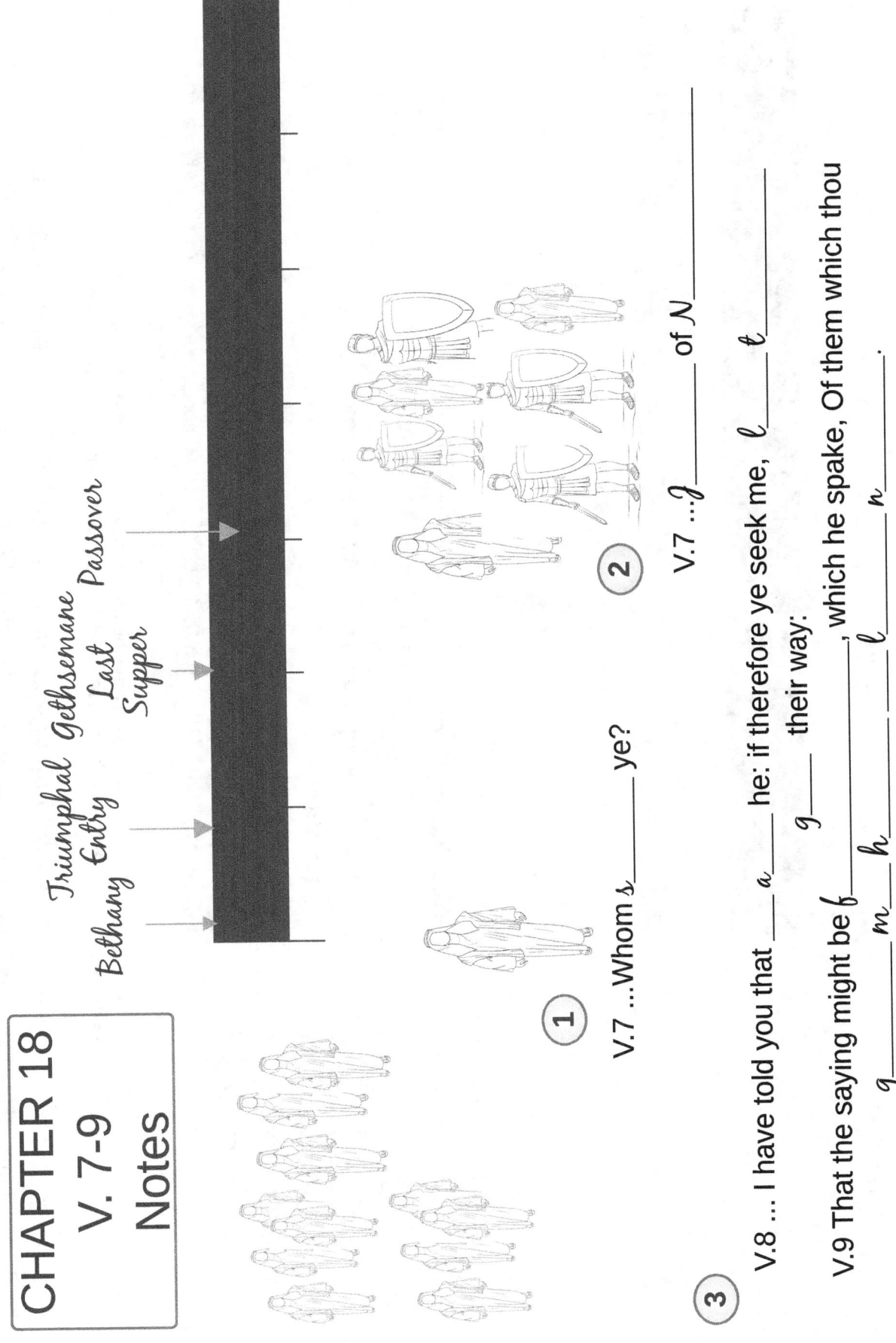

① V.7 ...Whom s_____ ye?

② V.7 ...J_____ of N_____

V.7 ...he: if therefore ye seek me, l___ t___ g_____ their way:

③ V.8 ... I have told you that ___ a_____

V.9 That the saying might be f_____, which he spake, Of them which thou
g_____ m___ h___ I ___ l___ n___.

CHAPTER 18
V. 10-12
Guide

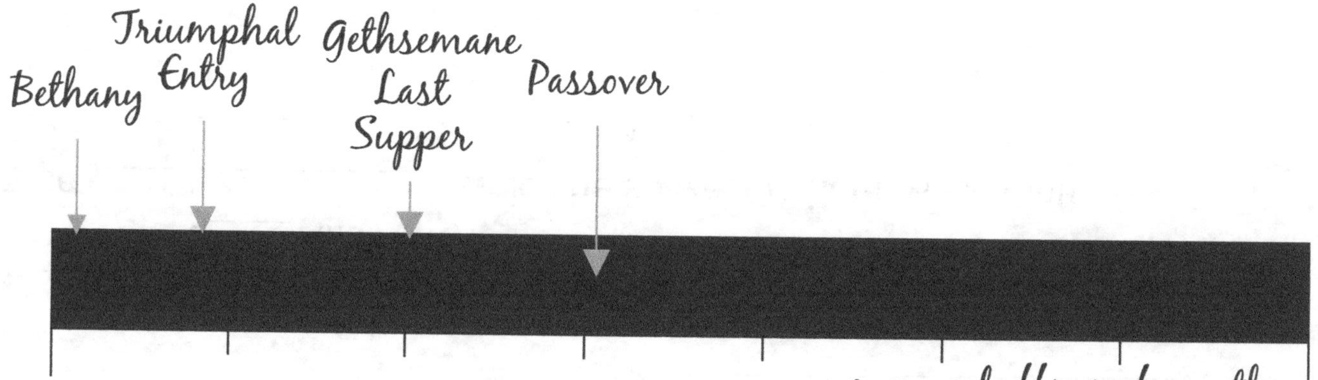

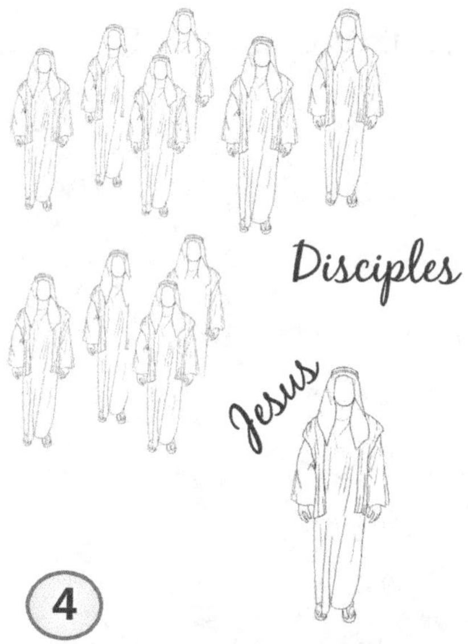

Triumphal Gethsemane
Bethany Entry Last Passover
Supper

men and officers from the
chief priest and Pharisee

Judas

① Simon Peter

V.10 Simon Peter

② V.10 Malchus the
high priest's servant,

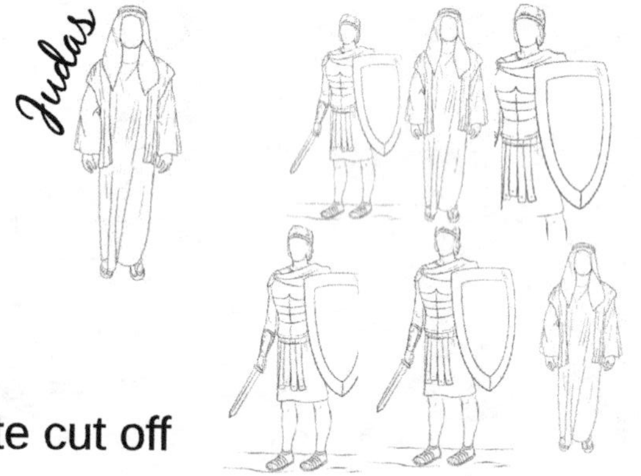

③ V.10 having a sword drew it, and smote cut off
his right ear.

This is not a verse against carrying a weapon. Jesus told Peter to put it
back into its sheath. He did not scold him for carrying one. The
purpose for not using it was so that Jesus could fulfill God's will in the
crucifixion. Later he told the disciples to buy a sword.

Luke 22:36 Then said he unto them, But now, he that hath a purse, let him take it, and
likewise his scrip: and he that hath no sword, let him sell his garment, and buy one.

Disciples

Jesus

④ V. 11 Put up thy sword into
the sheath: the cup which
my Father hath given me,
shall I not drink it?

⑤ V.12 Then the band and the captain and officers of the Jews took Jesus, and bound him,
Only after Peter put his weapon were they free to take Jesus and bound him.

CHAPTER 18
V. 10-12
Notes

Bethany
Triumphal
Entry
Gethsemane
Last
Supper
Passover

men and officers from the
chief priest and Pharisee

Judas

1

2

Disciples

Jesus

V.10 S _____
P _____

V.10 M _____ the h _____
priest's s _____,

3 V.10 h _____ drew it, and
smote cut off his r _____ e _____.

4 V. 11 Put up thy s _____ : the
c _____ which my Father
hath given me, shall I not
d _____ i _____ ?

5 V.12 J _____ the b _____ and the c _____ and o _____ of the
J _____ took Jesus, and bound him,

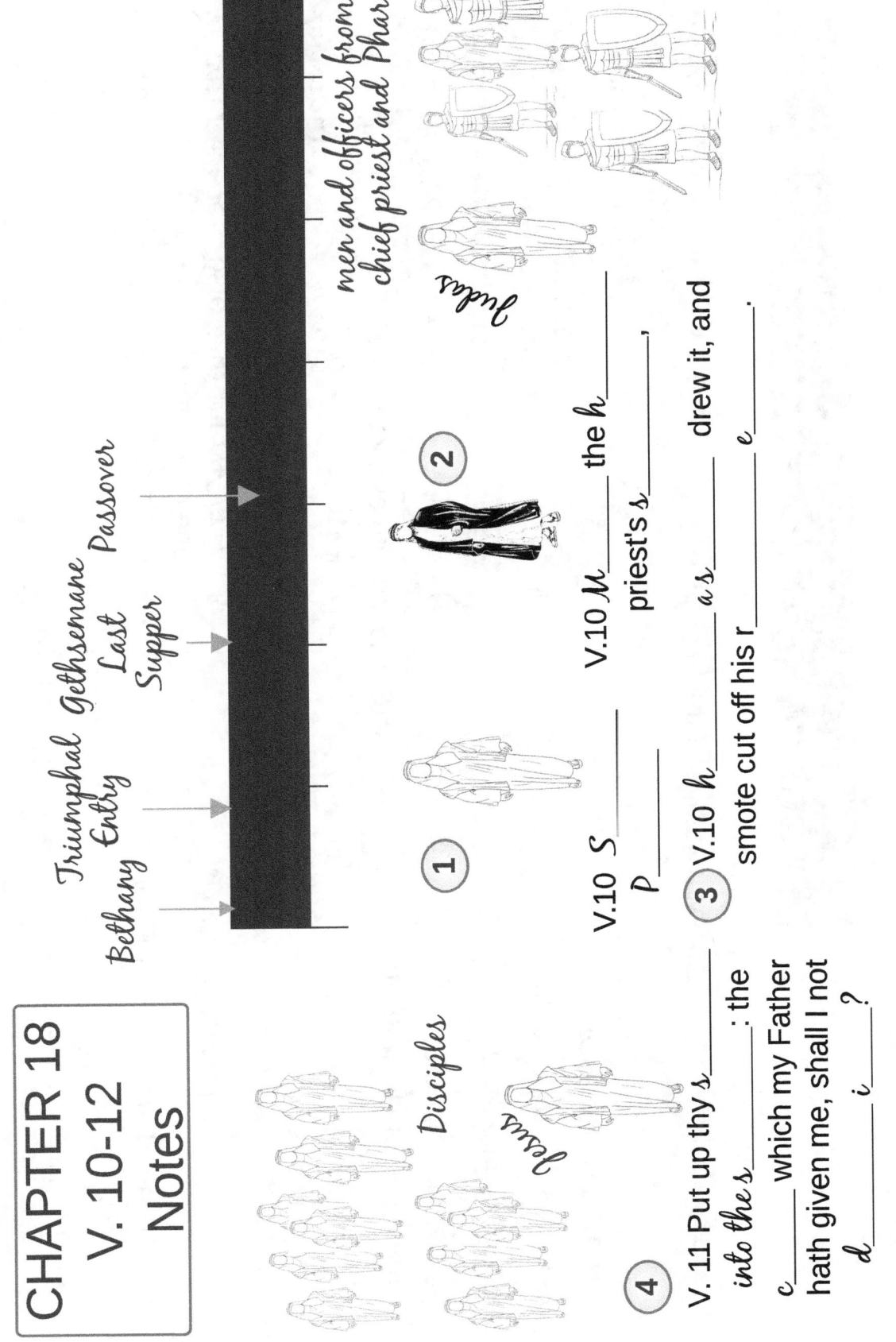

CHAPTER 18
V. 13-17
Guide

Bethany   Triumphal   Gethsemane
           Entry   Last   Judgment Hall
                                       Supper   Passover

6 V.15 *palace of the high priest.*

2 V. 13 for he was *father in law to Caiaphas,* which was the high priest that same year.

V. 14...which gave counsel to the Jews, that it was *expedient* that one man should die for the *people.*

3 Didn't know how true what he was saying? Thought the death of Jesus would save the nation and their positions in the corrupt government.

1 V13 And led him away to *Annas first;*

Jesus (bound)

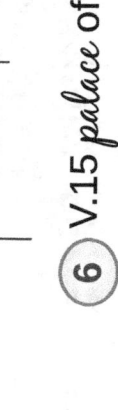

9 V. 17 *Art not thou also* one of this man's disciples?

damsel that kept the door
1st denial was to a woman

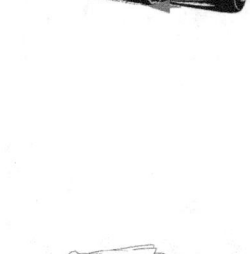

10 V.17 I am not.
1st Denial

5 V. 15 *another disciple: known unto the high priest,* and *went in* with Jesus

8 *spake unto her that kept the door, and brought in* Peter.

4 V.15 *Simon Peter*

7 V.16 stood at the door *without*
(*Without* is opposite of *within*.) means stood outside the door.

CHAPTER 18
V. 13-17
Notes

Triumphal Gethsemane
Bethany Entry Last Judgment Hall
Supper Passover

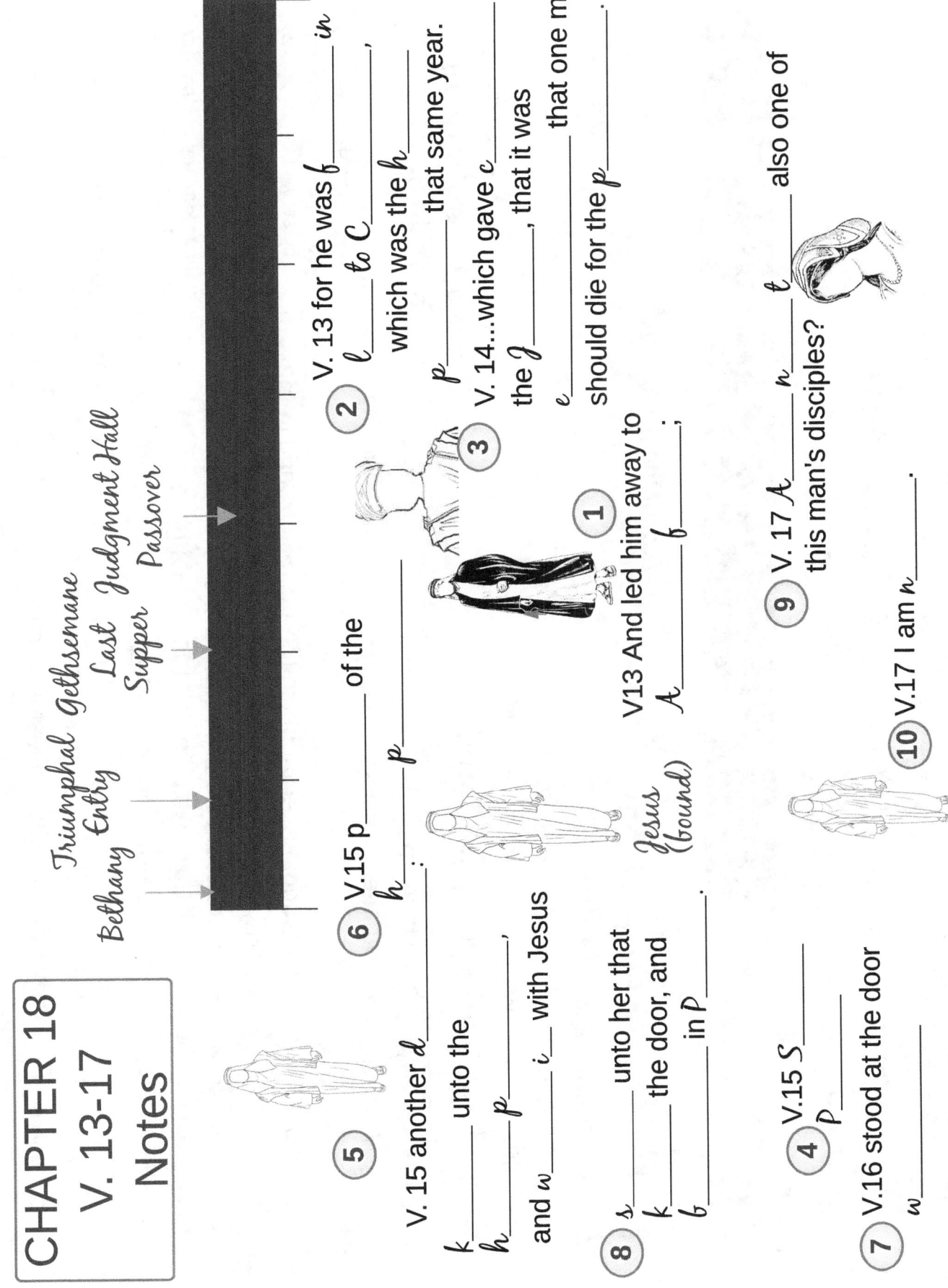

2 V. 13 for he was f_____ in_____,

l_____ to C_____,
which was the *h_____*
p_____ that same year.

3 V. 14...which gave c_____
the *J_____*, that it was
e_____ that one man
should die for the p_____.

1 V13 And led him away to
A_____
f_____ ;

Jesus
(bound)

5 V. 15 another d_____
unto the
k_____
h_____ p_____
and w_____ i_____ with Jesus

6 V.15 p_____ of the
h_____
p_____ :

8 s_____ unto her that
k_____ the door, and
b_____ in P_____ .

4 V.15 S_____
P_____

7 V.16 stood at the door
w_____

9 V. 17 A_____ n_____ t_____ also one of
this man's disciples?

10 V.17 I am n_____ .

CHAPTER 18
V. 18-23
Guide

Triumphal Gethsemane
Bethany Entry   Last   Judgment Hall
                Supper   Passover

palace of the high priest.

Caiaphas

Jesus (bound)

(2) V.19 The *high priest* then asked Jesus of his *disciples,* and of his *doctrine.*

John 15:20 Remember the word that I said unto you, The servant is not greater than his lord. If they have persecuted me, they will also persecute you: if they have kept my saying, they will keep yours also.

will look into a different fire of coals later.

(1) V.18 And the servants and officers stood there, who had made a fire of coals; for it was cold: and they warmed themselves: and *Peter stood with them, and warmed himself.*

(4) V.22...officers which stood by *struck Jesus with the palm of his hand*

(3) V.20 ...I spake openly to the world; I ever taught in the synagogue, and in the temple, whither the *Jews* always resort; and in *secret* have I said *nothing.* (Jesus went up to the feast in secret but he spoke openly when He got there.) V.21 *Why* askest thou me? ask *them* which heard me, what I have said unto them: behold, *they know* what I said. *Witnesses that know Jesus did nothing wrong.*

John 15:27 And ye also shall bear witness, because ye have been with me from the beginning.

(5) V.23 Jesus answered him, If I have spoken evil, *bear witness of the evil:* but if well, why smitest thou me?

CHAPTER 18
V. 18-23
Notes

Triumphal Gethsemane
Bethany Entry   Last   Judgment Hall
            Supper   Passover

Palace of the high priest

Caiaphas

Jesus
(bound.)

(1) V.18 And the s_____ and o_____ stood there, who had made a f_____ of c_____; for it was cold: and they warmed themselves: and P_____ s_____ w_____ t_____, and w_____ h_____.

(2) V.19 The h_____ then asked Jesus p_____ of his d_____, and of his d_____.

(4) V.22...o_____ which stood by s_____ J_____ with the p_____ of his hand

(3) V.20 ...I spake o_____ to the world; I ever taught in the s_____; and in the t_____, whither the J_____ always r_____; and in s_____ have I said n_____.

V.21 W_____ askest thou m_____? ask t_____ which h_____ me, what I have said unto them: behold, t_____ k_____ what I said. V.23 Jesus answered him, If I have spoken evil, b_____ w_____

(5) of the e_____: but if well, why smitest thou me?

CHAPTER 18
V. 24-27
Guide

Triumphal Gethsemane
Bethany Entry   Last   Judgment Hall
                Supper   Passover

Palace of the high priest

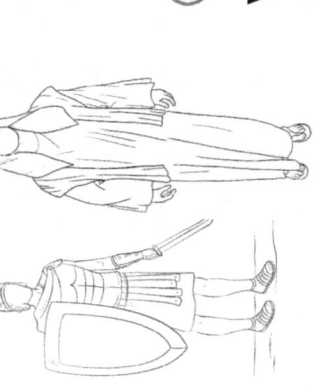

Jesus (bound)

servants and officers stood there... and Peter stood with them, and warmed himself.

① V.24 Caiaphas the high priest

② V.25 And Simon Peter stood and warmed himself. They said therefore unto him, Art not thou also one of his disciples? He denied it, and said, I am not. (2nd Denial)

③ V.26 One of the servants of the high priest, being his kinsman whose ear Peter cut off, saith, Did not I see thee in the garden with him?

④ V.27 Peter then denied again: and immediately the cock crew. 3rd Denial

All 3 times Peter denied Jesus in front of the servants that posed no threat. Not authorities or dignitaries.

In the presence of Jesus, Peter had the boldness to strike a servant of the high priest, without him Peter was fearful.

CHAPTER 18
V. 24-27
Notes

Triumphal   Gethsemane
Bethany Entry   Last   Judgment Hall
                  Supper   Passover

Palace of the high priest

servants and officers stood there... and
Peter stood with them, and warmed
himself.

Jesus (bound)

① V.24 C_____ the
        h_____ p_____

② V.25 And S_____ P_____ stood and w_____
h_____ . They said therefore unto him, A_____ n_____
t_____ also one of his d_____ ?
He d_____ it, and said, I am _____ .

③ V.26 One of the s_____ of
the high priest, being his
k_____ whose e_____
P_____ c_____ o_____ , saith,
Did not I see thee in the garden
with him?

④ V.27 P_____ then d_____ a_____ :
and i_____ the c_____ c_____ .

CHAPTER 18
V. 28-31
Guide

Triumphal Gethsemane Judgment
Entry Hall
Bethany Last Passover
Supper

1 V.28 Then led they Jesus from Caiaphas unto the hall of judgment

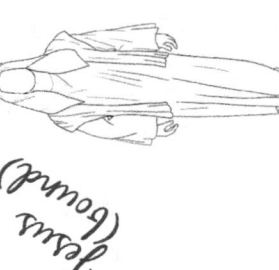

Jews (bound)

2 V.28 and it was early; and they themselves went not into the judgment hall, lest they should be defiled; but that they might eat the passover.

3 V.29 Pilate then went out unto them, and said, What accusation bring ye against this man?

4 V.30 They answered and said unto him, If he were not a malefactor, we would not have delivered him up unto thee. → Had no accusation. Only that He was a criminal.

Malefactor –criminal worthy of capital punishment.

5 V.31 Then said Pilate unto them, Take ye him, and judge him according to your law. The Jews therefore said unto him, It is not lawful for us to put any man to death: V.32 That the saying of Jesus might be fulfilled, which he spake, signifying what death he should die (Crucifixion was the means of capital punishment)

CHAPTER 18
V. 28-31
Notes

Triumphal Gethsemane   Last   Judgment Hall
Bethany   Entry   Supper   Passover

(1) V.28 Then led they J_____ from Caiaphas unto the h_____ of J_____

(2) V.28 and it was e_____; and they themselves went not into the J_____ h_____, lest they should be d_____; but that they might eat the p_____.

(3) V.29 P_____ then went out unto them, and said, What a_____ bring ye against this man?

Jesus (bound)

(4) V.30 They answered and said unto him, If he were not a m_____, we would n_____ have d_____ him up unto thee.

(5) V.31 Then said P_____ unto them, T_____ y_____ him, and J_____ him according to your law. The J_____ therefore said unto him, It is n_____ l_____ for us to put any man to d_____:
V.32 That the saying of Jesus might be f_____, which he spake, signifying what d_____ he should die.

CHAPTER 18
V. 32-38
Guide

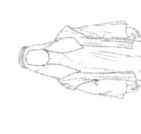

Judgment Hall

V.33 Then Pilate entered into the judgment hall again, and called Jesus, and said unto him, *Art thou the King of the Jews?*

V.34 Jesus answered him, Sayest thou this thing of *thyself*, or did *others* tell it thee of me? *Jesus doesn't answer the question immediately, but instead gives Pilate a chance to examine himself*

V.35 Pilate answered, Am I a Jew? *(How would I know?)* Thine own nation and the chief priests have delivered thee unto me: what hast thou done? *Again Jesus doesn't answer right away but goes back to the first question*

V.36 Jesus answered, My kingdom is not of this world: if my kingdom were of this world, then would my servants fight, that I should not be delivered to the Jews: but *now* is my kingdom *not* from hence. *(Jesus says plainly He has a kingdom)*

V.37 Pilate therefore said unto him, Art thou a king *then? Pilate doesn't dispute it. In his manner of speaking he is saying, "So you are a king then"* Jesus answered, *Thou sayest* that I am a king. To this end was I born, and for this cause came I into the world, that I should *bear witness* unto the *truth*. Every one that is of the truth heareth my voice. *Jesus is now answering Pilate's question, "what hast thou done?"* *(I came to this world to bear witness of the truth as I have just done to you. You now know the truth that I am a king but my kingdom is not of this world.*

V.38 Pilate saith unto him, *What is truth? Pilate found no fault in Jesus' claim that he came to bear witness of the truth. If Pilate would have seen the works of God, then he would know that the truth is a person not a philosophy.*

And when he had said this, he went out again unto the Jews, and saith unto them, I find in him no fault at all *(No one could prove Jesus was not bearing witness of the truth.)*

CHAPTER 18
V. 32-38
Notes

Pilate

Judgment Hall

Jesus

V.33 Then Pilate entered into the judgment hall again, and called Jesus, and said unto him, A_____ thou the k_____ of the Jews?

V.34 Jesus answered him, Sayest thou this thing of t_____, or did o_____ tell it thee of me?

V.35 Pilate answered, Am I a Jew? Thine o_____ n_____ and the c_____ p_____ have d_____ thee unto me: what hast thou done?

V.36 Jesus answered, M___ k_____ is not of this world: if my kingdom were of this world, then would my servants fight, that I should not be delivered to the Jews: but n_____ is my kingdom n_____ from hence.

V.37 Pilate therefore said unto him, Art thou a king t_____? Jesus answered, T_____ s_____ that I am a king. T___ t___ e_____ was I born, and for t___ c_____ came I into the world, that I should b_____ w_____ unto the t_____. Every one that is of the truth heareth my voice.

V.38 Pilate saith unto him, W_____ is t_____? And when he had said this, he went out again unto the Jews, and saith unto them, I find in him n___ b_____ a_____.

CHAPTER 18
V. 38-40
Guide

Triumphal Gethsemane
Bethany Entry   Last Judgment Hall
              Supper Passover

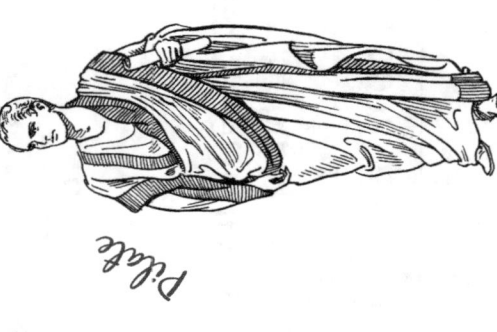
Pilate

Jews

V.40 Then cried they all again, saying, Not this man, but Barabbas. Now Barabbas was a robber.

Barabbas should have been crucified. Jesus was crucified in his place. We should die for our sins but Jesus died in our place.

V.38 he went out again unto the Jews, and saith unto them, I find in him *no fault in him at all*..
V.39 But ye have a *custom*, that I should *release* unto you *oone* at the *prisoner*: will ye therefore that I release unto you the *King of the Jews*?
Pilate confesses that Jesus is King of the Jews for the 3rd time.

CHAPTER 18
V. 38-40
Notes

Bethany   Triumphal   Gethsemane   Last   Judgment Hall
           Entry   Supper   Passover

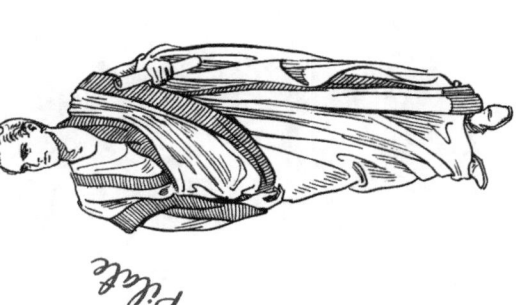

Pilate

Jews

1

V.38 he went out again unto the J_____, and saith unto them,
I find in him n___ f___ a___ a___ .
V.39 But ye have a *custom*, that I should r_____ unto you
o_____ at the p_____ : will ye therefore that I release
unto you the K_____ of the J_____ ?

2

V.40 Then cried they all again, saying, Not this man, but
B_____ . Now Barabbas was a r_____ .

Read John
Chapter 19

CHAPTER 19
V. 1-6
Guide

Bethany

Triumphal Entry

Gethsemane
Last Supper

Judgment Hall
Passover

④ V.2 soldiers

② V.1 Jesus

① V.1 Pilate

⑨ V.4 Behold, I bring him forth to you, that ye may know that I find no fault in him.
V.5 Behold the man!

pronounced Him innocent.

2nd time

John 3:14 And as Moses lifted up the serpent in the wilderness, even so must the Son of man be lifted up:

③ V.1 scourged him. *Many do not survive this beating.*

⑤ V.2 a crown of *thorns,* and put it on his head,

⑥ V.2 a purple robe,
Luke 9:29 and his raiment was *white* and glistering.

⑪ V.6 *Crucify* him, *crucify* him.

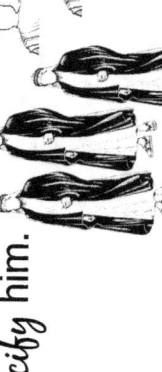

⑦ V.3 Hail, *King of the Jews!*

⑧ V.3 smote him with their hands.

⑩ V.6 chief priests and officers

CHAPTER 19
V. 1-6
Notes

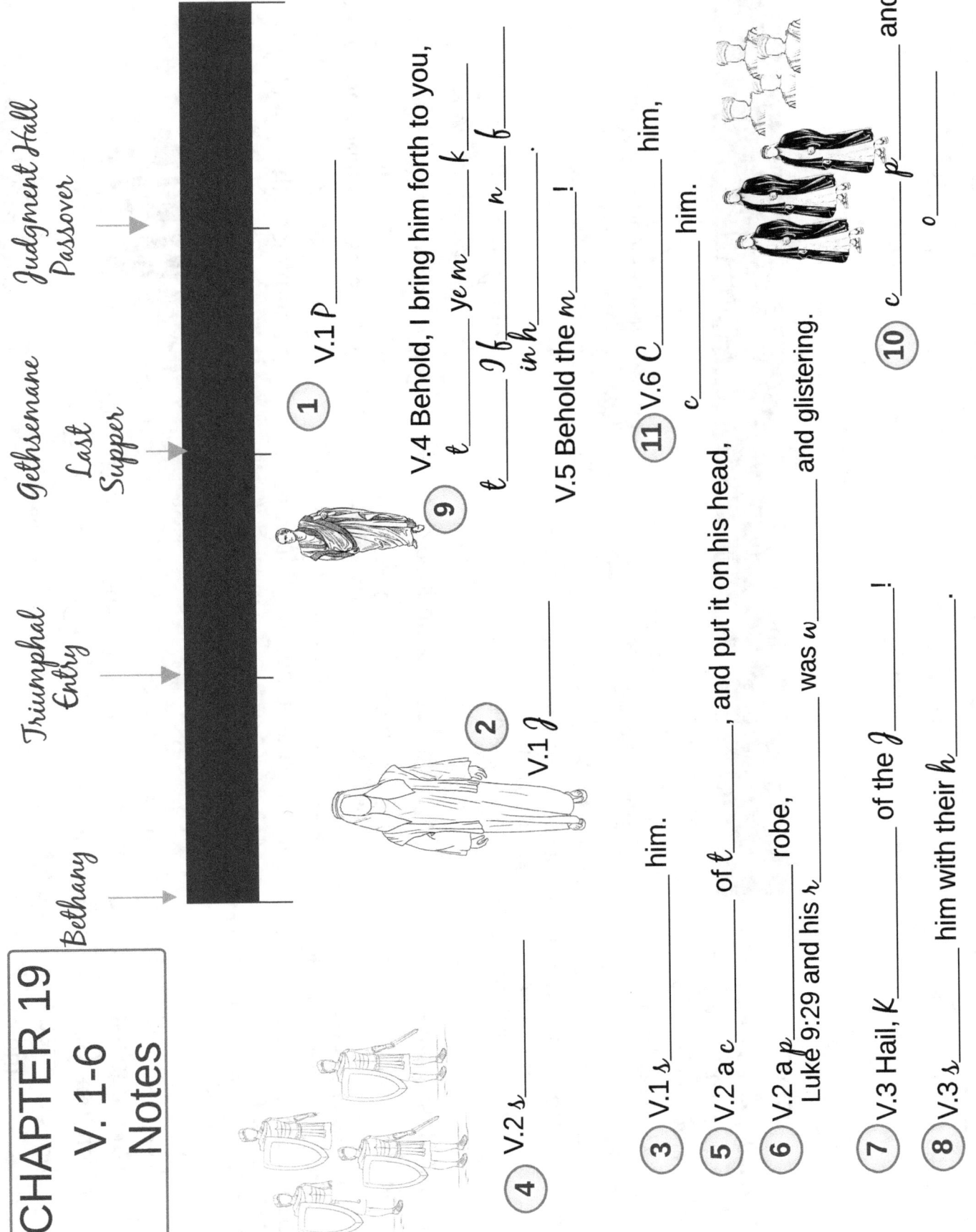

Bethany   Triumphal   Gethsemane   Judgment Hall
          Entry   Last   Passover
                       Supper

(1) V.1 P _____

(2) V.1 ƒ _____

(4) V.2 s _____

(9) V.4 Behold, I bring him forth to you,
   t _____ ye m _____ k _____ b _____
   t _____ I b _____ n _____ .
   in h _____

   V.5 Behold the m _____ !

(11) V.6 C _____ him,
    c _____ him.

and glistering.

(10) c _____ p _____ and
    o _____

(3) V.1 s _____ him.

(5) V.2 a c _____ of t _____ , and put it on his head,

(6) V.2 a p _____ robe,
    Luke 9:29 and his r _____ was w _____ and glistering.

(7) V.3 Hail, K _____ of the ƒ _____ !

(8) V.3 s _____ him with their h _____ .

CHAPTER
V. 6-12
Guide

Jesus

(scourged, crown of thorns, purple road, mocked and smote with the hands of soldiers)

Bethany — **Triumphal Entry** — **Gethsemane / Last Supper** — **Judgment Hall / Passover**

3 X's Pilate confessed *I find no fault in him.* (Serves as a witness) *John 18:38, 19:4,6*

(1) V.6 Take ye him, and crucify him: for *I find no fault in him.*

3rd time a witness that Jesus was innocent.

(2) V.7 We have a law, and by our law he ought to die, because he made himself the *Son of God.*

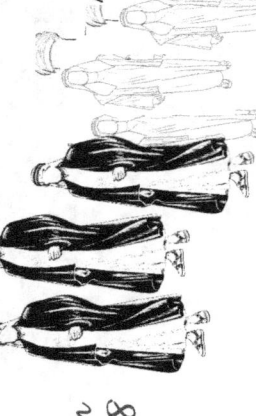

chief priests and officers

(3) V.8 When Pilate therefore heard that saying, he was *more afraid;*

→ Matthew 10:28 And fear not them which kill the body, but are not able to kill the soul: but rather fear him <u>which is able to destroy both soul and body in hell.</u>

V.9 But Jesus gave him *no answer.*

Isaiah 53:7 He was oppressed, and he was afflicted, <u>yet he opened not his mouth:</u> he is brought as a lamb to the <u>slaughter, and as a sheep before her shearers is dumb,</u> so he openeth not his mouth.

(4) V.9 *Whence art thou?*

Already told Him that His kingdom was not of the world.

(6) V.10 Speakest thou not unto me? knowest thou not that *I have power to crucify thee, and have power to release thee?*

No Blasphemy

See John 10:33-38

(8) V.12 And from thenceforth Pilate sought to release him: *Believed He was innocent.*

(7) V.11 Thou couldest have no power *at all against me, except it were given thee from above:* therefore he that delivered me unto thee hath *the greater sin.*

CHAPTER

V. 6-12

Notes

Bethany → Triumphal Entry → Gethsemane / Last Supper → Judgment Hall / Passover

Jesus

(scourged, crown of thorns, purple robe, mocked and smote with the hands of soldiers.)

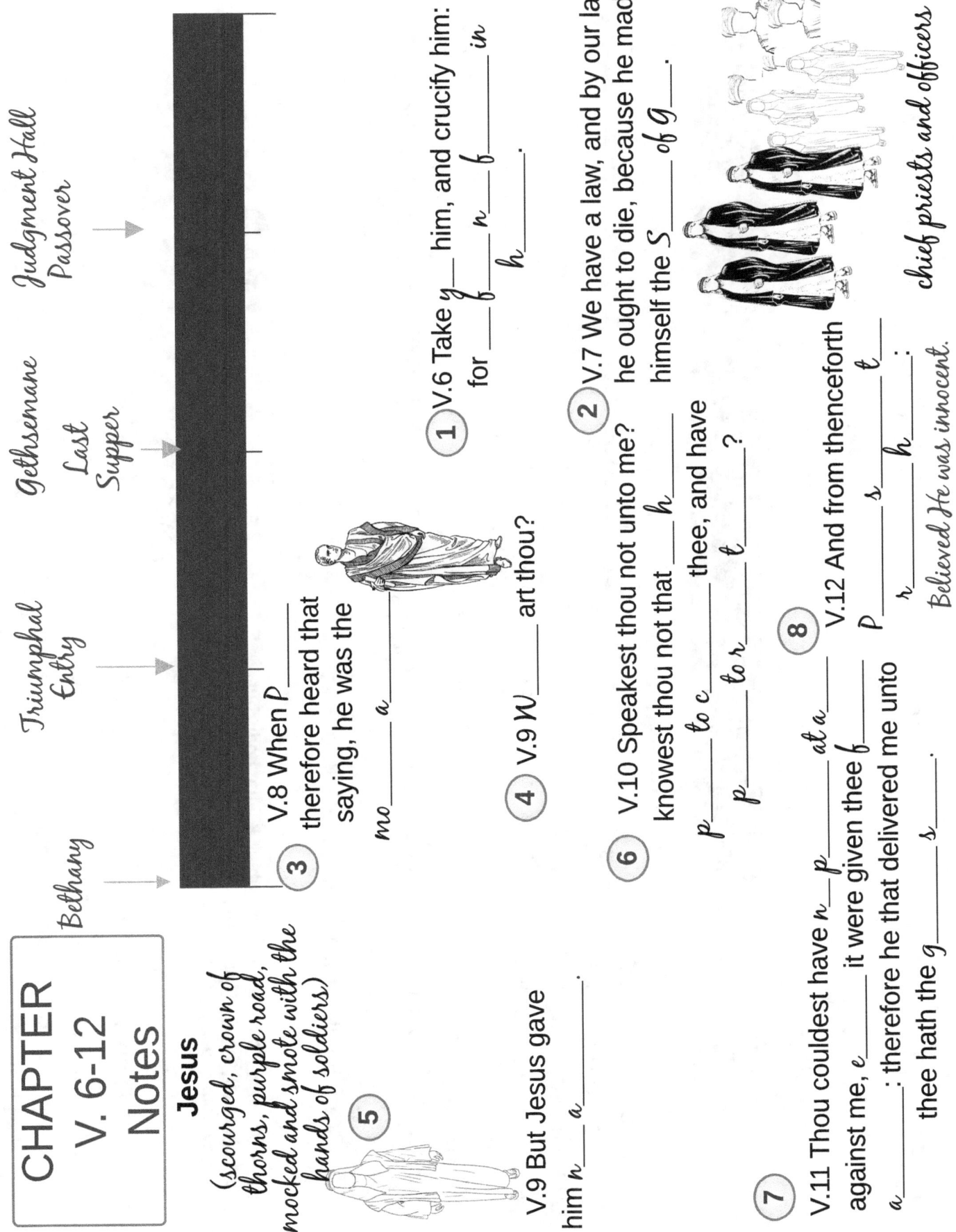

1 V.6 Take y____ him, and crucify him: for ____ b____ n____ b____ in ____ h____ .

2 V.7 We have a law, and by our law he ought to die, because he made himself the S____ of G____ .

3 V.8 When P____ therefore heard that saying, he was the mo____ a____ .

4 V.9 W____ art thou?

5 V.9 But Jesus gave him n____ a____ .

6 V.10 Speakest thou not unto me? knowest thou not that ____ h____ thee, and have p____ to c____ thee, and have p____ to r____ t____ ?

7 V.11 Thou couldest have n____ p____ at a____ against me, e____ it were given thee b____ ; therefore he that delivered me unto a____ thee hath the g____ s____ .

8 V.12 And from thenceforth P____ s____ t____ r____ h____ :

Believed He was innocent.

chief priests and officers

CHAPTER 19
V. 12-16
Guide

Bethany • Triumphal Entry • Gethsemane / Last Supper • Judgment Hall / Passover

(2) *that He made Himself the Son of God.*

V.13 When Pilate therefore heard that saying, he brought Jesus forth, and sat down in the judgment seat in a place that is called the Pavement, but in the Hebrew, *Gabbatha.*

Believes Jesus is the King of the Jews;

(6) V.15 Shall I crucify your *King?*

Matthew 10:28 And fear not them which kill the body, but are not able to kill the soul: but rather fear him which is able to destroy both soul and body in hell.

(8) V.16 Then *delivered* he him therefore unto *them* to be *crucified*. And they took Jesus, and led him away.

(3) V.14 And it was the preparation of the *passover*, and about the sixth hour:

Behold the Lamb of God

(4) V.14 Behold your *King!*
no longer saying Behold the Man; now calls Him a King.

John 16:7 Nevertheless I tell you the truth; It is <u>expedient</u> for you that I go away:

(5) V.15 *Away with* him, away with him, crucify him.

Rejected Jesus as King.

(7) V.15 We have *no king but* Caesar.

Pandering to Caesar so they can keep their power and position.

(1) V.12 If thou let this man go, thou art *not Caesar's friend:* whosoever maketh himself a king speaketh against Caesar.

Corrupt politicians is nothing new

chief priests and officers

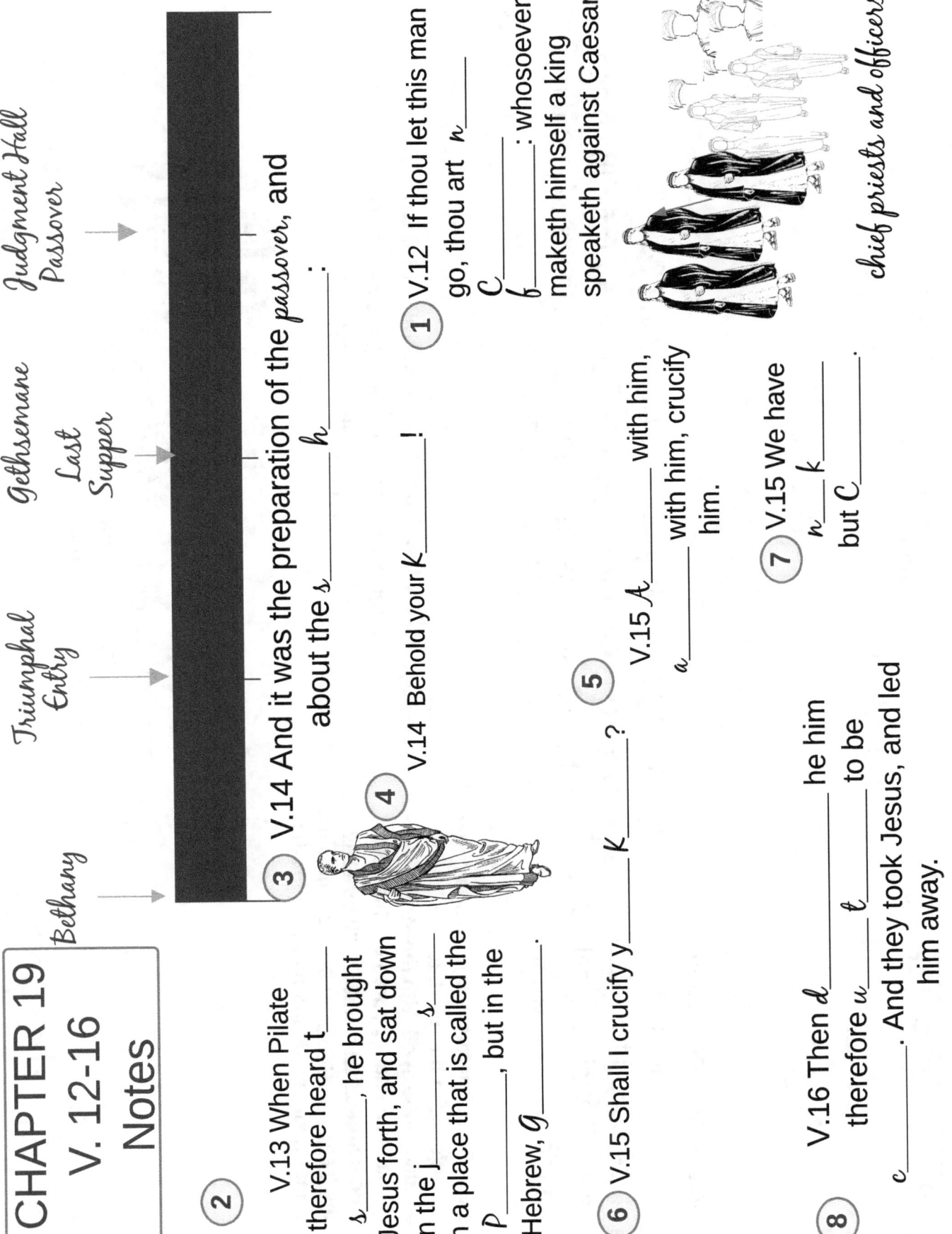

CHAPTER 19
V. 12-16
Notes

Bethany   Triumphal   Gethsemane   Judgment Hall
          Entry   Last   Passover
                       Supper

1 V.12 If thou let this man go, thou art n_____ C_____ f_____ : whosoever maketh himself a king speaketh against Caesar.

chief priests and officers

2 V.13 When Pilate therefore heard t_____ s_____, he brought Jesus forth, and sat down in the j_____ s_____ in a place that is called the P_____, but in the Hebrew, g_____.

3 V.14 And it was the preparation of the *passover*, and about the s_____ h_____ :

4 V.14 Behold your K_____ !

5 V.15 A_____ a_____ with him, with him, crucify him.

6 V.15 Shall I crucify y_____ K_____ ?

7 V.15 We have n_____ k_____ but C_____ .

8 V.16 Then d_____ he him therefore u_____ t_____ to be c_____ . And they took Jesus, and led him away.

CHAPTER 19
V. 17-22
Guide

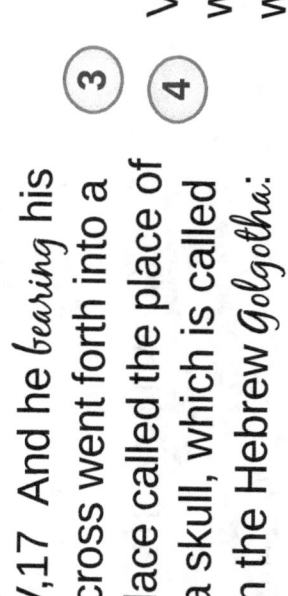

Malefactor

Jesus

King of the Jews

Malefactor

(1) V,17 And he *bearing* his cross went forth into a place called the place of a skull, which is called in the Hebrew *Golgotha:*

Isaiah 53:12 Therefore will I divide him a portion with the great, and he shall divide the spoil with the strong; because he hath poured out his soul unto death: <u>and he was numbered with the transgressors:</u> and he bare the sin of many, and made intercession for the transgressors.

(3) V.19 *Jesus of Nazareth* The *King of the Jews.*

(4) V.20 This *title* then read many of the *Jews:* for the place where Jesus was crucified was *nigh* to the *city:* and it was written in *Hebrew,* and *Greek,* and *Latin.*

written to all people

(2) V.18 Where they crucified him, and *two* other with him, on *either* side *one,* and *Jesus* in the midst.

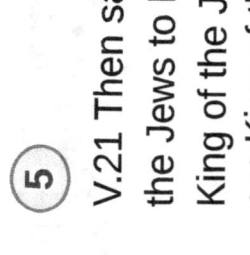

(5) V.21 Then said the *chief priests* of the Jews to Pilate, *Write not,* The King of the Jews; *but that he said,* I am King of the Jews.

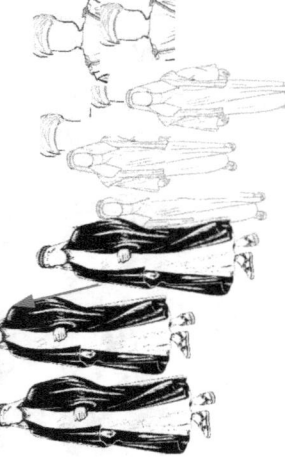

chief priests and officers

(6) V.22 Pilate answered, What I have *written* I have *written.*

CHAPTER 19
V. 17-22
Notes

1 V,17 And he b_____ his cross went forth into a place called the place of a skull, which is called in the Hebrew g_____.

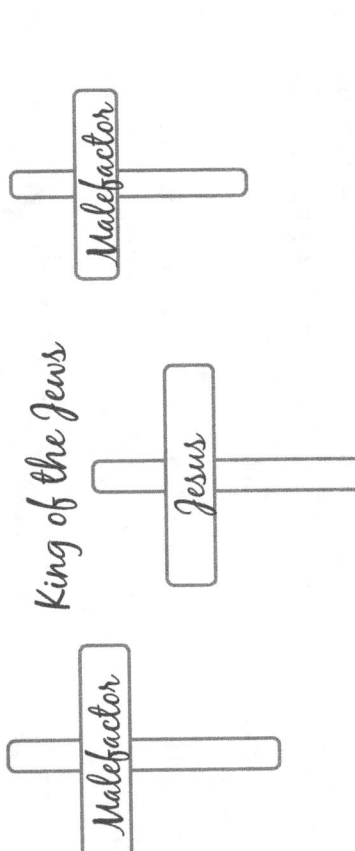

Malefactor Jesus Malefactor

King of the Jews

3 V.19 J_____ of N_____. The K_____ of the J_____.

4 V.20 This t_____ then read many of the J_____: for the place where Jesus was crucified was n_____ to the c_____: and it was written in H_____, and g_____, and L_____.

2 V.18 Where they crucified him, and t_____ other with him, on e_____ side o_____, and J_____ in the midst.

5 V.21 Then said the c_____ of the Jews to Pilate, W_____ n_____, The King of the Jews; b_____ that h_____ s_____, I am King of the Jews.

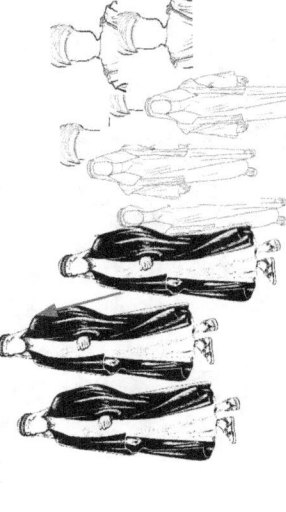

chief priests and officers

6 V.22 Pilate answered, What I have w_____. I have w_____.

CHAPTER 19
V. 23-27
Guide

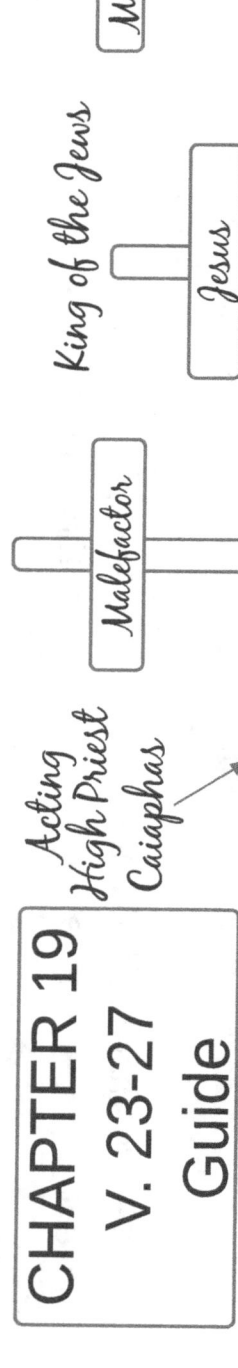

Acting
High Priest
Caiaphas

Matthew 26:65 Then the high priest rent his clothes, saying, He hath spoken blasphemy;

Did not realize what he had done was symbolic. Jesus was the true High Priest.

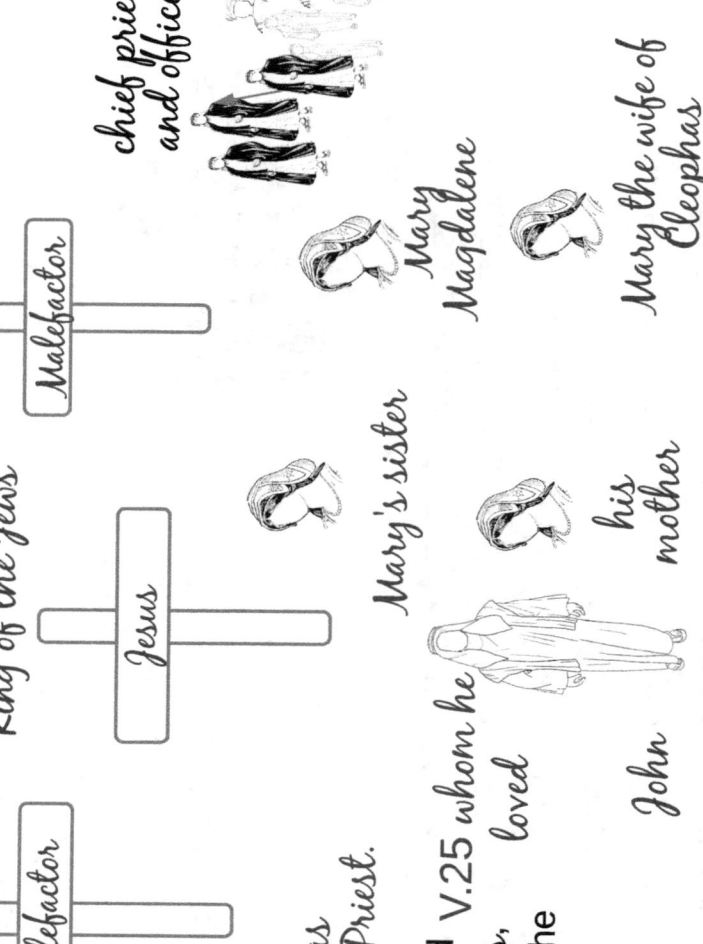

Malefactor

Jesus   King of the Jews

Malefactor

Malefactor

chief priests and officers

Mary's sister

whom he loved

Mary Magdalene

Mary the wife of Cleophas

John   his mother

V.23 Then the soldiers, when they had crucified Jesus, took his garments, and made *four parts*, to every soldier a part; and also his coat: now the coat was without seam, woven from the top throughout.

Exodus 39:23 And there was an hole in the midst of the robe, as the hole of an habergeon, with a band round about the hole, that it should not rend.

The robe of the High Priest was to be seamless and never to be rent. The garment was to be kept whole without blemish.

V.24 They said therefore among themselves, *Let us not rend it,* but cast lots for it, whose it shall be: that the scripture might be *fulfilled,* which saith, They parted my raiment among them, and for my vesture they did cast lots. These things therefore the soldiers did.

V.25 *whom he loved*

V.26 When Jesus therefore saw his mother, and *the disciple* standing by, *whom he loved,* he saith unto his mother, *Woman, behold the son!*

V.27 Then saith he *to the disciple,* Behold thy mother! And from that hour that disciple took her *unto his own home.*

John 2:4 Jesus saith unto her, Woman, what have I to do with thee? mine hour is not yet come.

His hour is come and now He answer's the question. Mary is not diety. She was His earthly mother but we are all equal in the family of God.

CHAPTER 19
V. 23-27
Notes

1

V.23 Then the *soldiers*, when they had crucified Jesus, took his *garments*, and made f_____

p_____, to every s_____ a p_____; and also his coat: now the coat was w_____

s_____, woven from the top throughout.

2

V.24 They said therefore among themselves,
L___ u___ n___ i___, but cast lots for
it, whose it shall be: that the s_____ might be
f_____, which saith, They parted my
raiment among them, and for my v_____
they did cast lots. These things therefore the soldiers did.

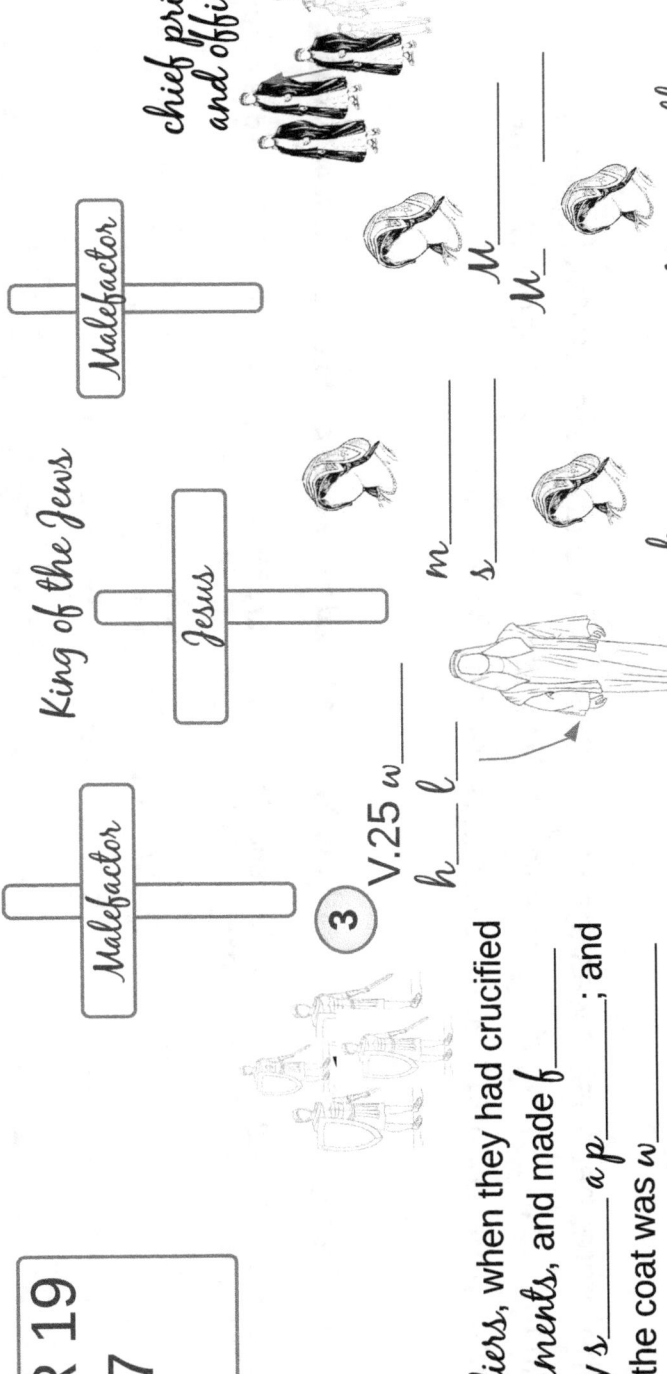

Malefactor

King of the Jews

Jesus

Malefactor

chief priests and officers

3 V.25 w_____ h_____ l_____

m_____
s_____

h_____
m_____

M_____
M_____

M_____
w_____ of
C_____ the

4

V.26 When Jesus therefore saw h_____ standing by,
m_____, and the d_____
w_____ h_____ l_____, he saith unto his
mother, W_____, b_____, t_____ s_____!
V.27 Then saith he t_____ t_____ d_____,
Behold thy mother! And from that hour that disciple
took her u_____ h_____ o_____ h_____.

King of the Jews

Malefactor

Jesus

Malefactor

CHAPTER 19
V. 28-31
Guide

so they may
believe a witness

1

V.28 After this, Jesus knowing that all things were now accomplished, that the scripture might be fulfilled, saith, I thirst. *(Fountain of living water. Emptied and poured out.)*

V.29 Now there was set a vessel full of vinegar: and they filled a spunge with vinegar, and put it upon hyssop, and put it to his mouth.

V.30 When Jesus therefore had received the vinegar, he said, It is finished: and he bowed his head, and gave up the ghost. *(Did not have His life taken from Him. He willing gave it).*

Psalm 69:21 They gave me also gall for my meat; and in my thirst they gave me vinegar to drink.

2

V.31 The Jews therefore, because it was the preparation, that the bodies should not remain upon the cross on the sabbath day, (for that sabbath day was an high day,) besought Pilate that their legs might be broken, and that they might be taken away.

(die quickly)

Deuteronomy 21:22-23 And if a man have committed a sin worthy of death, and he be to be put to death, and thou hang him on a tree:

His body shall not remain all night upon the tree, but thou shalt in any wise bury him that day; (for he that is hanged is accursed of God;) that thy land be not defiled, which the LORD thy God giveth thee for an inheritance.

A dead body would defile the land, so it could not remain overnight. Other symbols of the body of Jesus also was instructed not to remain so it would not corrupt and defile the land. Ex. the passover lamb, manna, and the feeding of the 5 thousand (they were instructed to gather up the fragments that nothing remain.)

CHAPTER 19
V. 28-31
Notes

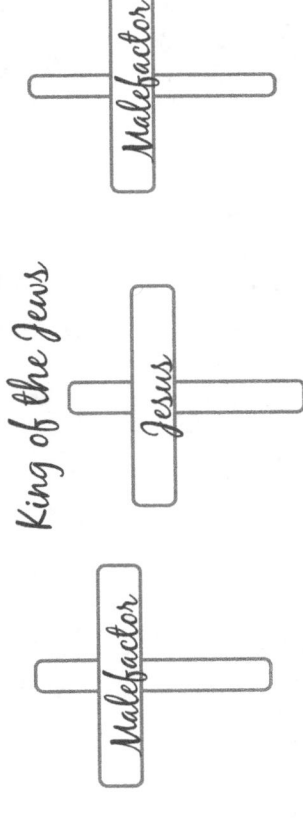

King of the Jews

Malefactor

Jesus

Malefactor

1

V.28 After this, Jesus knowing that all things were now accomplished, that the s_____
might be f_____, saith, ____ t_____.

V.29 Now there was set a vessel full of v_____: and they filled a s_____ with
v_____, and put it upon h_____, and put it to his m_____.

V.30 When Jesus therefore had received the vinegar, he said, I____ i____ f_____: and he
bowed his head, and g____ u____ the g_____.

2

V.31 The Jews therefore, because it was
the p_____, that the bodies
should n____ r_____ upon the
c_____ on the s_____
d_____, (for that sabbath day was an
h____ d_____,) besought Pilate that
their l_____ might b____ b_____,
and that they might be taken away.

CHAPTER 19
It is finished Guide

V.30 When Jesus therefore had received the vinegar, he said, *It is finished:* and he bowed his head, and *gave up the ghost.*

Hebrews 10:9 Then said he, Lo, I come to do thy will, O God. He taketh away the first, that he may establish the second.

Hebrews 9:16 For where a testament is, there must also of necessity be the death of the testator.

Old Testament ——→ *New Testament*

Old Testament

1Kings 6:13 And *I will dwell among* the children of Israel, and will not forsake my people Israel. 1Kings 6:14 So Solomon built the house, and *finished it.*

When the Old Testament temple was finished, God came to earth to dwell among the children of Israel.

It is finished

Jesus said, "It is finished and gave up the Ghost". Believers become the new temple where the Spirit of God dwells.

God dwells in the temple

New Testament

John 16:7 Nevertheless I tell you the truth; It is expedient for you that *I go away:* for if I go not away, the Comforter will not come unto you; *but if I depart,* I will send him unto you.

1Corinthians 3:16 Know ye not that ye are the temple *of God,* and that the *Spirit of God dwelleth in you?.*

CHAPTER 19
It is finished
Notes

V.30 When Jesus therefore had received the vinegar, he said, *It is finished:* and he bowed his head, and *gave up the ghost.*

Hebrews 10:9 Then said he, Lo, I come to do thy will, O God. He taketh away the first, that he may establish the second.

Hebrews 9:16 For where a testament is, there must also of necessity be the death of the testator.

Old Testament ———→ *New Testament*

Old Testament ———→

1Kings 6:13 And d_____ w_____ the children of Israel, a_____ and will not forsake my people Israel. 1Kings 6:14 So Solomon built the house, and f_____ i_____.

When the Old Testament temple was finished, God came to earth to dwell among the children of Israel.

New Testament ———→

John 16:7 Nevertheless I tell you the truth; It is expedient for you that g_____ a_____: for if I go not away, the Comforter will not come unto you; b_____ i_____ d_____, I will send him unto you.

1Corinthians 3:16 Know ye not that ye are the t_____ of G_____, and that the S_____ of G_____ d_____ i_____ y_____?.

The Holy Spirit could now come and indwell His children.

It is finished (diamond)

God dwells in the temple

CHAPTER 19
V. 32-37
Guide

Bethany

Triumphal Entry

Gethsemane
Last Supper

Crucifixion
Judgment Hall
Passover

Jesus was sacrificed on the cross for our sins. The Passover Lamb was only a shadow of Jesus, the true sacrifice.

The Passover Lamb was not to have it's bone broken.

Exodus 12:46 In one house shall it be eaten; thou shalt not carry forth ought of the flesh abroad out of the house; <u>neither shall ye break a bone thereof.</u>

John 1:29 The next day John seeth Jesus coming unto him, and saith, <u>Behold the Lamb of God</u>, which taketh away the sin of the world.

The Lamb of God

(1)

V.32 Then came the soldiers, and *brake the legs* of the *first*, and of the *other* which was *crucified* with him.

V.33 *But* when they came to *Jesus*, and saw that he was *dead already*, they *brake not* his legs:

(2)

V.36 For these things were done, that the *scripture should be fulfilled*, A *bone* of him shall *not be broken.*
Psalm 34:20 He keepeth all his bones: not one of them is broken.

V.37 And again *another scripture* saith, They shall look on him whom *they pierced.*
Zechariah 12:10 <u>and they shall look upon me whom they have pierced</u>, and they shall mourn for him,

CHAPTER 19
V. 32-37
Notes

Bethany

Triumphal Entry 10/27

Gethsemane
Last Supper

Crucifixion
Judgment Hall
Passover

The Lamb of God

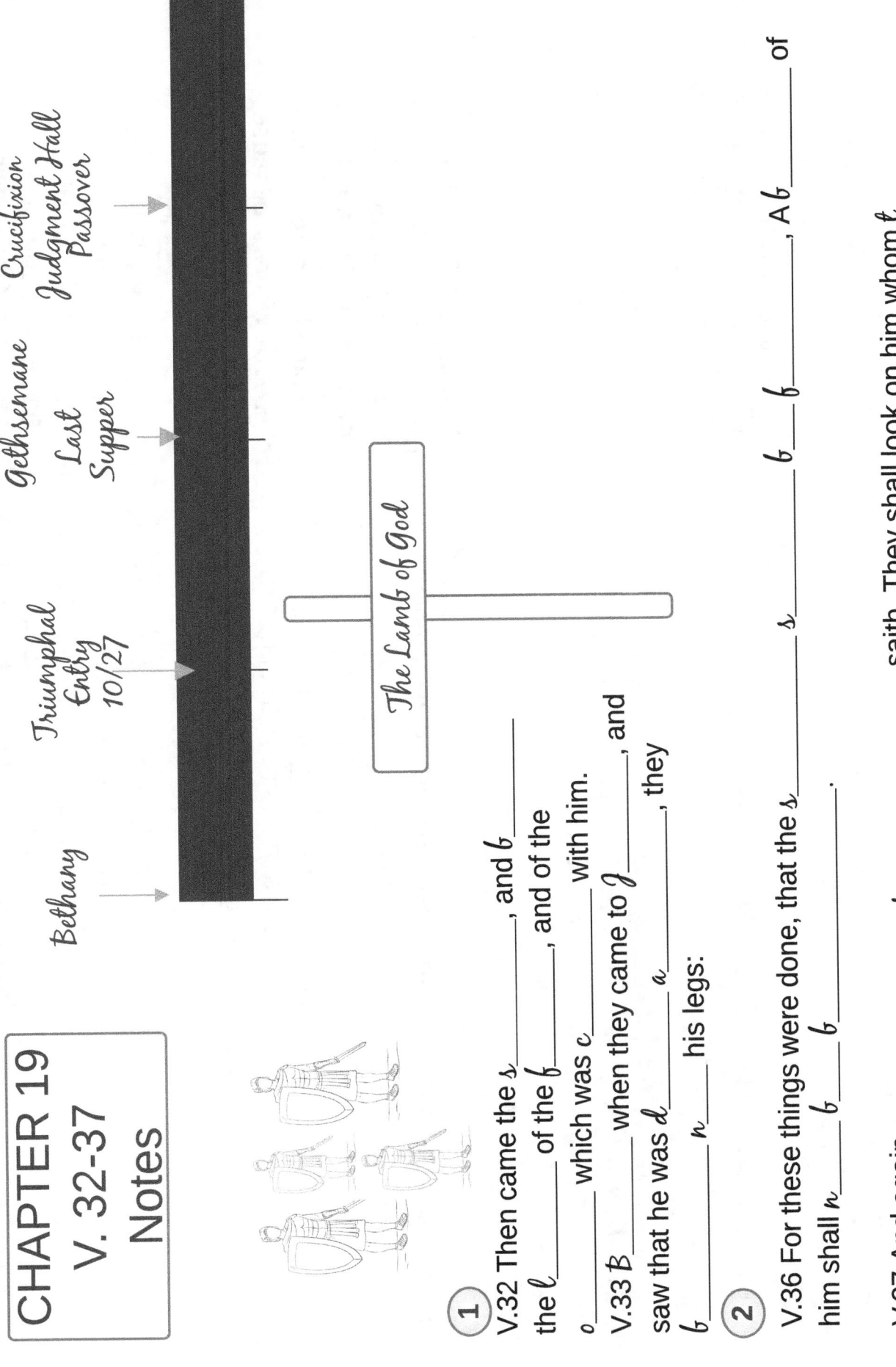

① V.32 Then came the s_____, and b_____ the l_____ of the f_____, and of the o_____ which was c_____ with him.

V.33 B_____ when they came to J_____, and saw that he was d_____ a_____, they b_____ n_____ his legs:

② V.36 For these things were done, that the s_____ s_____ b_____ b_____, A b_____ of him shall n_____ b_____ b_____.

V.37 And again a_____ s_____ saith, They shall look on him whom t_____ p_____.

CHAPTER 19
V. 34-35
Guide

Jesus Christ came by water and blood not just water as mankind is born.

The blood of Jesus looked unique to a degree that the soldier bare record.

Had it been a mere separation of the plasma from heart failure, the heart failure would have taken his life. But Jesus gave up the ghost. John 5:8 the blood and water beareth witness on the earth.

Jesus of Nazarath King of the Jews

The soldier beareth witness this is Jesus Christ when he saw the water and blood come forthwith.

V.34 But one of the soldiers with a spear pierced his side, and forthwith _came_ there out _blood_ and _water_.

V.35 And he that saw it _bare record_, and his record is true: and he knoweth that he saith _true_, _that ye might believe._

1 John 5:6 This is he that came by water and _blood_, even **Jesus Christ; not by water only, but by water and blood.**

And it is the Spirit that _beareth_ witness, because the Spirit is _truth._

John 5:7 For there are three that bear record in heaven, the Father, the Word, and the Holy Ghost: and these three are one.

John 5:8 And there are three that bear witness in earth, the Spirit, and the water, and the blood: and these three agree in one.

John 5:9 If we receive the witness of men, the witness of God is greater: for this is the witness of God which he hath testified of his Son.

CHAPTER 19
V. 34-35
Notes

Jesus of Nazarath King of the Jews

V.34 But one of the soldiers with a spear pierced his side, and forthwith c_____ there out b_____ and w_____.

V.35 And he that saw it b_____ r_____, and his record is true: and he knoweth that he saith t_____, t_____ g_____ m_____ b_____.

1 John 5:6 This is he that c_____ b_____ w_____ and **, even Jesus Christ; not by water only, but by water and blood. And it is the Spirit that** b_____ **witness, because the Spirit is** t_____.

CHAPTER 19
V. 38-42
Guide

V.38 And after this *Joseph of Arimathaea*, being a *disciple of Jesus*, but secretly for *fear of the Jews*, besought *Pilate* that he might *take away the body* of Jesus: and *Pilate* gave him leave. He came therefore, and took the *body of* Jesus.

V.39 And there came also *Nicodemus*, which at the first came to *Jesus by night*, and brought a mixture of *myrrh and aloes*, about an *hundred pound weight*.

V.40 Then took they the body of Jesus, and wound it in *linen clothes* with the spices, as the *manner* of the Jews is to bury.

(2) V. 38 *Pilate*

Both men had fear of the Jews knowing they were disciples. They were not afraid of the Roman Governor, Pilate.

(1) *Joseph of Arimathea*
V. 38

(3) *Nicodemus*
V. 39

Matthew 27:57 When the even was come, there came a <u>rich man of Arimathaea</u>,

Isaiah 53:9 And he <u>made his grave with the wicked, and with the rich in his death;</u> because he had done no violence, neither was any deceit in his mouth.

Isaiah 53:9 ... and <u>with the rich in his death;</u>

V.41 Now in the place where he was crucified there was *a garden;* and in the garden a *new sepulchre*, wherein was *never man yet laid.*

V.42 There laid they Jesus therefore because of the *Jews' preparation day;* for the sepulchre was *nigh at hand.*

for the Sabbath Day

Matthew 27:60 And laid it in his own new tomb, which he had <u>hewn out in the rock:</u> departed.

tomb was not polluted

Exodus 20:25 And if thou wilt make me an altar of stone, thou shalt not build it of hewn stone: for if thou lift up thy tool upon it, thou hast polluted it.

(4)

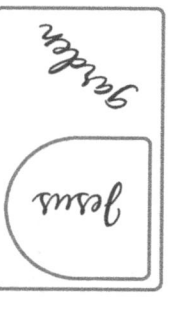

Jesus garden

CHAPTER 19
V. 38-42
Notes

V.38 And after this J_____ of A_____, being a
d_____ of J_____, but secretly for f_____ of the J_____,
besought P_____ that he might t_____ a_____ the body of Jesus:
and P_____ gave him leave. He came therefore, and took the b_____
of J_____.

V.39 And there came also N_____, which at the first came to J_____
by n_____, and brought a mixture of _____ and a_____,
about an h_____ p_____ w_____.

V.40 Then took they the body of Jesus, and wound it in l_____
c_____ with the s_____, as the m_____ of the Jews is to bury.

1 V.38

l_____
A_____

of_____

2 V.38

P_____

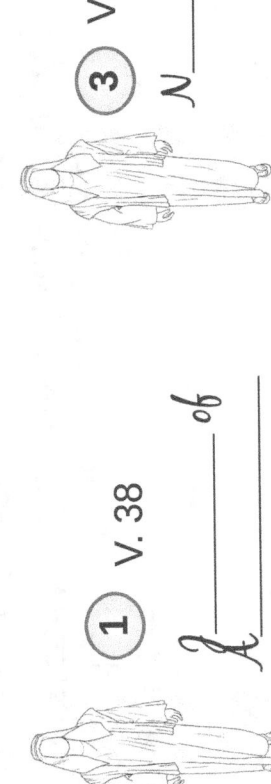

3 V.39

N_____

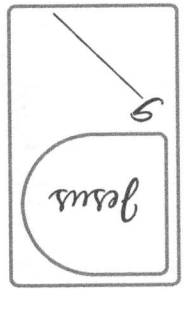

4

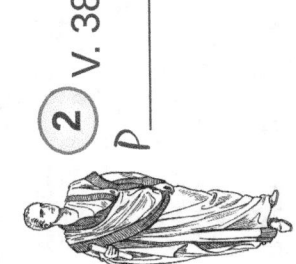

V.41 Now in the place where he was crucified there was a g_____; and in the garden a
n_____ s_____, wherein was n_____ man yet l_____.
V.42 There laid they Jesus therefore because of the J_____ p_____ d_____; for the
sepulchre was n_____ at h_____.

V. 41

Ye shall also bear witness Guide

Works

John 5:36 … the same works that I do, bear witness of me, that the Father hath sent me.

Holy Spirit

John 15:26 But when the Comforter is come, whom I will send unto you from the Father, even the Spirit of truth, which proceedeth from the Father, he shall testify of me:

Heaven

John 3:11 Verily, verily, I say unto thee, We speak that we do know, and testify that we have seen: and ye receive not our witness.

The People

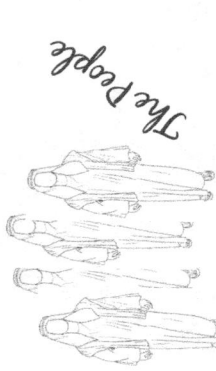

John 12:17 The people therefore that was with him when he called Lazarus out of his grave, and raised him from the dead, bare record.

Roman Soldier

John 19:35 And he that saw it bare record, and his record is true: and he knoweth that he saith true, that ye might believe.

John the Baptist

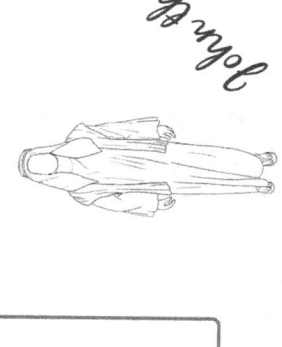

John 1:15 John bare witness of him

Prophecies

John 5:39 Search the scriptures; for in them ye think ye have eternal life: and they are they which testify of me.

The Father

John 8:18 … and the Father that sent me beareth witness of me.

Disciples

John 15:27 And ye also shall bear witness, because ye have been with me from the beginning.

Jesus

John 8:14 Though I bear record of myself, yet my record is true: for I know whence I came, and whither I go;

Ye shall also
bear witness
Notes

John 15:27 And ye also shall bear witness, because ye have been with me from the beginning.

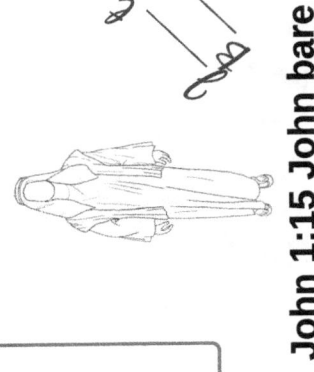

John 8:14 Though I bear record of myself, yet my record is true: for I know whence I came, and whither I go;

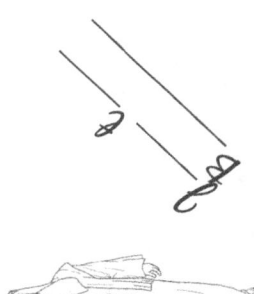

John 1:15 John bare witness of him

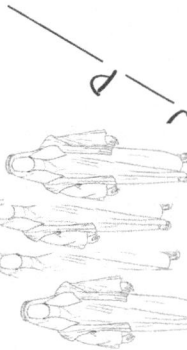

John 5:39 Search the scriptures; for in them ye think ye have eternal life: and they are they which testify of me.

John 8:18 ... and the Father that sent me beareth witness of me.

John 3:11 Verily, verily, I say unto thee, We speak that we do know, and testify that we have seen: and ye receive not our witness.

John 12:17 The people therefore that was with him when he called Lazarus out of his grave, and raised him from the dead, bare record.

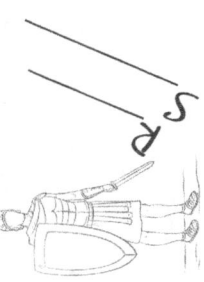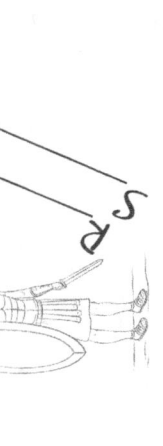

John 19:35 And he that saw it bare record, and his record is true: and he knoweth that he saith true, that ye might believe.

John 5:36 ... the same works that I do, bear witness of me, that the Father hath sent me.

John 15:26 But when the Comforter is come, whom I will send unto you from the Father, even the Spirit of truth, which proceedeth from the Father, he shall testify of me:

Read John
Chapter 20

CHAPTER 20
V. 1-10
Guide

Skeptics claim Jesus was not dead but only swooned. (Appeared to be dead). If so He could never had rolled the great stone away in such poor medical condition.

Garden

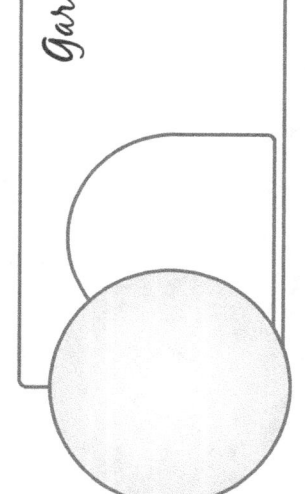

(2) V.1 seeth the stone taken away from the sepulchre.

did not go in at first

(1) V. 1 Mary Magdalene

See comments on next page about contradictions.

(4) They have taken away the LORD out of the sepulchre, and we know not where they have laid him.

(6) V.9 For as yet they knew not the scripture, that he must rise again from the dead.
V.10 Then the disciples went away again unto their own home.

Arrived first but did not go inside

Then went in after Peter..

(3) (John)

V.2 other disciple, whom Jesus loved,

graveclothes–defiled could not wear them into the Holy of Holies

(2) V.2 Simon Peter

(5) V.6 Then cometh Simon Peter following him, and went into the sepulchre, and seeth the linen clothes lie.
V.7 And the napkin, that was about his head, not lying with the linen clothes, but wrapped together in a place by itself.

(took it off and wrapped it up. (folded)
According to tradition–if a person wanted to signal they were coming back, they would fold their napkin.

The High Priest had 2 sets of clothes. On the Day of Atonement when he placed the blood on the mercy seat, the high priest wore ordinary linen garments and took off his priestly robes. Jesus changed clothes because He was getting ready to enter the Holy of Holies to place the blood on the mercy seat. This is why Mary mistook him for the gardener at first.

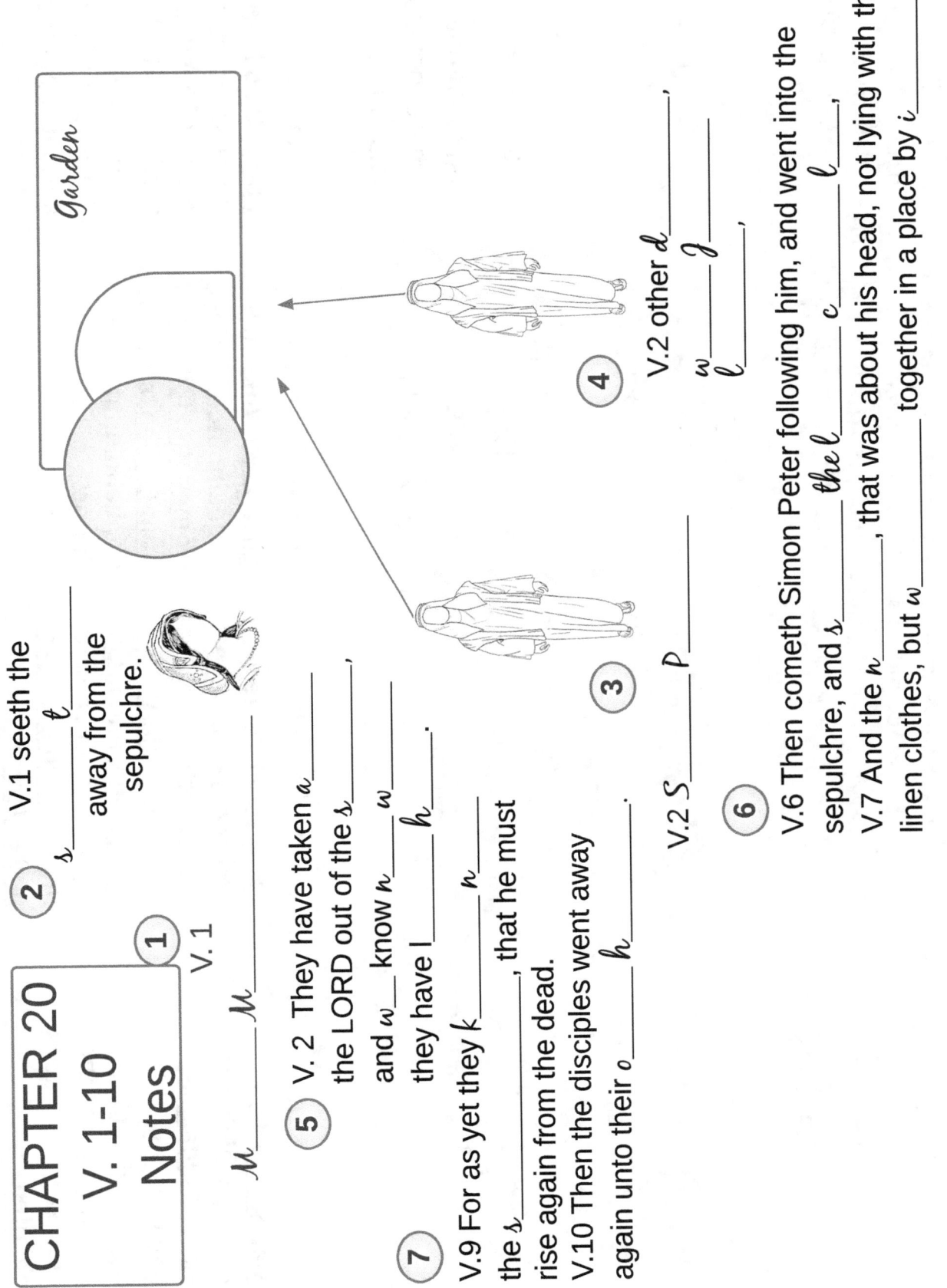

CHAPTER 20
V. 1-10
Notes

1 V. 1

M_____ M_____

2 V.1 seeth the

s_____ t_____ away from the
sepulchre.

5 V. 2 They have taken a_____
the LORD out of the s_____,
and w_____ know n_____ w_____
they have l_____ h_____.

7 V.9 For as yet they k_____ n_____, that he must
the s_____
rise again from the dead.
V.10 Then the disciples went away
again unto their o_____ h_____.

3 V.2 S_____ P_____

4 V.2 other d_____,
w_____ J_____
l_____,

6 V.6 Then cometh Simon Peter following him, and went into the
sepulchre, and s_____ the l_____ c_____ l_____,
V.7 And the n_____, that was about his head, not lying with the
linen clothes, but w_____ together in a place by i_____.

Garden

NO CONTRADICTIONS IN THE BIBLE
How many women were at the tomb?

Skeptics claim errors in the Bible because of the descrepancy among the gospels.

Answer: Not every gospel includes the name of each woman but it does not dismiss them as being present.

For example, My husband and son went to the ball game does not dismiss the fact their buddies also were there .

How many women at the tomb? Guide

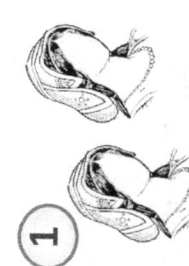

1

Matthew 28:1

Mary Magdalene

other Mary

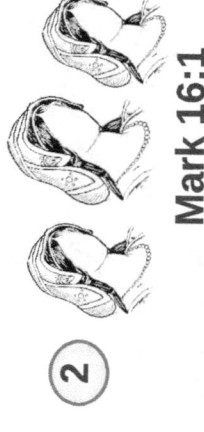

2

Mark 16:1

Mary Magdalene

Mary the mother of James

Salome

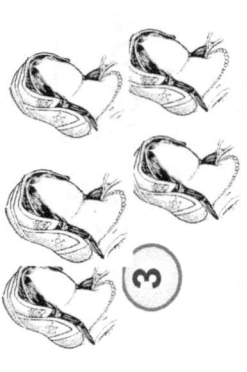

3

Luke 24:1,10

Mary Magdalene

Joanna

Mary the mother of James

other women

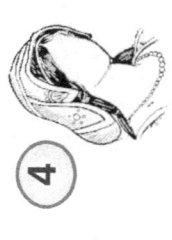

4

John 20:1-2

Mary Magdalene

and we know not where they have laid him.

*****Each gospel writer names the same women they named at the cross. *****

Matthew 27:56 Among which was <u>Mary Magdalene</u>, and <u>Mary the mother of James and Joses</u>, and the mother of Zebedees children.

Mark 15:40 There were also women looking on afar off: among whom was <u>Mary Magdalene</u>, and <u>Mary the mother of James the less and of Joses, and Salome;</u>

Luke 23:49 And all his acquaintance, and <u>the women that followed him from Galilee,</u> stood afar off, beholding these things.

John 19:25 Now there stood by the cross of Jesus his mother, and his mother's sister, Mary the wife of Cleophas, and <u>Mary Magdalene.</u>

NO CONTRADICTIONS IN THE BIBLE
How many women were at the tomb?

Skeptics claim errors in the Bible because of the descrepancy among the gospels.

Answer: Not every gospel includes the name of each woman but it does not dismiss them as being present.

For example, My husband and son went to the ball game does not dismiss the fact their buddies went with them.

How many women at the tomb? Notes

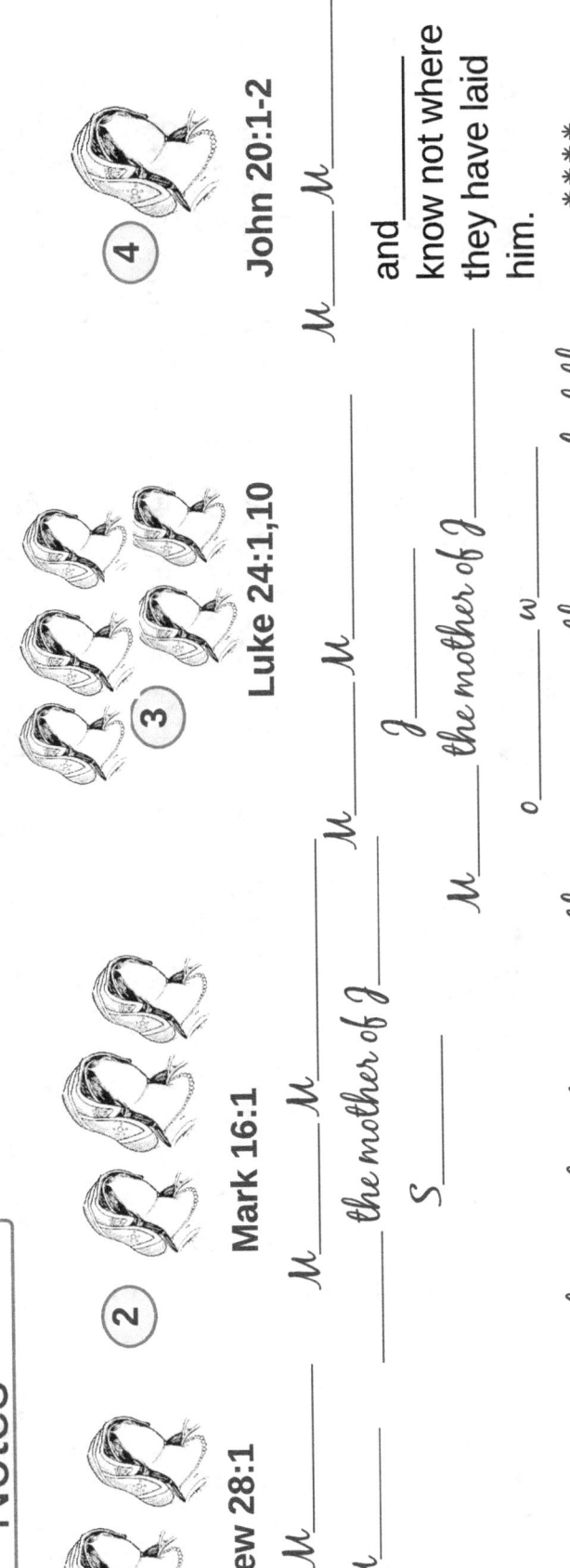

① Matthew 28:1

M_____ M_____

other M_____

② Mark 16:1

M_____ M_____ the mother of J_____

S_____

③ Luke 24:1,10

M_____ M_____

J_____

the mother of J_____

o_____ w_____

M_____

④ John 20:1-2

M_____ M_____

_____ and _____

know not where they have laid him.

***Each gospel writer names the same women they named at the cross. ***

Matthew 27:56 Among which was <u>Mary Magdalene,</u> and <u>Mary the mother of James and Joses,</u> and the <u>mother of Zebedees children.</u>

Mark 15:40 There were also women looking on afar off: among whom was <u>Mary Magdalene, and Mary the mother of James the less and of Joses, and Salome;</u>

Luke 23:49 And all his acquaintance, and <u>the women that followed him from Galilee,</u> stood afar off, beholding these things.

John 19:25 Now there stood by the cross of Jesus his mother, and his mother's sister, Mary the wife of Cleophas, and <u>Mary Magdalene.</u>

CHAPTER 20
V. 11-16
Guide

1 V.11 But *Mary* stood without at the sepulchre weeping: and as she wept, she stooped down, and looked into the sepulchre,

2 V.12 And seeth *two angels in white* sitting, the one at the head, and the other at the feet, where the *body of* Jesus had lain.

Garden

3 V.13 And they say unto her, *Woman,* why *weepest thou?*

4 V. 13 Because they have *taken away my LORD, and I* know not where *they have laid* him

5 V.14 And when she had thus said, she turned herself back, and saw Jesus standing, and *knew not that it was Jesus*

Didn't recognize Him in His glorified body.

My sheep hear my voice.

A Gardener because the High Priest wore ordinary linen clothes into the Holy of Holies.

7 V.15 She, supposing him to be the gardener, saith unto him, Sir, if thou have borne him hence, *tell me* where thou hast laid him, and I will take him away.

9 V.16 *Rabboni;* which is to say, *Master.*

6 V.15 *Jesus* saith unto her, *Woman, why weepest thou? whom seekest thou?*

Mary was seeking

8 V.16 Jesus saith unto her, *Mary.*

CHAPTER 20
V. 11-16
Notes

1 V.11 But M_____ stood without at the sepulchre weeping: and as she wept, she stooped down, and looked into the s_____,

2 V.12 And seeth t_____ a_____ sitting, the one at the head, and the other at the feet, where the b_____ l_____ of Jesus h_____.

Garden

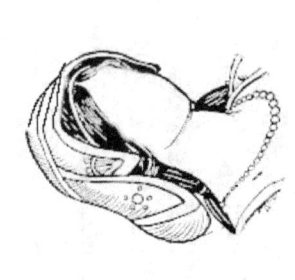

3 V.13 And they say unto her, W_____, why w_____ t_____?

4 V. 13 Because they have t_____ away my LORD, and I know not where t_____ l_____ have him

5 V.14 And when she had thus said, she turned herself back, and s_____ standing, and k_____ J_____ n_____ that it was J_____,

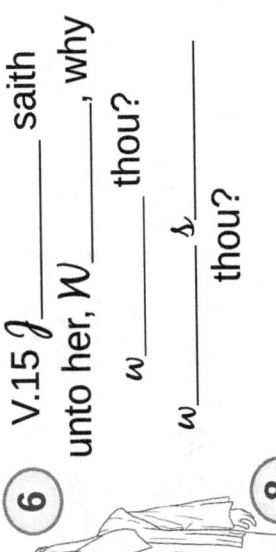

6 V.15 J_____ saith unto her, W_____, why w_____ s, thou? w_____ thou?

7 V.15 She, supposing him to be the g_____, saith unto him, Sir, if thou have borne him hence, t_____ m_____ where thou hast laid him, and I will take him a_____.

9 V.16 R_____; which is to say, M_____.

8 V.16 Jesus s_____ unto her, M_____.

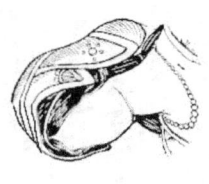
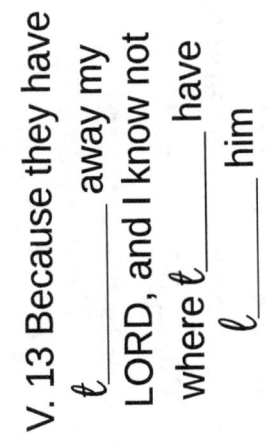

Jesus our High Priest

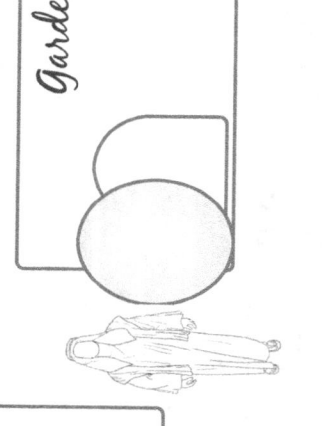

Garden

1

V.17 Jesus saith unto her, Touch me not; for I am not yet ascended to my Father: but go to my brethren, and say unto them, I ascend unto my Father, and your Father; and to my God, and your God.

Jesus told Mary not to touch Him. But just 8 days after (10 verses later) He told Thomas to reach hither his hand and thrust it into his side. Why was it ok for Thomas but not for Mary?

2

V.27 Then saith he to Thomas, Reach hither thy finger, and behold my hands; and reach hither thy hand, and thrust it into my side: and be not faithless, but believing.

Jesus, as the High Priest, appeared to Mary. He was on His way to heaven to place the blood on the mercy seat there. Before the High Priest could enter the Holy of Holies, he had to purify himself. If Mary touched Him, he would have been defiled. By the time, Jesus came to Thomas, He had already placed the blood on the mercy seat.

Hebrews 9:7 But into the <u>second</u> went the <u>high priest alone once every year, not without blood, which he offered for himself, and for the errors of</u> the people: (Second—was the Holy of Holies in the temple)

Hebrews 9:8 The Holy Ghost this signifying, that the <u>way into the holiest of all was not yet made manifest,</u> while as the first tabernacle was yet standing: (The holies of all was only a figure of heaven.

Hebrews 9:9 Which was a figure for the time then present, in which were offered both gifts and sacrifices, <u>that could not make him that did the service perfect,</u> as pertaining to the conscience;

Hebrews 9:11 <u>But Christ being come an high priest of good things to come, by a greater and more perfect tabernacle, not made with hands, that is to say, not of this building:</u>

Hebrews 9:24 For Christ is not entered into the holy places made with hands, which are the figures of the true; <u>but into heaven itself, now to appear in the presence of God for us:</u>

Leviticus 16:4 He shall put on the holy <u>linen coat,</u> and he shall have the <u>linen breeches</u> upon his flesh, and shall be girded with a <u>linen girdle,</u> and with the <u>linen mitre</u> shall he be attired: these are holy garments; therefore shall he wash his flesh in water, and so put them on.

——— Old Testament High Priest laws

If Mary touched Him, she would have defiled Him.

Jesus our High Priest

CHAPTER 20
V. 17
Notes

Garden

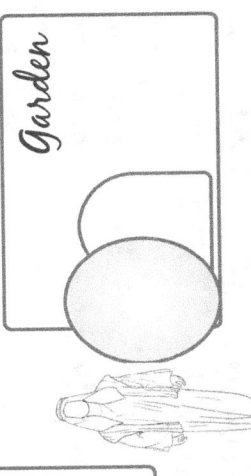

1 V.17 J_____ saith unto her,

T_____ m____ n_____; for I am

n_____ y_____ a_____ to my

F_____: but go to my brethren,

and say unto them, I ascend unto my

Father, and your Father; and to my

God, and your God.

2 V.27 Then saith he to Thomas, Reach

hither thy finger, and behold my hands;

and r_____ h_____ t_____ i___ i_____

h_____, and t_____ i___ i_____

m_____ s_____: and be not faithless, but

believing.

CHAPTER 20
V. 18-23
Guide

Luke 7:47
forgiven much

1 V.18
Mary Magdalene

The 12 disciples were there except for Judas and Thomas

remit means to forgive or pardon.

2
V.19 Then the same day at evening, being the *first day of the week*, when the *doors were shut* where the disciples were assembled for fear of the Jews, came *Jesus* and *stood* in the *midst*, and saith unto them, *Peac* be unto you.

3
V.21 Then said Jesus to them *again*, *Peace* be unto you: as my Father hath sent me, even so send I you.
V.22 And when he had said this, he *breathed* on them, and saith unto them, Receive ye the *Holy Ghost*.
V.23 Whose soever sins *ye remit*, they are remitted unto them; and whose soever sins ye *retain*, they are retained.

speaking to the Disciples

Acts 2:1 And when the day of Pentecost was fully <u>come</u>, they were all with one accord in one place.
Acts 2:2 And suddenly there came a <u>sound</u> from heaven as of a rushing <u>mighty wind</u>, and it filled all the house where they were sitting.
Acts 2:3 And there appeared unto them cloven tongues like as of fire, and it sat upon each of them.
Acts 2:4 <u>And they were all filled with the Holy Ghost</u>, and began to speak with other tongues, as the Spirit gave them utterance.

John 15:16 Ye have not chosen me, but I have chosen you, and ordained you, that ye should go and bring forth fruit, and that your fruit should remain: <u>that whatsoever ye shall ask of the Father in my name, he may give it you.</u>

CHAPTER 20
V. 18-23
Notes

1 V.18

𝓜_____

𝓜_____

2 V.19 Then the same day at
evening, being the 𝒇_____, when
the 𝒹_____ 𝓌_____ 𝓈_____
where the disciples were
assembled for fear of the Jews,
came 𝒥_____ and 𝓈_____
in the 𝓂_____, and saith untc
them, 𝒫_____ be unto you.

3 V.21 Then said Jesus to them
𝒶_____, 𝒫_____ be unto you:
as my Father hath sent me, even 𝓈_____
𝓈_____ 𝓎_____.
V.22 And when he had said this, he
𝒷_____ on them, and saith unto
them, Receive ye the 𝓗_____
𝒢_____.
V.23 Whose soever sins 𝓎_____
𝓇_____, they are remitted unto
them; and whose soever sins ye
𝓇_____, they are retained.

Eight days after Jesus told Mary not to touch Him, He told Thomas to thrust His hand into His side.

Jesus, as our High Priest, had already been to heaven and placed the blood on the mercy seat. It was ok to touch Him now.

V.27 Then saith he to Thomas, Reach hither thy finger, and behold my hands; and reach hither thy hand, and *thrust it into my side: and be not faithless, but believing.*

V.28 And Thomas answered and said unto him, My *LORD* and my *God.*

V.29 Jesus saith unto him, Thomas, because thou hast seen me, thou hast believed: *blessed* are they that have *not seen,* and yet have believed.

V.30 And many other signs truly did Jesus in the *presence of his disciples,* which are not written in this book:

All disciples, except John, was martyred for preaching the Gospel and proclaiming that Jesus was the Son of God. They knew it to be true!!! John died of old age on the Isle of Patmos

V.31 *But* these are written, that ye might *believe that Jesus is the Christ, the Son of God;* and that believing ye might have life through his name.

The Scriptures were written so that we (who have not seen Him) might believe.

V.27 Then saith he to Thomas, Reach hither thy finger, and behold my hands; and reach hither thy hand, and t_____ it i_____ m_____ s_____: and be n_____ b_____, b_____.

V.28 And Thomas answered and said unto him, M___ L___ and m___ G___.

V.29 Jesus saith unto him, Thomas, because thou hast seen me, thou hast believed: b_____ are they that have n___ s_____, and y___ h_____ b_____.

V.30 And m_____ o_____ s_____ truly did Jesus in the p_____ of his d_____, which are not written in this book:

V.31 B_____ these are w_____, that y___ m_____ b_____ that J_____ is the C_____, the S___ of G_____; and that b_____ y___ m___ h_____ l___ t_____ h___ n_____.

Read John Chapter 21

CHAPTER 21
V. 1-2
Guide

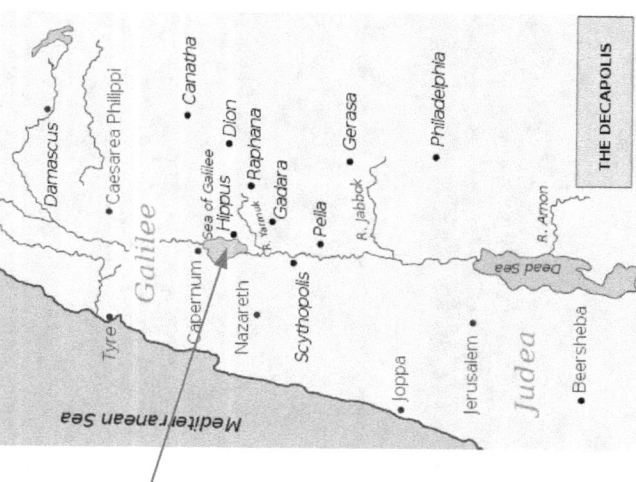

John 6:1 After these things Jesus went over the <u>sea of Galilee, which is the sea of Tiberias.</u>

Same place as
1. He first met them and said "Follow Me:
2. the Miracle of feeding the 5000
3. Walked on the water

V.1 After these things Jesus shewed himself again to the disciples at the sea of Tiberias; and on this wise shewed he himself. (how it happened)

V.2 two other of his disciples.

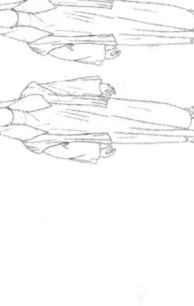

V. 2 sons of Zebedee,
(James and John.)

Luke 5:10 <u>And so was also James, and John, the sons of Zebedee</u>

V.2 Simon Peter

V.2 Thomas called Didymus

V.2 Nathanael of Cana in Galilee

CHAPTER 21
V. 1-2
Notes

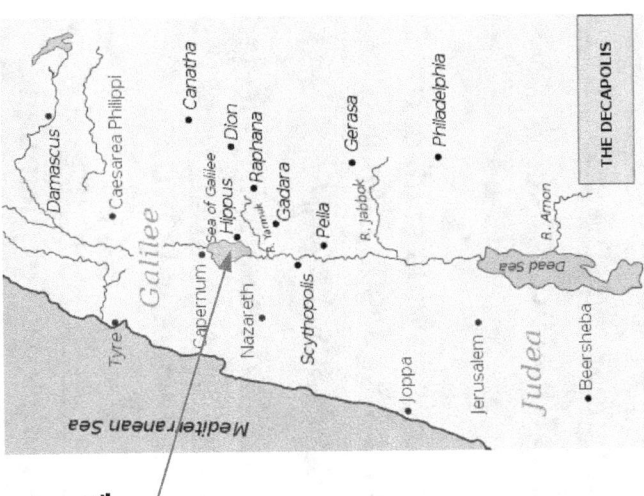

John 6:1 After these things Jesus went over the <u>sea of Galilee, which is the sea of Tiberias.</u>

V.1 After these things J_____
shewed himself again to the
d_____ at the s_____ of
_____ T_____;
and on _this_ w_____ shewed he
himself.

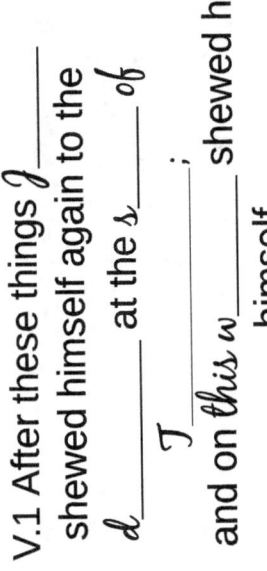

V.2 S_____ P_____

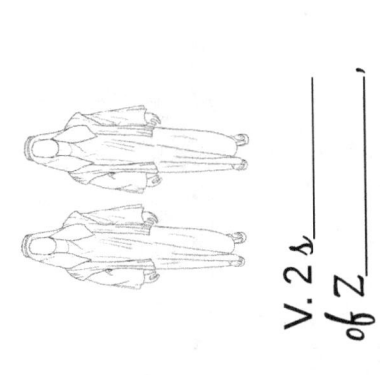

V. 2 s_____
of Z_____

V.2 J_____
c_____
D_____

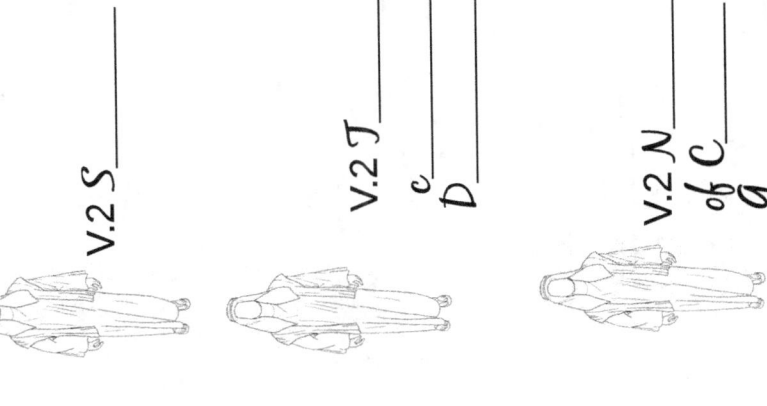

V.2 N_____
of C_____ in
g_____

V.2 t_____
o_____ of h_____ .
d_____

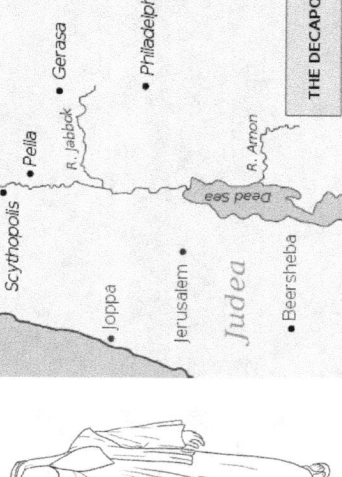

THE DECAPOLIS

CHAPTER 21
V. 3-4
Guide

Sea of Tiberias
He first met James & John
Feeding of the 5000
Jesus walks on water

John 6:27 Labour not for the meat which perisheth,

same place

(2) V.3 I go a fishing.

(3) V. 3 and that night they caught nothing.

(1) V.3 Simon Peter

Thomas

Nathanael

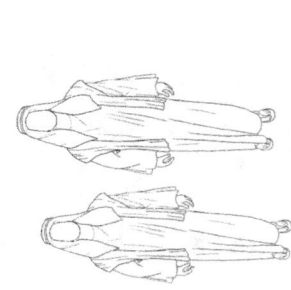

James and John

2 other disciples

(4) V.4 *But when the morning was now come, Jesus stood on the shore: but the disciples knew not that it was Jesus. (After the resurrection, Jesus reveals himself.*

John 20:14 And when she had thus said, she turned herself back, and saw Jesus standing, and <u>knew not that it was Jesus.</u> (Mary)

John 20:20 And when he had so said, <u>he shewed unto them his hands and his side. Then were the disciples glad, when they saw the LORD.</u>

Luke 24:31 <u>And their eyes were opened, and they knew him;</u> and he vanished out of their sight.
(Emmaus Rd)

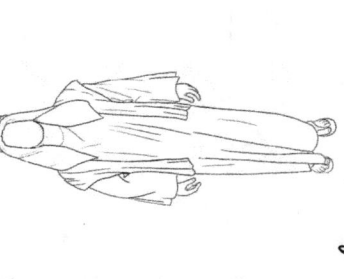

CHAPTER 21
V. 3-4
Notes

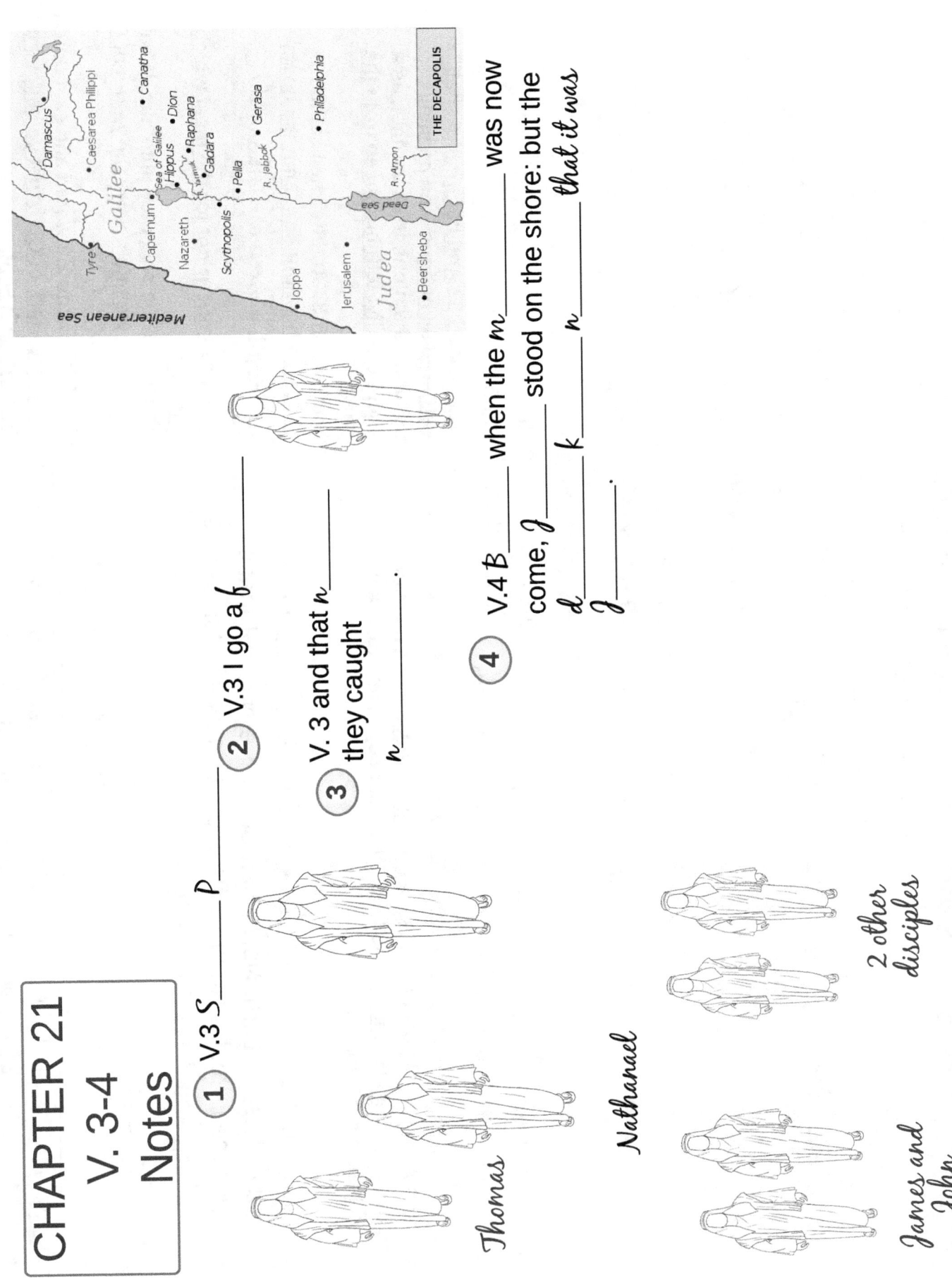

(1) V.3 S_____

P_____

(2) V.3 I go a f_____

(3) V. 3 and that n_____
they caught
n_____ .

(4) V.4 B_____ when the m_____ was now
come, J_____ stood on the shore: but the
d_____ k_____ n_____ *that it was*
J_____ .

Thomas

Nathanael

James and
John

2 other
disciples

THE DECAPOLIS

Damascus

Caesarea Philippi

Canatha

Dion

Raphana

Sea of Galilee

Hippus

Gadara

Capernum

Yarmuk

Gerasa

Nazareth

Pella

R. Jabbok

Scythopolis

Philadelphia

Galilee

Tyre

Mediterranean Sea

Joppa

Jerusalem

Judea

R. Arnon

Dead Sea

Beersheba

CHAPTER 21
V. 5-7
Guide

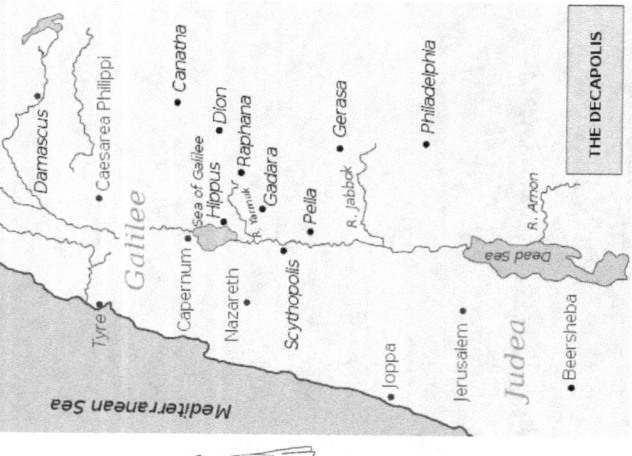

THE DECAPOLIS

Same shore as the feeding of the multitudes (John 6:23-29)

I go a fishing.

They were laboring for the meat which perisheth

(1) V.5 Then *Jesus*

(2) v. 5 Children, have ye any *meat?*

(3) V.5 *No.*

(4) V.6 Cast the net on the *right side* of the ship, and ye shall find.

(5) V.6 They cast therefore, and now they were not able to draw it for the *multitude* of fishes

(The multitudes represents souls.)

Rev. 7:9 After this, I beheld, and, lo, a **great multitude**, which no man could number, **of all nations**, and kindreds, and people, and tongues, stood before the throne, ...

(John)

(6) V.7 Therefore that *disciple whom Jesus loved* saith unto *Peter*, It is the Lord. Now when Simon Peter *heard* that it was the Lord, he girt his fisher's coat unto him, (for he was *naked*,) and did *cast himself into the sea.*

Nakedness is always associated with shame. Peter was shamed because he denied Jesus three times. This is the same sea that he began to sink when he tried to walk on the water to Jesus. Now seeing that Jesus had risen from the dead, he heard that it was the Lord and cast himself into the sea without fear.

Matthew 25:32 <u>And before him shall be gathered all nations</u>: and he shall separate them one from another, as a shepherd <u>divideth his sheep from the goats:</u>
Matthew 25:33 And he shall set the sheep on his right hand, but the goats on the left. *(Sheep are the saved)*

John 6:27 <u>Labour not for the meat which perisheth.</u> ...
John 6:28 Then said they unto him, What shall we do, that we might work the works of God? *(They went a fishin)*
John 6:29 Jesus answered and said unto them, <u>This is the work of God, that ye believe on him whom he hath sent.</u>

CHAPTER 21
V. 5-7
Notes

Same shore as the feeding of the multitudes (John 6:23-29)

THE DECAPOLIS

① V.5 Then J_____

② V. 5 Children, have ye any m_____?

③ V.5
N_____

④ V.6 Cast the net on the r_____ s_____ of the ship, and ye shall find.

V.6 They cast therefore, and now they were _____

⑤ not able to draw it for the m_____ of fishes

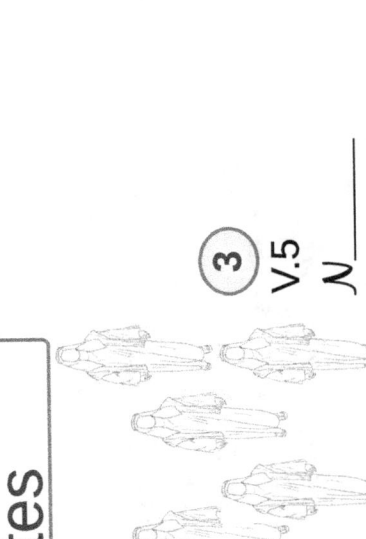

⑥ V.7 Therefore that d_____ w_____ J_____ saith unto P_____, It is the Lord. Now when Simon Peter h_____ that it was the Lord, he girt his fisher's coat unto him, (for he was n_____,) and did c_____ h_____ into the s_____.

CHAPTER 21
V. 8-11
Guide

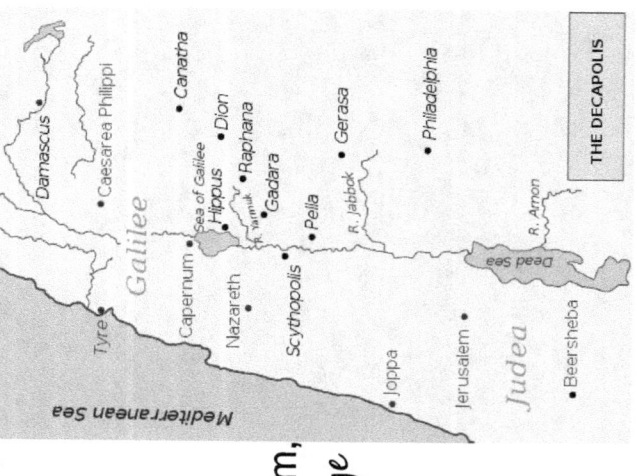

THE DECAPOLIS

1 V.8 And the other disciples came in a little ship; (for they were not far from land, but as it were two hundred cubits,) *dragging the net with fishes.*

3 V.10 *Jesus* saith unto them, Bring of the *fish* which ye *have now caught.*

Jesus is the bread of life

Fish	bread

V.9 **2** *fire of coals*

Jesus had caught fish (souls) during His ministry and now He is getting ready to send the disciples so they can bring fish (souls) also.

4 V.11 *Simon Peter* went up, and drew the net to land full of great fishes, an *hundred and fifty and three:* and for all there were so many, yet was *not the net broken*

153 represents the number of nations *on earth at that time.*

Peter was now looking into a set of coals now kindled by the Holy Spirit

Holy Spirit represented by the Kindled coals
2 Samuel 22:9 There went up a smoke out of his nostrils, and fire out of his mouth devoured: coals were kindled by it.

John 18:18 And the servants and officers **stood there, who had made a fire of** coals**; for it was cold: and they warmed themselves: and** Peter stood with them**, and warmed himself.**

CHAPTER 21
V. 8-11
Notes

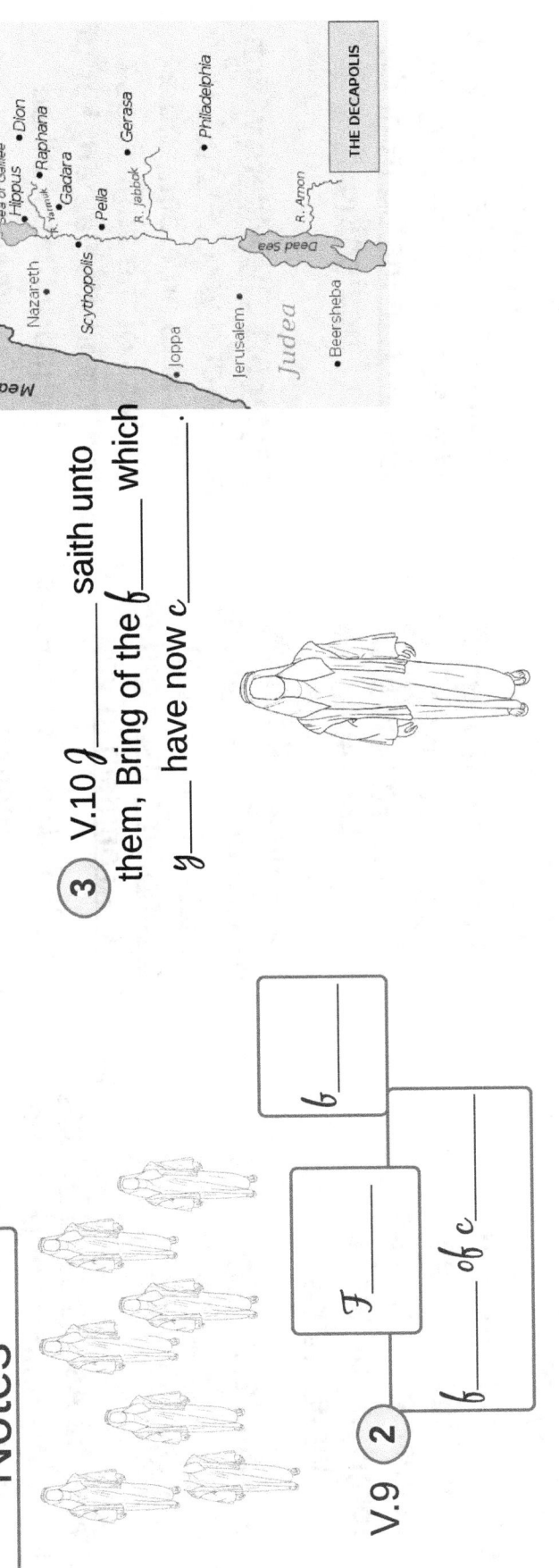

THE DECAPOLIS

(1) V.8 And the other disciples came in a little ship; (for they were not far from land, but as it were two hundred cubits,) d_____ _the_ n_____ with f_____.

(2) V.9

F_____

b_____ of c_____

b_____

(3) V.10 J_____ saith unto them, Bring of the f_____ which y_____ have now c_____.

(4) V.11 S_____ P_____ went up, and drew the net to land full of g_____ f_____, an h_____ and f_____ and t_____ : and for all there were so many, yet was n_____ the n_____ b_____.

Jesus fed them in the same place He fed the multitudes (on the shore of the Sea of Tiberias)

V.12 Jesus saith unto them, *Come and dine. And none of the disciples durst ask him, Who art thou? knowing that it was the Lord.*

Didn't recognize Him in His glorified body.

V.13 Jesus then cometh, and taketh *bread,* and giveth them, and *fish* likewise.
V.14 This is now the *third time* that Jesus shewed himself to his *disciples,* after that he was risen from the dead.

Lovest thou me?

V. 15
Feed my lambs

1 John 2:12 I write unto you, little children, because your sins are forgiven you for his name's sake.

1 John 12:13 ..little children, because ye have known the Father.

1Peter 2:2 As newborn babes, desire the sincere milk of the word, that ye may grow thereby:

Peter was being instructed to feed all the sheep. The little children, the strong young men and the elders (fathers).
John had written to the same groups according to spiritual maturity in 1-3 Epistles of John

V. 16
Feed my sheep

1 John 12:14 young men, because ye have overcome the wicked one.

1 John 12:14 I have written unto you, young men, because ye are strong, and the word of God abideth in you

1Peter 5:5 Likewise, ye younger,

V. 17
Feed my sheep

1 John 2:13 I write unto you, fathers, because ye have known him that is from the beginning.

1Peter 5:1 The elders which are among you I exhort, who am also an elder, and a witness of the sufferings of Christ, and also a partaker of the glory that shall be revealed:

CHAPTER 21

V. 12-17

Notes

V.12 Jesus saith unto them, C_____ and d_____ .

And none of the d_____ durst ask him, W_____ art

t_____ ? k_____ that it was the L_____ .

V.13 Jesus then cometh, and taketh b_____ , and giveth them, and f_____ likewise.

V.14 This is now the t_____ t_____ that Jesus shewed himself to his d_____ , after that he was risen from the dead.

Lovest thou me?

V. 15

J_____ my l_____

V. 16

J_____ m_____ s_____

V. 17

J_____ m_____ s_____

CHA-PTER 21
V. 18-23
Guide

Jesus was telling Peter when you were young you clothed yourself and went where ever you wanted to go but when you are old you will be bound and carried to the cross with outstretched hands.

Prophecy can only come from heaven

① V.18 Verily, verily, I say unto thee, When thou wast young, thou girdest thyself, and walkedst whither thou wouldest: but when thou shalt be old, thou shalt stretch forth thy hands, and another shall gird thee, and carry thee whither thou wouldest not.

V.19 This spake he, signifying by what death he should glorify God. And when he had spoken this, he saith unto him, Follow me.

Same place when Jesus said to him "Follow me" when he first met him.

② V.20 Then Peter

③ V. 20 seeth the disciple whom Jesus loved following; which also leaned on his breast at supper, and said, Lord, which is he that betrayeth thee?

John

④ V.21 Peter seeing him saith to Jesus, Lord, and what shall this man do?

John Lives

⑤ V. 22 Jesus If I will that he tarry till I come, what is that to thee? follow thou me.

Peter died crucified upside down in Rome in 67 AD.

⑥ V.23 Then went this saying abroad among the brethren, that that disciple should not die: yet Jesus said not unto him, He shall not die; but, If I will that he tarry till I come, what is that to thee?

John did see the visions of the 2nd coming of Jesus. He writes of this in the Book of the Revelation.

CHA-PTER 21
V. 18-23
Notes

1

V.18 V_____, v_____, s_____ unto thee, When thou wast y_____, thou g_____ t_____, and walkedst whither thou w_____: b_____ when thou shalt be o_____, t_____ shalt s_____ forth thy h_____, and a_____ shall g_____ thee, and c_____ thee w_____ thou w_____ n_____.

V.19 This spake he, s_____ by what d_____ he should g_____ g_____. And when he had spoken this, he saith unto him, F_____ m_____.

2

V.20 Then P_____

3

V. 20 seeth the disciple w_____ J_____ l_____ following; which also l_____ on h_____ b_____ at s_____, and said, Lord, w_____ is he that b_____ thee?

4

V.21 P_____ seeing him saith to Jesus, L_____, and what shall t_____ m_____ d_____?

5

V. 22 J_____ If I will that he t_____ till I come, what is that to thee? f_____ t_____ m_____.

6

V.23 Then went this saying abroad among the brethren, that that d_____ should n_____ d_____: yet J_____ s_____ not unto him, H_____ s_____ n_____ die; but, If I will that he t_____ t_____ c_____, what is that to thee?

Who is the disciple whom Jesus loved?

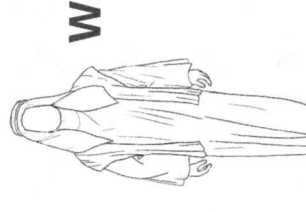

John 21:20 Then Peter, turning about, seeth the disciple whom Jesus loved following; which also leaned on his breast at supper, and said, Lord, which is he that betrayeth thee?

John 21:23 Then went this saying abroad among the brethren, that that disciple should not die: yet Jesus said not unto him, He shall not die: but, If I will that he tarry till I come, what is that to thee?

V.24 This is the disciple which testifieth of these things, and wrote these things: and we know that his testimony is true.

1. John wrote the Gospel of John which testifies of these things.

2. Jesus did not say that John would not die but his disciples said John would not die. John did die but was the only disciple that was not martyred. He died of old age.

3. The Gospel of John is the only Book in the Bible that uses the phrase "the disciple whom Jesus loved." John felt like Jesus loved him most and wrote this of himself.

V.25 And there are also many other things which Jesus did, the which, if they should be written every one, I suppose that even the world itself could not contain the books that should be written.

Amen.

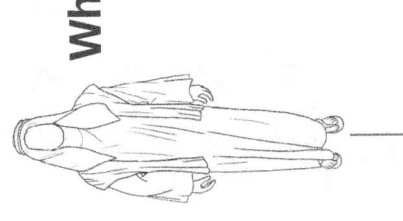

CHAPTER 21
V. 24-25
Notes

Who is the disciple whom Jesus loved?

V.24 _J_____ _is the d_____ _which t_____ _of t_____
_t_____, and _w_____ _t_____ _t_____ ; and we know that his
testimony is true.

V.25 And there are also _m_____ _o_____ _t_____ which Jesus did, the which, if they
should be written every one, I suppose that even _the w_____ _i_____ _could n_____
_the b_____ that should be written.
_c_____ _A_____ .

There is so much more!

CommonPeopleBibleStudies.com

Free Printable Lessons and Videos
Same format used in this book!
Great for individual and small group studies

Common People Bible Study Guides
Currently available on our website
- The Gospel According to John
- The Book of Ruth
- I,II,III John
- The Book of I Kings
- The Book of Obadiah

Coming Soon! Online Courses for the Common People Bible Study Guides

Join our email list to receive new lessons as they are published.